Common Place
Toward Neighborhood and Regional Design

New
Communities
Charrette

LAKE
SAMMAMISH

LAKE

Sand Point
Charrette

WASHINGTON

University District
Charrette

Seattle Commons
Charrette

Interbay
Charrette

Kingdome
Charrette

PUGET

Winslow
Charrette

SOUND

A Samuel and Althea Stroum Book

Common Place

Toward Neighborhood and Regional Design

Douglas Kelbaugh

University of Washington Press   Seattle and London

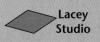

Lacey
Studio

This book is published with the assistance of a grant from the Stroum Book Fund, established through the generosity of Samuel and Althea Stroum

The writing was supported by a grant from the
Graham Foundation for Advanced Studies in the Fine Arts

Copyright © 1997 by the University of Washington Press
Printed in Hong Kong

Library of Congress Cataloging-in-Publication Data

Kelbaugh, Douglas
    Common place : toward neighborhood and regional design /
Douglas S. Kelbaugh.
        p.   cm.
    Includes bibliographical references and index.
    ISBN 0-295-97590-3 (alk. paper)
    1. Planned communities—Washington (State)—Seattle Region.
I. Title.
HT169.57.U62S45   1997
307.76'8'0979772—dc20   96-42311
                                                                CIP

The paper used in this publication meets the minimum requirements of American National Standard for Information Sciences—Permanence of Paper for Printed Library Materials, ANSI Z39.48-1984.

Cover: View toward downtown Seattle, by Doug Kelbaugh. Water-color wash of ink drawing photocopied onto water-color paper—a rendering technique appropriate to the fast pace of a design charrette, in this case, Interbay 2020.

For my father, John Calvin Kelbaugh, 1912–1994,
who contributed in knowing and unknowing ways

Contents

Foreword

This book arrives at a critical time for our region and other metropolitan regions around the country. We are at a watershed in the development of regional community. Decisions we make today, or fail to make, will determine how well the American metropolis will avoid the pitfalls of increasing sprawl, congestion, pollution, and social isolation that threaten to overwhelm it. Clearly, protecting what we value in this and other regions and building a better future for ourselves and our children will require changes in our current practice of community building.

Common Place provides a useful tool for planning at many levels. The chapters on theory help explain how we arrived at our present predicament. The case made against sprawl is a compelling call to action. But this book is more than a condensation of twentieth-century design theory. As an architect, urban designer, and educator, Doug Kelbaugh provides a valuable resource for the citizens of our region by demonstrating how community values and desires can be translated into real physical possibilities. This book's emphasis on core values also speaks to the core values of our citizenry: we see ourselves as the guardians of cities within a natural environment that is very much worth protecting.

It has always been my belief that planning must engage the full spectrum of the community in a profound discussion of its values and aspirations as a whole. In Seattle, we engaged in such a discussion over a period of several years during the development of our Comprehensive Plan. Through our public process our community began to confront the prospects of change and grapple with the uncertainties about the future. Many of the charrettes outlined here were helpful in the process because they addressed major projects, such as the Commons, Sand Point, Interbay, University District, and the Kingdome, that would have an impact on the city and the region. The charrette format also allowed residents from diverse backgrounds to participate in the design of their future.

Too often community groups can agree on what they don't want—neighborhood disruption, displacement, continued dependence on the automobile—but have a more difficult time developing a shared vision for the future they do want. This book demonstrates the power of design and images in any effort to create a shared vision or preferred future for our community. Indeed, this book is so powerful and so accessible that it will serve to inspire citizens to develop their own visions for their communities.

Norman B. Rice, Mayor of Seattle
President of the U.S. Conference of Mayors

Common Place

Toward Neighborhood and Regional Design

Introduction

I could start by stating that this book is about the salvation of the American metropolis, but that would be stretching it. It is about incremental steps—some small, some large—to save and improve upon America's urbanism and one of its best cities. It is offered up with equal parts of chauvinism and alarm. There is civic pride and hope in Seattle, but there is also fear and disintegration. Its region, especially at the periphery, is going the way of every American metropolis. Modern technology—primarily the automobile—and contemporary economic, cultural, and social forces continue to erode and spread out the city. Not only is the modern metropolis at risk, Modernism itself is in deep trouble

This book is about bringing a greater sense of community and coherence to neighborhood and region. It champions physical structure that is simultaneously more diverse, more sustainable, and more legible than megazoned suburban sprawl or underutilized urban areas. It is also about our social physique and about bringing meaning to architecture and a sense of place to communities. It touches on commerce and how our market economy needs repair if it is going to produce true wealth, as it has so fruitfully done in the past. It touches on Critical Regionalism, or how a region can maintain and architectually celebrate its identities and its differences. It touches on typology or how the built environment can be physically and spatially understandable and cohesive—a prerequisite to individual and shared meaning in our lives. It also touches on postmodern urban theory, design, and practice, especially the New Urbanism. Lastly, it illustrates all of this in a series of design workshop, or charrette, proposals for the Seattle region that are also topical in other metropolitan areas.

Common Place is a collection of linked essays, design projects, and policy proposals. It is a sandwich. The front and back slices are more theoretical and written in a more personal voice than the middle, which is a factual description of specific projects and sometimes recapitulates the voice of other designers. The essays have been written and rewritten over many years for many audiences: urban designers, architects, urban planners, landscape architects, developers, transportation planners, housing consultants, energy consultants, city officials, environmentalists, planning board members, civil engineers, bankers, real estate lawyers, design educators, and concerned citizens. Because the book is written for a range of readers, both lay and professional, some may find that it reads unevenly. Some reviewers of the manuscript have suggested that it would be better presented as two books, one for academics and design professionals, the other for citizens and community leaders. For me, an attempt to bridge and connect to both audiences is worth the risk of reaching neither with a signal that is either too strong or too weak. Books that narrow the gap between theory and practice, professionals and lay people, are needed more than ever. As scientific and technical subjects become more arcane and opaque for everyday citizens, and as governments and institutions become more open and egalitarian, there is a greater need for popularizing the esoteric and theorizing about the popular.

Most of the ideas offered here have been kicking around for some time, either in academia or on the street, or both. Some of the charrette designs have already been published, although in a limited way. What is new and of special interest is the way the material has been presented or re-presented, integrating ideas from a number of sources—ideas that have been separated by discipline and perforated by the media. I have striven to be clear and to make complex ideas, theories, and designs as accessible as possible in words and images.

Roughly speaking, Part I is about the ideas, principles, and theory that undergird the specific designs presented in Part II. The shortest section, Part III, is about the policies needed to realize the ideas and designs presented in the first two parts. Appendix A offers practical advice on how to organize a charrette. Some readers may want to focus on one or two sections. Design professionals from anywhere in the western world should find Part I and Part II particularly engaging. Those from the Seattle region may get more out of Part II. Policy makers, elected officials, lawmakers, and interested citizens, including those who consider themselves environmentalists, would especially benefit from reading chapters 1, 4, and 10, as well as perusing Part II and Appendix A. Those who read every chapter should find themselves rewarded with a broad perspective and vision for the American metropolis in general and the Seattle region in particular.

ABOUT THE TITLE

The words in the title are the most carefully chosen in the book. "Common Place" was selected because it offered both a high and a low reading. The word "common" has many meanings. They range from "relating or belonging to the community at large" to "familiar" to "coarse or vulgar." "Place" is an abstract word with even more meanings, several of which have to do with a particular location in physical space. Together, the two words are meant to evoke a physically defined realm, either public or private, that is mutually understood, shared, and shaped by its inhabitants. When elided into the single word "commonplace," an entirely different meaning is suddenly available to the reader: ordinary, unremarkable, or even trite. This double meaning is important to the book, which tries to champion the everyday and the typical as much as the monumental and which, no doubt, has its share of trite observations.

The book is about "regional" design in Seattle. It is simultaneously about *regionalist* design, that is, how *any* region can go about understanding, designing, and developing itself. However, it does not prescribe universal or global solutions per se. As Wendell Berry has said, "Properly speaking, global thinking is not possible."[1] This book is about how we should behave and dispose ourselves as households, as neighborhoods, and as a region. It also reminds us that, although everyone lives in a region, only some of us are lucky enough to live in a "neighborhood," which is why "toward" is the operable preposition. Toward is a word with a polemical ring and an echo of Le Corbusier's famous tract so familiar to architecture students.

Neighborhoods are the integers of cities. Without neighborhoods, cities are much less coherent and livable, however beautiful they may be. They integrate the daily functions of life—living, working, playing, schooling, worshipping and especially shopping. With their centers and edges, they also provide a physical focus and common ground for local social life. If individual structures are the building blocks of streets and streets are the building blocks of neighborhoods, then neighborhoods are the building blocks of cities. They are indispensable to urban community. They have been with us for a long time, sometimes and some places known by other names such as quarter, district, precinct, or zone. Over a remarkably broad spectrum of place, culture, and time, neighborhoods have served the same purpose and been about the same size—roughly a half mile on a side or about 150 acres. Their populations vary tenfold, from fewer than 2,000 inhabitants in America to as many as 20,000 in Paris, for instance. But what seem to be constant about traditional neighborhoods are two things: their size, determined by what is a comfortable walking distance, and their ubiquity.

This book is about one region as well as regionalism in general. Unlike most books published in this field, it seeks a broad spectrum of readers from a particular metropolitan region as well as a narrow stratum of specialists from across the country. To be true to its first mission, the text is full of proper nouns that name particular people and particular places in the Seattle region, however parochial that may make passages for readers from other regions.

"Design" I have saved for last, because its meaning is less obvious in this context. When it is qualified by "regional," another intentional double reading is introduced into the title. Regional design can reflect regional architecture, i.e., design that expresses regional characteristics, or it can refer to regional planning, i.e., the overall layout of the region. Both readings apply, the first to Critical Regionalism in chapter 2 and the second to the design work in Part II. "Design" was chosen over "planning" to convey the idea that a region must be physically designed in three dimensions rather than only two. The city can be thought of as a gigantic design problem, as a big building. As architectural historian Vincent Scully points out, the city should be designed like a house. It should always be scaled for and understandable to human beings. Even the region should be legible, with clearly defined edges and centers. It is hard to experience the entire Seattle metropolitan region at one time, even from an airplane. (Only the Blue Angels fly wide and fast enough to tie a ribbon around it.) But it is possible to know where you are relative to mountains and water, cores and open space.

"Design" is used because this book illustrates the work of architects and urban designers rather than urban, city, or regional planners. Most of the charrette participants—the professionals, the faculty members, and the students—were architects, although landscape architects and students were involved in later charrettes. A number of urban planning faculty and students also participated, as occasionally did developers and artists. Despite the lack of involvement of practicing urban planners per se, many of the charrettes dealt with a project scale considered since the mid-century more the realm of urban planning than architecture. Architects have been active at this scale before—from Renaissance and Baroque town planning to early twentieth-century visions such as Garden City by Ebenezer Howard, Broadacre City by Frank Lloyd Wright, and Radiant City by Le Corbusier. Landscape architects, too, have been thinking and designing more and more at a larger scale, whether it be a habitat, ecosystem, or bioregion.

Urban planners are trained in mapping, demographics, statistics, transportation, land use, and economics. In the 1970s, many of the planning schools moved away from teaching the three-dimensional shaping of the physical environment toward analysis and policy. Planners are better equipped to answer the locational questions of *where* development should go, while architects and urban designers can better answer the design questions of *what* development should be like. Landscape architects can often answer both locational and design questions, because of their understanding of natural systems from the

6

micro to the macro scale. They know regions and open space—from wetlands to watersheds—and have provided critical leadership in the understanding, conservation, and restoration of the environment.

Architecture, landscape architecture, and urban design are different from urban planning in a basic way. They are three-dimensional. There are many two-dimensional master plans in this book, but they are not the usual urban planner's mosaic of land-use colors. They are delineated with the actual footprints (and shadows) of proposed buildings. These footprints represent building types with which architects are intimately familiar. Also, the many three-dimensional drawings, renderings, and models in the book are more characteristic of designers than planners. These graphic devices are essential for helping professionals and lay people alike to understand and respond to proposed plans. Indeed, they have been spectacularly absent until recently from much of the debate about growth management and comprehensive planning.

Designers have the ability to be visually imaginative and creative. They are comfortable envisioning new places and illustrating them in ways that non-designers can understand. Because they must detail a building design to the nearest eighth of an inch and specify its every material and component, the visions of architects are usually grounded to some degree in reality. Designers are also used to making trade-offs and weighing costs with benefits—often without all the data. The mark of a good designer, unlike a scientist, is the very ability to make final decisions *without* all the requisite information, because it is rarely all available at the proper time. Nor are all the data necessary, because good design is about getting most of the answers mostly right. It is not about perfection. Holding a great number of design variables up in the air as long as possible and bringing them together synergistically at the last possible minute are a skill and talent needed for design. They are especially necessary in charrettes.

ABOUT UNDERLYING VALUES

A word about the values that underlie these studies—the ones that are so basic that they usually go unstated by the author. There are at least three fundamental values and ideas that frame the book.

The first is *community*. Without community, we are all doomed to private worlds that are ultimately selfish and loveless. As our society becomes more privatized and our culture more narcissistic, the need and appetite to be part of something bigger than our individual selves grow. Organized religion and individual spiritual development answer this need and calling for many people. For some people, however, belonging to a community may be the highest expression of this spiritual need. People are social animals, and our need to share and to love makes community a *sine qua non* of existence. On the other hand, humans also have a fundamental need to express themselves as individuals, to individuate themselves psychologically and socially, even to excel and rise above the crowd. A community must simultaneously nurture both a respect for group values and a tolerance for individuality, even eccentricity. This is the paradox of community that will forever require readjustments.

Few humans would deny the value of community, as well as of mutual respect and tolerance. But some contemporary sages question the notion of traditional community. They posit that communities of interest, including ones enabled by modern electronic communications, have supplanted what used to be communities of propinquity and place. This is not a new notion in America. Alexis de Tocqueville observed in his early nineteenth-century classic *Democracy in America*: "Americans of all ages, all stations of life, and all types of disposition are forever forming associations . . . religious, moral, serious, futile, very general and very limited, immensely large and very minute."

It is an undeniable fact that telecommunications and computers have changed our lives in many ways. However, it is not evident that they have reduced our need for physical community. Indeed, living with a computer screen in your face all day and a telephone in your ear, with radio or CD in the background, is no substitute for physical community. As the poet and pundit Gary Snyder likes to say, the Internet is not a community because you can't hug someone on it. The World Wide Web may prove antithetical to community by providing anonymous sources with instantaneous access to vast audiences to which they are not accountable. Never have such hidden voices had such access to such a large audience. Electronic sniping on the information highway is not public discourse, any more than a website is an Italian piazza. If anything, electronic communications have increased the human need for traditional neighborhoods with buildings you can kick and neighbors to whom you can wave or frown.

To quote Bart Giamatti, former president of Yale University and of baseball's National League:

> Over millennia, this refinement of negotiation—of balancing private need and public obligation, personal desire and public duty, and keen interests of the one and the many into a common, shared set of agreements—becomes a civilization. That is the public version of what binds us. That state is achieved because city dwellers as individuals or as families or as groups have smoothed the edges of private desire so as to fit, or at least work in, with all the other city dwellers, without undue abrasion, without sharp edges forever nicking and wounding, each refining an individual capacity for those thousands of daily, instantaneous negotiations that keep crowded city life from becoming a constant brawl or ceaseless shoving match.[2]

Society must strive to be both tolerant and just enough to allow minority groups and subcultures to coexist with dignity and in peace. Achieving this tolerance is easier said than done, as America has found after centuries of trying. It is becoming an even bigger challenge as more and more Americans grow up without firsthand experience and skills in city living. "There are now several generations of Americans who have no idea or experience of the kinds of tolerance and cooperation which are implicit in higher density neighborhoods or communities."[3]

Community must deal with the full range of human nature, including its own dark side. If it projects its own pathologies onto an outside enemy or stigmatized minority, it has not fully faced up to itself and is in collective denial. More typically, the unity in community is bought at the price of making enemies, who are sure to return the favor. They will get even some day, as the chain reaction of intolerance and injustice continues. If this is the inevitable human condition, the question arises as to what is the most hospitable scale for social and political unity and the least hospitable scale for enmity. As you will see, this book presents the case that neighborhood and region are the most sensible and equitable scales of community and governance in the emerging American metropolis.

The second fundamental is *sustainability*. It remains the most succinct term for another unassailable value. Hard to define precisely, it has a lot to do with living within your means in a way that allows future generations a good and decent life. Sustainability also involves respect and reverence for life itself—for the billions of living things that have taken billions of years to evolve, for that miraculous web of plants and creatures that truly passeth all understanding. If it is not human responsibility to protect all life, it is certainly our responsibility not to mess it up. Humans have long been cavalier and rogue members of the natural order. Now their technology and population have grown so gargantuan that they are the planet's greatest threat. It would probably not be an exaggeration to say that most species on this planet other than human beings are in decline. It is not plants and animals that have fouled up the world, but the wanton, rapacious habits of homo sapiens.

We're not going to change human nature. However, we can reform human values, habits, and institutions. We can shift paradigms and transform culture. Among other urgent changes, we must change industrial commerce so that it can coexist with the natural environment. As "green" architect William McDonough puts it, we need a second industrial revolution. This will not happen unless the market economy starts factoring the true and total cost of commodities into prices. Otherwise, we're not sustained, as false cues and distorted signals from the marketplace accelerate us unknowingly but inexorably to our demise.

Sustainability, alas, is not enough. As Paul Hawken says in his book *The Ecology of Commerce*, "The dirty secret in environmentalism is that sustainability is an insufficient objective . . . we have also probably already passed the point where present planetary resources can be relied on to support the population of the next forty years. Any viable economic program must turn back the resource clock and devote itself actively to restoring damaged and deteriorating systems—restoration is far more compelling than the algebra of sustainability."[4] We may also have to turn back the population clock. The planet is expecting another 4 billion babies over the next thirty years. Somehow we've got to come to grips with overpopulation, which is probably *the* ultimate question facing humanity. Denis Hayes, of Seattle's Bullitt Foundation, has been an articulate spokesperson for population control and has proposed an international birthrate that would reduce world population within the next century.

We must rely on current income, that is, living efficiently within the ebb and flow of energy from the sun and plants. One of the keys to living within our current means is old fashioned Yankee ingenuity and frugality. Killing as many birds with as few stones as possible (I should probably say photographing as many birds with as little film as possible, but it doesn't ring as true) is the key to efficiency for me. That's why passive solar architecture had me totally in its thrall from the oil embargo of 1972 until I moved to cloudy Seattle in 1985. Passive solar heating, cooling, and lighting are a holistic, natural way to go about tempering the daily and seasonal cycles of climate. Unlike active solar systems, they are integrated into the architecture rather than added on. The Trombe Wall that I lived behind for a decade supports the roof as well as heats the rooms. The only moving parts in the system are the sun and the occupants. Its primitive yet elegant simplicity encourages straightforward architecture and living.

Another contemporary example of multivalent, efficient design is the greenway. These riparian corridors and their flood plains can fulfill many goals simultaneously. They can act as a city edge; provide community recreation and amenity with walkways, bikeways, parkways, outdoor rooms, and views; serve as wildlife habitat corridors and detention and retention ponds for controlling floods; work as filtration systems for polluted runoff; and be a source of water, beauty, and rejuvenation.[5] A last example of this synergy is the alley with garage apartment. Simultaneously, it provides affordable housing for a tenant, a second-income stream for the owner, enclosed parking for both party's vehicles, alley surveillance, a corridor for utilities and garbage pick-up, and a place to work and play. It is this kind of thinking and designing that to me is savvy, exciting, *and* sustainable.

The third bedrock issue is *order*. Certainly a major role, perhaps the major role, of human beings in the universe is helping to bring order and meaning to it. As entropy runs down and exhausts the physical universe, is there an equal and opposite life force creating order? And if so, is it a metaphysical, spiritual order that humans contribute to or even are entrusted with? Or is it simply a physical order? And is it something discovered or created? Although these questions are unanswerable, they give us enough pause to realize that humankind and other intelligent life may be collectively playing a critical role in the cosmos. If this is the case, we need to do our job of bringing order to the world, just as billions of other organisms are faithfully and flawlessly doing their jobs. They are, after all, constantly toiling, if not exactly on our behalf, at least to our benefit—whether it be through photosynthesis or eating our garbage. Nobody does more with less than nature, and its sublime efficiency seems to be a sustained one. We could not ask for a better model for ordering architecture and engineering, urban design, and city planning. Inherent in this discovery and creation of order is meaning. Human beings seem set on finding out not only what makes things work but why they work and why it should matter. They are forever looking for questions as well as answers, in what appears to be an endless spiritual quest for the meaning in life and of life.

Although cities are inherently messy and chronically unfinished, bringing order to them is clearly a big part of bringing order to our world. They are about to be where most of our species dwell. After thousands of years of a world population that was almost exclusively rural and only hundreds of years of one that was predominantly rural, the majority of the peoples of the world will live in urban areas early next century. The United Nations predicts that by 2025 our species will be over 60 percent urban.[6] At this historic moment in civilization—the urban/rural equinox—it behooves us to better understand, plan, design, and build cities.

Sometimes urban order is enhanced in single, giant steps, but usually it comes slowly and after many trials and errors. A city needs both many little moves and a few big ideas. It can't be all organic or all monumental. Seattle, like many gridiron cities, started out with an overarching pattern, but has been fleshed out (with a few exceptions like the University of Washington campus and the Olmsted Plan) in small, organic steps. This organic urbanism is the appropriate mode of development in our political economy, but it can be enhanced by having key centers, districts, corridors, axes, and edges more intentionally designed. This book is about bringing greater order to key places.

Gradual reformation is sometimes more difficult to bring about than quick or cataclysmic revolution. Like building maintenance, it is less exciting and creative than building anew. Incremental change, whether social or physical, is, however, often more lasting than radical or revolutionary change. It is usually the appropriate mode of improvement in a society that is more right than wrong, which is on balance what I believe to be the case in most parts of America and in Seattle. It also seems the correct stance in a city, especially its residential neighborhoods. Contrary to design and planning theory that prevailed for much of this century, where people make their home is not the place for avant-garde or radical experiments. Dwelling is an essentially conservative act and neighborhood is an essentially fragile condition. As long as they are more good than bad, more hopeful than hopeless, both need to be guarded jealously and changed carefully.

I suppose there are other bedrock values that I am omitting. Certainly liberty or freedom is sacred to my position—so sacred that I will let it pass without elaboration. Equality is also so very basic to any American's inherited values that it scarcely needs mention. However, I think it is perhaps the most elusive of these values. It is not so difficult to assure everyone of equality in the eyes of the law. But to assure egalitarian status in the eyes of other people is a very ambitious ideal. Human beings seem very canny and persistent about reasserting their individual or group superiority. Egalitarianism is also more abstract than community, sustainability, order, and liberty, and if history is any measure, it seems the hardest value to realize. Maintaining true political and social equality takes constant vigilance.

These are all consciously taught and learned values. There are also the less consciously transferred values that we inherit from our families, before society gets a chance to temper them. For me, the Calvinist respect for industry, thrift, and moderation has come down from my parents and grandparents as surely as it has unconsciously. Honesty and fair play are essential to this view of life, because commerce won't sustain itself without trust in the marketplace and honesty in government.[7] Frugality and economy are bodily reflexes for many Protestants. Comfort is fine; but downright luxury and profligacy are not.

ABOUT THE BOOK

There is a growing group of design and planning professionals and environmentalists and a surprisingly large number of government officials and developers who are increasingly pointed and unanimous in their critique of the contemporary metropolis. People drawn from this group have helped organize and have participated in design charrettes. Some have a long history of community activism and reform-minded design. Many design team leaders addressed community design in the 1960s, energy in the '70s and regionalism in the '80s. They have added urban design and town planning to their focus during the '90s. During the last three decades this group has gone full circle. They have taken on a widening and concentric ring of concerns. It has been a fast ride for the generation that came of age in the Vietnam era: the sixties' anti-war and civil rights militancy replaced the complacency of the

Eisenhower decade; the seventies' energy, preservation, and environmental movements overtook the civil rights movement; the eighties' softening of energy prices and boom mentality pulled the rug out from under the energy movement and added impetus to the consumptive lifestyle, while female and gay rights came to the foreground; and the nineties' credit-card hangovers and government deficits brought on downsizing in first the private and then the public sector, while underscoring the costs of suburbia and the disinvestment in our inner cities.

Is this an upper middle class, liberal movement? The urban poor have long experienced the economic, social, and environmental problems that now beset the suburbs. Why, they rightfully ask, have suburbanites waited so long to raise a hue and cry? Before suburbia was visited by decaying infrastructure, noise, crime, gridlock, and low-paying jobs, there was little upper middle class concern for these issues. The lower classes have an undeniable case that should strike humility into the hearts of suburbanites, who come lately to crime control, traffic calming, noise abatement, job development, etc. These are old problems for the urban poor and working class. These underclasses should not be further ignored because the political muscle and investment have shifted to the suburbs. This confluence of interests offers an historic opportunity. Now that different classes have more problems in common, there is an opportunity to build broader coalitions and more community solidarity. There is more of a feeling that everyone is in this dilemma together. Although there is still an unfinished agenda for social justice, the clicking environmental clock and population time bomb have brought a new urgency to working together.

At this moment in American history, design professionals have a particularly compelling message. Physical design has been left out of the policy and political debate so long that designers are becoming more vocal and assertive. In Seattle, the growing chorus of voices for reform includes not only design professionals but government officials, university faculty and students, environmental groups, community groups, and some developers. The legislative and executive branches of state, county, and municipal government have been particularly active in growth management. Any state that can enact a Growth Management Act as ambitious as Washington's, any region that can produce a study as compelling as Vision 2020, and any city that can produce a Comprehensive Plan as progressive as Seattle's is serious about visionary change.

THE DESIGN CHARRETTE

"Charrette" is a French word meaning wagon, used by architecture students at the old Ecôle des Beaux Arts in Paris. Students worked round the clock to a deadline, even to the point of running after and jumping on the wagon that was dispatched by the professor to the student quarter to pick up their drawings. To be *en charrette* was to draw to the very last moment. The word has been revived in recent years to describe a design workshop in which designers work intensively on a problem and present their findings and proposals in a public forum. In the early years of the University of Washington charrettes, I had to explain the word to almost everyone, including design professionals. Now it is a popular word in Seattle, overworked and becoming diluted. Sometimes it is applied to any design meeting of over four hours!

What exactly is a design charrette? The short answer is that it is an illustrated brainstorm. The long answer that has emerged at the University of Washington is that it is a five-day intensive workshop in which competing teams of advanced students led by design professionals develop different design solutions for the same project and present them at a public review. The design professionals and students represent the architecture, landscape architecture, urban design, and planning disciplines of the College of Architecture and Urban Planning. The charrette typically deals with an urban design issue of social and civic importance. There are three basic types: ones that test new public policies or design ideas on real sites, ones that respond to requests for help from neighborhood groups or government agencies, and ones that explore a particularly glaring problem or opportunity presented by a specific site. Some charrettes are hybrids, for example, testing a new idea on a site that is underutilized. They are meant to advance feasible but creative solutions to issues for real clients and users, as opposed to being a theoretical or pedagogic exercise for the sake of faculty or students.

Befitting a public university, the UW charrettes have always served a public agency, organization, or institution and resisted requests from private parties. The projects are usually sited in the Seattle region, although two have been in Italy. The sites are often open or underutilized areas from five to five hundred acres in size, where there is room to exercise a full range of design imagination and creativity and there is less political and physical complexity than in the midst of an existing neighborhood. These brainstorms have consistently generated imaginative ideas and proposals that conventional design consulting would be unlikely to produce.

Each charrette produces drawings and slides of four design solutions, a booklet delineating the project, and publicity for the project, including a public presentation attended by hundreds of citizens and officials. The public presentation is sometimes on campus and sometimes on or near the site, depending on location and sponsorship. There are always follow-up presentations to community groups. The charrettes are published and aired widely by the local media. Sometimes they precipitate the commissioning of consultant studies and/or actual projects. But mostly charrettes generate and illustrate visions for the public and provide a large gene pool of ideas for discussion and dissemination.

Public and private funds have been generously contributed to underwrite these workshops, which have cost as little as $5,000 and as much as $50,000 to organize, conduct, and document. Typically, four to eight guest design professionals are brought to campus to lead four teams. The UW's contribution is administration, support staff, research assistants, and use of the facilities. In addition, several faculty and some fifty students donate the first week of the Spring Quarter to the charrette. See Appendix A for details on how actually to organize and execute a design charrette.

Perhaps the best way to further introduce the complex mix of material covered in this book is to answer the questions of where the charrettes took place, when, and why.

Where?

The book is about the Seattle region, although many of its ideas should be transferable to other regions. It is a good place for these efforts because it still holds out the possibility of a livable and sustainable metropolis. It is still early enough to avoid some of the disastrous modes of development that have been the ruin of many an American city and region. As Lester Brown, president of the Worldwatch Institute, declares, "the Pacific Northwest is the proving ground for sustainability—human progress that does not harm the earth."[8]

The Seattle region covers a large area. It stretches 100 driving miles from Olympia in the south to Arlington in the north and 50 highway and ferry miles from North Bend in the east to Bremerton in the west. It is broken up by hills and water, which generally have a north-south grain. This topography makes for difficult east-west travel and for a linear, north-south conurbation. Whether Tacoma and Olympia are included or whether they have a separate identity is always a question. The U.S. Census Bureau puts them in the same CMSA (Consolidated Metropolitan Statistical Area) as Seattle, but historically they are large and distinct enough to want mention in the region's placename (or at least to keep Seattle's name from being the sole namesake). "Puget Sound Region" or "Puget Sound Basin" (but not "Pugetopolis," please) could be used as an umbrella term, but it is not the way the area is known nationally or internationally. Nor is "Seattle-Tacoma" or "Sea-Tac" very satisfying phonetically or demographically (given the difference in economic clout, cultural activity, and population). On the other hand, the City of Seattle currently represents less than 20 percent of the region's population and may eventually dwindle to as little as 10 percent. This lopsided situation already prevails in Boston and Pittsburgh, two of America's other most livable regions that are known by the name of their central city. A region needs a clear identity. The "Seattle Region" seems the briefest, best name.

The Seattle Region is an almost perfect place to practice regionalism. It is large in area, but not so large as to feel endless or boundless. It is large and diverse in population, with 3.3 million people already in the Seattle-Tacoma-Bremerton CMSA. The six counties (King, Pierce, Snohomish, Thurston, Kitsap, and Island) in the CMSA will reach toward 5 million within the next generation or so. This is large enough to support high quality civic, cultural, medical, and educational institutions, as well as professional sports, outstanding ballet, opera, symphony, theater, modern dance, public art, art museums, art galleries, antique and craft galleries, bookstores, and restaurants. But it is not so large or polyglot as to be overpowering and bewildering.

Importantly, there is the international trade to keep this culture cross-pollinated and flourishing. The successful ports of Tacoma and Seattle (which should merge rather than compete) continue the long trading tradition of the region. They are well positioned and respected in the world of maritime and aviation commerce as we enter the Asian Century, which is sure to be played out in increasing measure around the vast ocean rim on which Seattle is strategically perched.

There is also the strong economic base to keep culture nourished. Boeing, Weyerhaeuser, and Microsoft are only the biggest and bluest chips in a growing array of companies headquartered in the region. Seattle is fortunate to have a particularly large number of small companies. Of the 28 major league baseball cities, Seattle has the second fewest number of companies with 500 or more employees.[9] Software, medical research, biotechnology, microbrewing, coffee-roasting, bread-baking, movie-making, and clothing companies are some of the small, new economic engines pulling the region toward economic and cultural diversity and strength. Some of these engines, such as the software and biomedical ones, are no longer small or regional but are national and international players. Even Seattle brewers, bakers, and baristas are going national. Replacing imports and generating exports are a healthy sign for a region's economic base (although at the expense of some other region).[10] It will tend to raise the whole tide of prosperity. It has also made many young millionaires, some of whom seem to be developing the philanthropic ethic that historically has tended to be relatively anemic in this region.

On top of these and other assets, there are the natural wonders and the ecological riches of the area. There are three national parks close at hand. The pristine water, mountains, and vast wilderness constitute a healthy ecosystem and provide recreation, regeneration, and beauty. We must be careful not to let companies (or owners of professional sports teams) that start or move here mine these riches—just like they used to mine coal, cut timber, or deplete fisheries—and then move on to greener pastures. Local lifestyle and amenity may be exploited by corporations in the twenty-first century as natural resources were in the twentieth.

The vast and beautiful natural areas clearly separate our metropolitan area from other regions. Portland, Seattle, and Vancouver are happily distanced so as not to merge and blur as the Boston to Washington megalopolis on the East Coast does. They are part of the bioclimatic region that stretches from Northern California to British Columbia and from the Pacific Ocean to the Rocky Mountains. Yet, the Cascadia region (or Georgia Basin, if you're from British Columbia) is clearly separated by mountains and a great distance from the Inland Empire to the east and California to the south. Our common geographic and natural fortune should be more consciously linked, as many Vancouverites, Seattleites, and Portlandians have been aggressively promoting.

These charrettes attempt to fill in some of the holes and take advantage of some of the opportunities in the Seattle metropolitan area. Each site and program was carefully chosen, although the availability of funds sometimes determined the particular year a topic would be picked. The criteria varied from time to time but there were several that were nonnegotiable: the charrette had to deal with a problem of significant enough size and scope to warrant the use of so many designers and resources; the location and topic had to make sense in environmental and regional planning terms; and the sponsors had to be not-for-profit. If it answered an urgent need or jumped on a promising opportunity, so much the better. If the charrette was likely to influence the course of actual development, better yet. Outside funding was also a prerequisite. In the early years, willing sponsors were harder to find than in later years, when interested communities and agencies sometimes competed to be selected for a University of Washington charrette.

The charrettes have run the gamut. They have suggested development where there is a hole in the fabric (the Kingdome charrette), where there are underutilized and underpopulated areas (the Lacey Studio and the Seattle Commons, Sand Point, Winslow, and University District charrettes), and empty land where entirely new or different opportunities may exist (Interbay and New Communities charrettes). As more charrettes were convened, it slowly became clear that there were varying types of target areas that needed different interventions. It also became clear that there was an essential difference between an infill strategy and the clearance/urban renewal strategy of the previous generation. The resulting typology is specific to the Seattle Region, but it is probably also generic to other American metropolitan areas. Its five-part classification forms the structure of Part II of the book:

1. **City Center**, the Central Business District or downtown of a city, e.g., Seattle, Tacoma, Bellevue, Bremerton, or Everett. There are two charrettes on downtown sites presented in Part II.
2. **Urban Neighborhood**, e.g., Seattle's Capitol Hill, Columbia City, Ballard; Tacoma's North End, Hilltop, etc. In many cases, these were once streetcar suburbs, a.k.a. first-ring suburbs. Over the decades a countless num-

ber of the University of Washington's design studios have studied problems and opportunities in these neighborhoods, especially their commercial centers. One charrette and related studio about the University District is included in Part II.

3. **Suburb**, from Lacey to Lynnwood, Silverdale to Sammamish. One charrette and two studios on the suburbs are documented in Part II. (*The Pedestrian Pocket Book*, edited by the author and published by Princeton Architectural Press in 1989, discusses another University of Washington charrette and illustrates the Pedestrian Pocket suburban infill strategy in great detail.)

4. **Small Town**, such as Monroe, Auburn, and Steilacoom. These are formerly rural towns that now find themselves within the orbit of the metropolitan region. The small town charrette focuses on Winslow, the commercial center of Bainbridge Island. (Towns in rural areas outside the metropolitan region do not fall within the scope of this book. See the work of Randall Arendt, Robert Yaro, William Morrish, and Catherine Brown for guidance in rural and small town development.)

5. **New Town**, e.g., Mill Creek, Northwest Landing, and other proposed stand-alone communities that are too large or too remote to be considered infill. More idealized than infill development, new towns are often built on greenfield sites as satellites of the city beyond the urbanized area. However, they can be built on large sites in the city, sometimes called a new-town-in-town. There are two charrettes and one studio on new towns covered in Part II. One site is near downtown Seattle and one beyond its urban growth boundary.

Although there are other ways to slice the metropolitan project (simply urban, suburban, and exurban, for example), a decade of charrettes and studios has suggested this structure as the most helpful in understanding, designing, and planning this region. Because the contemporary metropolis in North America does not vary that significantly, this taxonomy may obtain in most of them. In any case, it must be interpreted for specific locales.

When?

The University of Washington design charrettes started in 1985. (Teams led by Joseph Esherick, Henning Larson, and Lucien Kroll explored housing for the homeless, but a lack of surviving documentation has precluded this early charrette's inclusion in the book.) Since then there has been a charrette the first week of every Spring Quarter, plus an extra one during the summer of 1987 in Civita di Bagnoregio, Italy. All are included in Part II of this book, with the exception of the 1986 and 1987 charrettes in Italy, the 1988 Pedestrian Pocket charrette, and the 1989 Public Restroom in Downtown Seattle charrette.

The planning horizon for the various charrettes is typically twenty to thirty years. The appropriate time to act on proposed designs varies, from immediately to soon to eventually. The five suggested types of development are already happening around the country. Downtown infill and redevelopment (once known as urban renewal and model cities) have been around since World War II, although usually for the worse. Urban neighborhood infill is happening unevenly and continually, especially in neighborhood commercial zones. The proposed forms of suburban infill and redevelopment are now being built in such places as Laguna West outside Sacramento, Kentlands outside Washington, D.C., Harbor Town in Memphis, and Northwest Landing next to DuPont, Washington. There has been very little suburban redevelopment, where existing subdivisions, shopping malls, or office parks are actually torn down and reconfigured as a new generation of denser development. Small town infill and redevelopment go on all the time, but often in accidental ways. New Town, an old and frequently utopian American tradition, has had a spotty track record in this country compared to Europe since World War II. Nonetheless, it now has a renewed role to play in the realization of the metropolitan project.

Why?

The reason for compiling these charrettes in a book is the same reason they were held in the first place: the planning efforts for a region need the benefit of creative physical design in their formative stages. Neighborhoods, towns, cities, and regions should not be planned, or even zoned for that matter, by abstract policies and nonvisual formulae drafted by lawyers, lawmakers, and bureaucrats without the help of design professionals. Such methods have led to zoning codes as thick as the local telephone book. Among other flaws, these codes inadvertently prohibit building a traditional town or neighborhood. To build anything resembling "Main Street" or "Elm Street" in many American municipalities is actually now against the law!

Planning a region should not be done *ex novo*; it is an interactive process that involves illustrating and testing proposed policies and laws in three dimensions before they are adopted. It is not only a question of designers and planners validating policies and laws; it is also very much a question of design *formulating* policy. Design is more than a service to be bought by the pound or the hour and plugged in at the appropriate time in a problem-solving process. It is too powerfully integrative and formulative to be withheld until all the policy and programming are in place.

CHARRETTE'S SYNDROME

Design charrettes can brainstorm a problem in a way that can liberate latent and inevitable possibilities. They can reveal what a project's site and program want to be, as well as illustrate what special interest groups and stakeholders desire. Because design charrettes look at problems holistically, their results are less likely to fall prey to specialized thinking and political tinkering. They kill many birds with one stone: they help the community solve problems and build consensus; they test new ideas and policies that are generated within the community, the design professions, or the university; they seize on forgotten places and nascent opportunities; they build the community's understanding of itself; in the case of university-sponsored charrettes, they bring to town and campus leading designers who would otherwise be unaffordable, and they stimulate and bring together faculty and students while putting to good use university resources and expertise.

Design charrettes can be hosted by community groups, universities, or other institutions. Universities and their schools of architecture and planning are peculiarly well suited for charrettes because of their studio facilities and legions of students. Design and planning students can also participate in charrettes organized by off-campus groups, as happened in the Winslow charrette. In any case, charrettes are not academic exercises. They directly engage reality—real sites, real neighborhoods, real time, and real constraints. They can bring the best local and national brains and talent to these engagements.

Charrettes are productive because the designers are captive. There are large multidisciplinary teams in place for days with the expertise and judgment available to make the long chain of decisions that constitutes design. The deadline insures that decisions will not be postponed, as they tend to be in normal design work while awaiting input from other parties. In an ideal charrette, all the parties are there. Perhaps they are even convened on the actual site in question. Almost without exception, the teams accomplish a remarkable amount of work in a remarkably short period. True, a charrette is short-lived, episodic, and sometimes subject to fatal wrong turns or truncated thinking forced by a clock that ticks much faster than normal. And community involvement is sometimes a logistical challenge. This is especially true when vacant or underutilized sites are studied, because they lack a strong or clear neighborhood constituency. In other cases, community representatives have joined the design teams.

The chemistry of both collaboration with teammates and competition between teams always seems to unleash ideas that would otherwise remain overlooked in slower paced, more linear design methods. The confusion of a charrette—at times rife—can give rise to fertile creativity. The workshops generate many bad ideas along with many good ones. The results of this compressed and febrile creativity must be widely and carefully reviewed. Charrettes, by their very nature, tend to encourage a no-holds-barred approach. Because they focus hard on a single place and want to make sure all the cards are played, design teams are sometimes loath to leave out any promising ideas. They assume that the charrette represents a given project's moment in the spotlight. As a consequence, many ideas must be edited or discarded; the surviving ones need to be reworked and refined. This book is an invitation to that ongoing process.

There is a deeper worry that underlies the charrettes and the book: a fundamental dissatisfaction and alarm with the direction that metropolitan development has taken in recent decades. It has degraded the natural environment and diminished the human community. While the citizenry may disagree on what constitutes salvation and what is possible for the future, there is a growing understanding that we cannot continue to spread ourselves endlessly across the countryside, to live by and for our automobiles, to produce tons of waste and pollutants for every man, woman, and child. We are sucking the planet dry of energy and resources, and letting our established communities wither. There is, however, a fundamental optimism radiated by the charrettes. The whole project is predicated on the belief that the right land use, the right transportation, the right design at the right scale at the right time will go a long way toward solving society's problems.

Since the charrettes began, the stakes got much higher when the U.S. Census Bureau estimated that more people will move to Washington State than to forty-seven other states between 1995 and 2020. Only Texas and Florida, both considerably larger in population and buildable area, are predicted to have more in-migration. Some pundits predict that this region will be *the* fastest growing area in the country—an exhilarating but potentially devastating trajectory. This population boom, even if less than estimated, will have enormous effects on the Seattle region, which will be its epicenter. We must act thoughtfully and decisively, or life will be far more degraded than enhanced by this rapid growth. There are some difficult trade-offs ahead and our choices are not going to please everyone. Even if most citizens are against sprawl, they are also against density—leaving society at one of those arterial traffic ligts in suburbia, where turning left takes forever and continuing straight leads to more nowhere.

PART I   THEORY

"What! No theory?
That's like an organism without a head!"

—Claus Seligman, UW Professor of Architecture, at a faculty meeting

CHAPTER 1

Paved with Good Intentions
Suburbia and the Costs of Sprawl

"The influence of the . . . car and the new . . . highways is reflected in the decline of so many of the old communal centers . . . the cities of the region are rapidly growing together."—Roderick McKenzie, a sociologist describing the Puget Sound region in 1929

We are a culture of production and consumption. We produce and consume so much because we borrow so much. We borrow from the past when we burn fossil fuels and clear cut ancient forests. We borrow from the present when we overfertilize the land and overfish the oceans. And we borrow from the future when we bequeath government deficits and chemical toxins to our children. Put less gently, we are robbers: by plundering the planet's savings account and squandering its income, we rob future generations of a good and decent life and maybe of life itself.

THE FIRST TO SPRAWL

No phenomenon embodies and sponsors our predicament more than suburban sprawl does at this point in our history. Only recently have cities begun to sprawl.

Since the first cities of the ancient Near East, cities have existed to define a center. The Egyptian hieroglyph for the city was a cross inscribed in a circle—the idea of a crossroads or center combined with that of a defined border. In Hellenistic and Roman times the very form of the classical city expressed the idea of a center around which a hinterland was organized; later, the Renaissance used the techniques of linear perspective along great boulevards to reinforce the meaning and dominance of the core. . . . The coming of the global trading city and the 19th-century industrial city did not contradict but reinforced the desire to create classical urban space at least at the city's core.[1]

The United States is the first nation to distribute its metropolitan populations at extremely low densities across the countryside, to achieve that unlikely mix of both sprawl and congestion. The American metropolis is far less dense than its counterparts in Europe, Asia, and other parts of the world— about a third as dense as metropolitan Paris and a thirtieth as dense as metropolitan Hong Kong! And it is getting less dense every year.

Why are we the first suburban culture in history, with more people residing in the suburbs than in the city or country? An underlying reason for spreading out is the historical propensity of Americans to depend on expansion, growth, and the new start as a way to solve difficult problems. Westward expansion across a vast continent provided a giant safety valve. Abundant natural resources supplied inexpensive building materials. Compared to other cultures, Americans opted for bigness over quality—big houses with big rooms, quickly constructed on big parcels of land. They also opted for newness, perpetually starting over again, rather than sticking it out in the old place and reworking it until they got it right. Waste, largeness, obsolescence, and impermanence were not worrisome. There was plenty of room and resources; and no reason to crowd together in small dwellings in tightly packed communities.

Our agrarian roots and pioneer spirit held the promise of generous acreage and commodious homes. There were no compelling reasons for permanence, frugality, or sustainable practices. In fact, there were social and political pressures to be free of these restraints and shed the tight and oppressive European or Asian models of dwelling and community from which many of our forebears emigrated or escaped.

Another factor in the American way of life is physical mobility. The typical household now moves more frequently than it votes for president or watches the summer Olympics. This transience has deterred the investment in housing of more permanent construction, which is less expensive in the long run than shorter-lived buildings. This mobility is amplified by the easy ownership of automobiles and the vast highway and interstate system. Both have made it more convenient and attractive to move to and commute to pastures that are presumably greener. Moving is not the physical ordeal today that it once was when, for instance, the farmhands migrated westward in the 1930s, so vividly depicted in *The Grapes of Wrath*. Whether for executives being shuffled around by national corporations or for migrant workers, modern vehicles and highways have made migration much easier—with an inevitable dissipation in the sense of community.

An underlying reason for spreading out is the historical propensity of Americans to depend on expansion, growth, and the new start as a way to solve difficult problems.

Public Enemy No. 1: Cheap Land

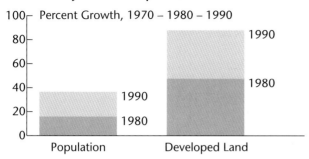

Percent Growth, 1970 – 1980 – 1990

Public Enemy No. 2: Cheap Gasoline

Percent Growth, 1970 – 1990

Like most American metropolitan areas, land in the Seattle region is being developed much faster than population is growing, meaning that our pattern of settlement is getting even less dense. On the other hand, Portland expects a 77 percent increase in population but only a 6 percent increase in land area between 1990 and 2040—thanks to its urban growth boundary.

The number of vehicles owned and the miles we drive them are increasing more than twice as fast as population in the Seattle region and many other metropolitan regions. Until gasoline is properly priced in America, this unsustainable trend will continue.

Charts published by Puget Sound Regional Council, Washington State Institute for Public Policy, Jan., 1990.

Automobiles and automobility are by now deeply rooted in American culture. There is now one motor vehicle for every licensed driver, nearly twice as many per capita as a generation ago. Cars and trucks are a major part of our modern folklore, mythology, movies (e.g., *American Graffiti, Hud, Batman, Road Warrior*), art world (Cadillac Ranch, the Fremont Troll), music (The Beach Boys, Don McLean), sports world (Indy racing, stockcar racing, drag racing), entertainment world (demolition derby, monster trucks), styling world (car shows), and media (TV and magazine advertising, Click 'n Clack). They are also fundamental to our economy, providing many jobs in designing, manufacturing, repairing, servicing, and fueling cars—not to mention the need for roads and bridges, police, insurance, etc. Automobiles are objects of desire as well as of mobility and represent some of the more beautiful and refined industrial designs of the century. Their bodies, grilles, headlights, and tailfins titillate us everywhere we go.

Automobile names "are the single largest set of discriminated nouns in English. . . . The typical 26-year-old American man can name 12 to 20 colors, maybe 15 fruits, but he can name 60 or 70 cars and tell you something about most of them."[2] Americans also put a lot of money where their mouths are. Young people spend 4 billion dollars a year customizing their cars, not to mention what they spend to buy them in the first place. We are not going to exorcise automobiles from our culture in the foreseeable future. Nor do we have to. We can, however, tame these metallic monsters and return them to an expeditious and pleasurable mode of travel, rather than the addictive answer to our restlessness.

Our national restlessness seems to go hand in hand with the local traffic we have come to expect daily on our crowded roads. Gone is the sheer joy of driving—the exhilaration of acceleration and the wind-in-the-hair, heart-in-the-mouth thrill of moving effortlessly and fast along an open highway. Life on the run has become the norm, and the transportation network is overloaded. Gridlock is no longer just a rush-hour phenomenon. It occurs much of the time in much of the metropolis here and abroad. "In the 1950s a similar situation faced two other cities, Tokyo and Seoul. Tokyo opted for a mass transportation system which today is respected the world over. Seoul went for more roads; today the city has twenty-eight lane highways and traffic jams that would impress even a Manhattan taxi driver."[3]

Not long ago the Southern California Association of Governments, including some thirty municipalities around Los Angeles, commissioned a computer simulation of traffic in the year 2010. It modeled many possibilities, among them, double-decking highways, additional lanes, expanded bus and rail transit service, and staggered work hours. They concluded that nothing that could be done to add capacity to the system would have a lasting effect on congestion—except for one strategy that was not a transportation fix per se. Mixed-use neighborhoods, because they eliminate the need for trips in the first place, were found to offer a permanent solution to traffic congestion!

American metropolises have managed to do the impossible: to sprawl at very low densities *and* choke themselves with traffic congestion at the same time. If we are going to make metropolitan areas that are more livable, more affordable, and more sustainable, we need new paradigms and mixed-use models that do not perpetuate sprawl and that recognize its economic, social, and environmental costs. Peter Calthorpe and Henry Richmond have succinctly summed up the situation:

> Unrestrained sprawl around our cities is generating profound environmental stress, intractable traffic congestion, a dearth of affordable housing, loss of irreplaceable open space, disinvestment in our inner cities, and life-styles which burden working families and isolate elderly and singles. We are using land planning strategies which are 40 years old and no longer relevant or affordable to today's culture. We are still building World War II suburbs as if families were large and had only one breadwinner, as if jobs were all downtown, as if land and energy were endless and as if another lane on the freeway would end traffic congestion. It is time to overhaul the American dream, returning to the values and patterns of our traditional towns—diversity, community, frugality, and human scale. We must move back from cul de sac subdivisions to elm street neighborhoods, from drive-through commercial strips to main street communities, quite simply from segregated sprawl to places more like traditional American towns.[4]

A PRIMER ON COSTS

Some thoughts on the nature and definition of costs may be helpful before tallying the costs of sprawl. There are two important distinctions to be made for the purposes of this book. First, there is the distinction between *public* costs and *private* costs. Public costs, a.k.a. social costs, are the ones borne by all of society, or at least by a large group or class within it. These costs are exacted primarily through government taxation or through collective sacrifice or loss. Private costs are the ones paid in the market by individuals for goods and services.

There is also the distinction between *cost* and *price*. Price is the numerical value affixed to goods and services by the market. It is driven by supply and demand, although often modified by taxes or subsidies. Cost, sometimes referred to as true cost, is the fully reckoned cost of providing goods or services. It includes both direct and indirect costs. Direct costs include expenditures by the supplier for items such as design, supplies, raw material, manufacturing, packaging, transportation, advertising, sales, transaction fees, and profit. Indirect costs include environmental and social costs or subsidies that are not reflected in the price. They are often called externalities, a term that also can refer to either costs or benefits that accrue to a third party. External costs refer to measurable costs, such as environmental clean-up or disposal costs, and to less quantifiable costs or losses, such as degradation of the quality of life; loss of comfort, convenience, or time through congestion, crime, or negligence; or outright loss of life. These externalities are borne by individuals or society or both.

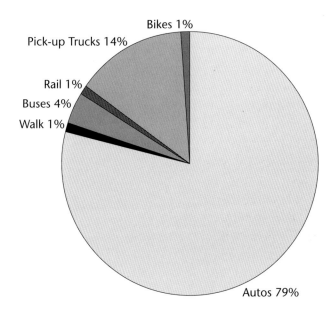

Pick-up Trucks 14%
Bikes 1%
Rail 1%
Buses 4%
Walk 1%
Autos 79%

"The price of private vehicle travel in the United States is very low. Private vehicle users do not pay directly for the pollution they generate or the congestion they impose on other travelers. Police and other emergency services, maintenance of local roads, and many other parts of the transportation system are supported indirectly by property and other taxes. Gasoline taxes, vehicle-registration fees, driver's license fees, and automobile taxes are lower here than anywhere in the developed world. Parking is offered free to most workers and shoppers. Given the extent of subsidies to private vehicle use, we should not be surprised that other forms of transportation cannot compete. . . ." (Genevieve Giuliano, "The Weakening of the Land Use/Transportation Connection," *On the Ground*, Summer, 1995, pp.13-14; pie chart, p. 4.)

However brilliant and quick the market may be at establishing price for a given transaction, it is not very good at determining cost including externalities. In a more perfect market, the true and total cost would be more accurately reflected in the price. A closer correlation between cost and price would serve to assign the costs for goods and services to the actual beneficiaries of those goods and services. Although there may be cases or times when society decides it is advantageous to favor or penalize a particular enterprise, sector of the market, or segment of the population, a society has a greater chance of equity and sustainability when market prices square with true costs. Without such accountability, society or an economic unit within it can make foolish decisions and transactions. This is one of the main reasons that the eastern block of European countries, whose centrally planned and managed economies failed to factor in environmental pollution, ruined vast reaches of their environment. Even if the pricing for small items is below cost, it can result in small environmental deficits that can accumulate into disastrous results. The everyday use of millions of underpriced aerosol cans, for example, has quickly helped to open a baldspot in the planet's ozone layer. Underpricing can result in false savings and deep risks.

Lastly, there are subsidies. These are attempts, usually by the public sector but also by the private sector (in the form of charitable contributions), to benefit a particular industry, institution, region, or segment of the population. This assistance can be through grants, services, or tax relief. Sometimes they are out in the open and well known (e.g., the National Endowments for the Arts and the Humanities or agricultural price supports) and sometimes they are hidden and hard to trace (e.g., the oil depletion allowance; defense contracts that aid corporate research and development; military commitments that benefit a particular foreign investment; reduced tuition at state universities). Government subsidies are often hidden because special interest groups have successfully lobbied for favorable policies, taxes, or tariffs that are too subtle, complex, or numerous for the average citizen to follow. Private gifts and grants are often publicly acknowledged, but they, too, are sometimes anonymous or secret for the sake of the donor and/or the recipient. Because subsidies, including many to suburbia, are often hard to understand and track, it is important that we account for them publicly.

THE ECONOMIC COSTS OF SPRAWL

Government subsidies have played a large role in promoting low-density suburban development. The federal income tax deduction for home mortgage interest payments has had a powerful impact on home ownership, raising it to among the world's highest rates—65 percent, almost double the turn-of-the-century rate. Seattle has one of the highest rates, if not *the* highest, in

The economic costs of highway construction are measured in millions of dollars per mile; the environmental costs are sometimes beyond measure.

the nation. However, this tax policy has tended to encourage the construction of detached single-family houses, most often in suburbs. This single tax provision costs the federal treasury an estimated $50 to $90 billion a year, making it in effect the broadest and most expensive welfare program in the U.S.A. Earlier this century, the federal government intervened after the Great Depression to bail out the banks that were financing suburban homes. Later, FHA loan guarantees made long-term and low-interest mortgages available to homebuyers, who were for the most part purchasing new homes in suburbia.

Another often cited subsidy is the federal road building program, which promoted automobile usage almost to the exclusion of rail transit. The interstate highways that radiate from and ring our central cities have made inexpensive land on the urban fringe suddenly accessible. It is estimated that revenues raised at the federal and state levels from vehicle use covers only 60 percent of the cost of building and maintaining roads and bridges.[5] Federal grants have allowed the extensive construction of sewers for suburbia. The federal policy that allows businesses to write off the expense of providing free parking to their employees, who don't have to declare it as income, is a growing subsidy. The post–World War II policy of federal, state, and many municipal governments to decentralize their own offices and facilities has also encouraged sprawl. American defense policy also spurred defense contractors to locate new plants outside the city centers. In general, the perceived threat of nuclear attack during the Cold War prompted federal policies that favored decentralization.

Some subsidies are less obvious. Federal energy subsidies such as the oil depletion allowance and support of nuclear and hydroelectric power are examples. They have helped provide the apparently cheap energy required for operating a typical suburban household—whether it be the oil, gas, or electricity to heat a large freestanding suburban house or the gasoline to power the ten automobile trips made per day by the typical suburban household. This incredible rate of automobile usage is perhaps the most damning of all suburban statistics. There are virtually no work or shopping trips taken by foot or by bus or rail in the suburbs, and there are few pedestrians on the sidewalks, should sidewalks exist. Work commutation to, from, and within suburbia is relatively cheap. Over time, the price of commuting has dropped dramatically. "Turn-of-the-century streetcar commuters spent about 20% of their daily wages on the work trip; urban auto commuters now spend about 7%."[6]

A subsidy of another kind is the profound cost paid by the American people in highway deaths and injuries. Automobiles are the leading cause of death among Americans aged fifteen to twenty-four.[7] Although the death rate per motor vehicle mile is way down (perhaps as much as eight times) since pre–WWI rates, the much greater number of miles driven has cancelled out

The biggest perpetuator of sprawl is zoning that segregates different land uses into large, single-use zones that are monocultures, i.e., all garden apartments, all single-family houses, all retail, all office. Large arterials separate these areas like rivers, impassable to pedestrians and often gridlocked for automobiles.

this prodigious achievement. Northwest Environment Watch's Alan Durning has made a very provocative argument in *The Car and the City* that, despite higher crime rates in the inner city, the suburbs are the more dangerous place to live. This is because sururbanites "drive three times as much, and twice as fast, as urban dwellers. All told, city dwellers are much safer."[8] Far more people are killed and injured in automobile accidents than by violent crime in this and other regions of the country.

Probably the least obvious government subsidy is that part of our defense budget used to maintain secure sources of oil. This indirect subsidy sometimes takes the form of war, as it did in the Persian Gulf, with its consequent loss of life and property. The defense of distant oil fields and shipping lanes is a high cost not paid at the gas pump. Durning's compelling book goes on to point out that our security interests in the Middle East added about $40 billion to our annual military budgets during the 1980s. All these energy subsidies result in massive income redistribution—from people who drive less to people who drive more, from city residents to suburban residents, and from poorer households to richer households.

The availability of cheap land and the subsidized roads, sewers, and utilities that serve it have probably been the biggest causes of the rise of *homo suburbus* and the suburban lifestyle and economy. Underpriced land has reduced the capital cost of the suburban home and underpriced fossil fuels have reduced the operating costs of suburban living. And the subsidized infrastructure has veiled the cost of low-density suburban zoning. Together, arti-

We are constructing three freestanding communities where we used to have a single, integrated one: a town.

ficially cheap land, infrastructure, and transportation have masked the costs of suburban housing. They have fooled us into thinking we can afford this wasteful pattern of settlement.

Because the home and the workplace are entirely separated from each other, often by a long auto trip, suburban living has grown to mean a complete, well-serviced, self-contained residential community, a complete, well-serviced place of work such as an office park, and a self-contained mall for shopping. In a sense, we are constructing three freestanding communities where we used to have a single, integrated one: a town. Three communities cost more than one; there is not only the duplication of infrastructure but often of services, institutions, and retail, not to mention a parking space or garage for every car as it shuttles from one community to the other.

As the cost of suburban development and the role of subsidies are becoming better understood, communities are forcing developers to pay impact fees or some equivalent assessment. These fees are for off-site improvements such as roads, sewers, and schools. They are usually passed on to the housing buyer or renter in the form of higher prices and rents. In a sense they are paid by the developer on behalf of the future residents, although there is also evidence that the farmers who sell the land to developers are being forced to absorb some of the impact fees by dropping their asking prices. This "concurrency" requirement that the developer pays up front for cost incurred by the development has not yet become fully accepted by the real estate development community. Many developers want to repeal or reduce impact fees and assessments.

Impact fees, however, are usually not high enough to cover the marginal costs of providing off-site infrastructure for new suburban developments. Researchers at Florida State University estimate that the true cost of sewer service alone to a new home ranges from $2,700 to $25,000—far higher at the upper end of the range than most impact fees, which are also meant to offset road, utility, school costs, etc. This means that new homes, which are usually purchased by more affluent households, are subsidized by poorer households. These studies also suggest that the premium for providing services to three-unit per acre sprawl located ten miles out is $48,000 per house, or twice that of a twelve-unit per acre development closer in.[9] Moreover, none of these figures reflects environmental costs and other economic externalities. The assignment of infrastructure costs to the developer shifts some of society's costs to the private sector, where additional capital must be raised. Developers take large risks and should be rewarded accordingly. However, they should not be allowed to socialize all the risks and privatize all the gains. Their profits, which can be obscenely high when cheap land is upzoned and developed, should be more heavily assessed when local governments absorb many of the costs and reduce many of the risks.

The ancient, ongoing shell game between the public and private sectors, between society and the individual, and between buyer and seller must be recognized as essentially a zero-sum game. While the shell game can be made more economically equitable among the players, it can never represent a net savings to society. Concurrency is part of a legitimate political and moral question of economic fairness—do those who benefit pay their fair share? It is also a question of economic feasibility. Suburban development is too expensive in absolute terms for the combined means of government and its citizens. Suburban sprawl is bankrupting local and state governments. The economy of sprawl also may be contributing in unrecognized ways to the federal deficit. Yet we continue to subsidize suburbia.

There is growing consensus that suburban land use and transportation patterns are not economically sustainable—at least not at their present scale and pace. This is not to say that suburbia or the automobile is destined to disappear. Suburban living may remain the preferred alternative for many. The option for citizens to live at lower densities can be maintained, but the full costs of such lifestyles should be more equitably distributed and more accurately reflected in higher purchase prices or rents. Suburban residents of the future should have to pay their way and not expect society to continue to shoulder the indirect costs.

For those who are willing and able to pay the higher premium to live in arcadia, more environmentally benign ways to dwell in single-family homes at lower densities must be developed. More sensitive ways to insert single-

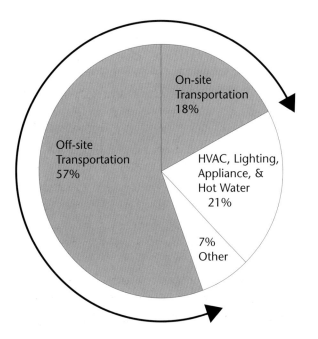

Transportation consumes more than three times as much energy as heating, lighting, and cooling buildings in a typical suburban community. More energy-efficient building stock is important but not as critical as reforming the transportation system. (National Association of Home Builders, *Planning for Housing*, 1980.)

family homes into rural settings without degrading the environment are also needed. First, homes can and should become smaller to reflect not only true construction and land costs but also shrinking households. (Between 1960 and 1990, American houses grew in area by 50 percent while household size shrunk from 3.4 to 2.7 persons.) Second, detached dwellings on large lots should utilize passive solar heating and cooling, as well as composting toilets, xeriscaping, organic gardening, green construction, and more efficient vehicles. Lastly, rural development should take care of open space, agriculture, habitat, wetlands, and other critical areas.

Not only is suburban sprawl expensive in and of itself, it usually adds to the economic woes of the inner city. Suburban investment is often matched by urban disinvestment. While this may be less true of Seattle, where the middle class flight from the city is less pronounced than in East Coast cities, there are increasing signs of withdrawal from the region's largest city. Tacoma is in deeper decline, as is Bremerton. Downtown Everett is not exactly booming. There is only so much money to go around and the older, central cities are hemorrhaging capital to their suburban fringes. This makes the economic cost of sprawl even higher: there is the savings foregone by leaving behind an underutilized physical and institutional infrastructure. It's not only the redundant schools and roads, sewers and utilities. Building new firehouses, libraries, police stations, and parks outside our cities when they are already in place in our urban neighborhoods is economically redundant.

THE ENVIRONMENTAL COSTS OF SPRAWL

Our continent has tolerated wasteful and rapacious American settlement patterns for several centuries. The land, air, and water have been vast enough to absorb our excesses and our wastes. Indeed, nature was once feared as the world of the heathen and even of the devil. Then it was something to be subjugated and tamed, first by farmers with their plows and then by engineers with their railroads, highways, bridges, canals, and dams. By the end of the twentieth century, we have gone from thinking of the wilderness as threatening and evil to thinking of it as threatened and sublime. We have taken short-sighted advantage of its forgiving size and abundance. We have liquidated our environmental trust fund in the currency of pleasure, convenience, profit, or environmental indifference and become the world's greatest polluters per person. We can no longer foul our planetary nest at the present rate; nor can we continue to live the environmental lifestyle to which we are accustomed.

"The United States is the world's largest polluter of the atmosphere, alone emitting nearly one fifth of the world's greenhouse gases annually (which means that we're contributing roughly four times our per capita share to global warming). . . . In the Northwest as in North America overall, our rapidly expanding automobile fleet is the largest greenhouse gas producer."[10] The other major cause of greenhouse pollution is the high vehicle miles traveled associated with sprawl. A week of 25-mile commutes to and from work plus weekend errands typically pumps 2 forty-pound sacks of carbon into the air shed. (A car that averages less than the national norm of 21.5 MPG adds even more carbon dioxide to the atmosphere through the tailpipe and through losses at the refinery.) Government policies have attempted to cut fuel consumption by increasing the fuel efficiency of cars and trucks rather than reducing sprawl. The new car fleet went from 13 MPG in 1973 to 29 MPG in 1989, but has since fallen. This improvement was impressive but was outstripped by the explosive growth in use of internal-combustion vehicles and was well below what was technically possible for Detroit. Ironically, the U.S. transportation sector may burn more and more fuel because of, not in spite of, improvements in fuel efficiency.

Air pollution is a symptom of sprawl that cannot be cured without treating the underlying malady. Despite more stringent tailpipe emission standards, traffic increases are predicted to make air pollutants even worse in the future. Traffic congestion not only increases the production of pollutants but it also wastes gasoline. Reducing highway congestion by building more metropolitan highways is self-defeating and ineffectual: they add to sprawl and generate more and longer trips. We must reduce the *need* for trips by mixed-use land planning. We also need planning that encourages ride-sharing and carpooling, which means mixed-use workplaces where passengers can reach lunchtime destinations by foot.

Most cars on the roads carry only one person; currently only 13 percent of commuters share a private vehicle, down from 20 percent in 1980.[11] We have so much extra room in our cars, it has been estimated that everyone in Western Europe could fit in them with us.[12] High Vehicle Miles Traveled is, after all, an index of economic and social dysfunction; it illustrates that people are not where they want or need to be and therefore must get in a car and drive.

Telecommuting from home by phone, fax, and computer can never replace face-to-face interaction. Nonetheless, it can provide significant relief to the congestion, fuel consumption, and air pollution that results from commuting. In some cases, employers are notifying their white collar employees that they will no longer provide an office. AT&T expects that "one half of its 123,000 managers will be telecommuting within five years. It is estimated that by the turn of the century, involuntary telecommuting could encompass over 30 million information workers."[13] Whether voluntary or not, bringing work back home to domestic space could ultimately build a greater sense of community. Having the breadwinner home with the bread-

High Vehicle Miles Traveled is, after all, an index of economic and social dysfunction; it illustrates that people are not where they want or need to be . . .

Carpooling is not a new urgency. During World War II it was thought to be a significant enough economic factor to mount a national campaign. Now we realize it is also a significant environmental factor, worthy of another campaign.

baker means more balanced neighborhoods. In some households, it could mean more and healthier family life.

Whether it be the preservation of clean air, open space, wetlands, wildlife habitat, clean water, or scenic views, environmental stewardship will cost us money—a great deal of money, as exemplified by the multibillion dollar bill to clean up toxic wastes. As stated earlier, our market economy efficiently determines price, but is notoriously weak in acknowledging hidden costs. It doesn't assign costs to intangible losses such as air pollution and oil spills. Clean-up costs are actually counted as "economic activity" and add to our GNP (as do health care costs and hospital stays!). When the costs of a clean environment are added to the direct and indirect economic costs of low-density development, sprawl becomes even less tenable. And there are many other well-known environmental pathologies of sprawl, such as a lowered water table, excessive stormwater run-off, and loss of agricultural land, that are beyond the scope of this book.

THE SOCIAL COSTS OF SPRAWL

The social costs of suburbia are the most elusive but also the most explosive. The flight of the middle class from city to suburb is a well-documented demographic shift in America. The census now counts half of the U.S.A.'s population as suburban, up from a third in 1960 and a quarter in 1950. Since the 1950s, racial tensions have caused the "white flight" to suburban communities, schools, and social institutions. Indeed, scholars such as Kenneth Jackson in his *The Crabgrass Frontier* argue that race may have been the major factor in this demographic shift, at least in the nation's large eastern cities. But now middle class African Americans, Latinos, and Asian Americans are moving in large numbers to the suburbs.

Racial tension notwithstanding, homebuyers often seek out like-minded neighbors and retreat into familiar and secure surroundings. "Sociologists take the rural-urban migration of the nineteenth century to be the result of economic compulsion, but the twentieth century exodus into the suburbs tends to be explained by the notion of a 'search for environment.'"[14] Anthony Downs of the Brookings Institute points out that "there is the temptation of the most successful Americans to 'secede' from the society of the majority, and especially of low-income households, by withdrawing into exclusive enclaves inhabited only by other economically prosperous people like themselves: this temptation is especially prevalent in suburban communities."[15]

Not only is this voluntary social withdrawal common in suburbia, there is often outright opposition to low-income and higher-density housing. There are several reasons, articulated again by Anthony Downs:

The first reason [for the opposition] is that most Americans do not want to live in neighborhoods with people poorer than themselves for social reasons. They want to establish and reinforce their own social and economic status by living with others whose socioeconomic levels are as good as or better than their own. Also, many Americans believe that poorer households have different values and behavior patterns—such as a greater propensity to commit crimes. And many whites associate poorer households with ethnic groups they dislike, such as blacks and Hispanics. That may not be ethical, but it is widespread.

As a result of this widespread view (plus our use of the trickle-down process to house the poor), we establish a definite social economic hierarchy of residential neighborhoods within every metropolitan area. This enables people of each socioeconomic level to live together, and it therefore benefits the vast majority—at least in their own eyes. It also compels the very poorest households to live together in extremely poor areas.

The poor are legally excluded from higher-income communities by local laws that deliberately raise housing costs there. This creates severe disadvantages for their life chances and those of their children. Hence it is a fundamentally unjust arrangement.

Wealthier residents also resist lower-income housing because they fear their property values will be reduced. Homeowners dominate suburban electorates, and their primary assets are their homes. In fact, homeowners want housing prices in their towns to rise, not fall, since that increases the value of their main assets. They believe letting lower-priced homes into their communities will reduce property values there.[16]

Household Composition in 1990

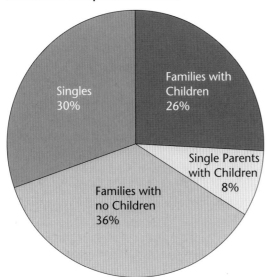

The housing market tends to overbuild for some household types and underbuild for others. This chart, based on U.S. Census Bureau figures, vividly illustrates one of the more surprising demographic shifts: the overwhelming number of households in America are *not* nuclear families with children—the families for whom suburbia was originally conceived. Barely one in four new households has two parents with children! Among *new* households formed in the 1980s, singles (and unrelated individuals) made up 51 percent, single parents with children were 22 percent and families with and without children were only 27 percent.

Living on cul-de-sacs in monocultural, gated subdivisions and communicating with telephone, fax, and computer may be more comfortable but is a long-term recipe for social disaster.

Rigid social hierarchy and exclusivity are exactly what many colonists and later immigrants sought to escape when they came to America. We would be better sustained if our communities were more mixed in socioeconomic, racial, and ethnic terms. It is better to take out our differences with our fellow citizens on a day-to-day basis in mixed communities, where we rub shoulders in a true public realm with everyone, including people we don't understand and don't like. Many small face-to-face encounters, however unpleasant, are better than infrequent but cataclysmic violence, whether it be mugging or civil insurrection. Living on cul-de-sacs in monocultural, gated subdivisions and communicating by telephone, fax, and computer may be more comfortable but is a long-term recipe for social disaster.

A recent market study found that 50 out of 50 of the most recent market rate projects in suburban New York City were gated.[17] This is an extreme case, but real estate agents speculate that a third of all new development in Southern California in the last five years has been gated and regulated by private covenants.[18] These private worlds are free from random encounters, encouraging not only social aloofness but an unwillingness to support public schools, parks, even roads. This kind of separation breeds ignorance and misunderstanding and builds tension. This tension, allowed to fester long enough, is likely ultimately to erupt in violence and confrontation. In more than a symbolic sense, the price of suburban insularity was the rioting in the inner city neighborhoods of Los Angeles.

Violent crime is not limited to the inner city. The most obvious signs of social malaise—youth violence and substance abuse—are becoming more widespread in suburbia. If adolescents are any measure of social health and if stable and cohesive communities generate less pathological behavior in youths, there is reason to believe there are problems brewing in the suburbs. "Nothing really local is left, and there is nothing to distinguish one town from the next. It is ironic to notice, as we sacrifice coherence and sense of place, that a major preoccupation of youth gangs is with marking territory, with defining their 'place.' . . . If we tour through large sections of the Lynnwoods, the Bellevues and the Federal Ways, we might well ask 'Why *wouldn't* a kid join a gang, growing up here?'"[19] Although suburbs do not in and of themselves cause gangs and youth violence, their lack of physical coherence, public space, local businesses, and palpable identity surely contribute to social trauma and failure in the suburbs.

Not only is civil and criminal violence tragic and traumatic, it is economically counterproductive—in the cost of clean-up and rebuilding but also in the cost of the law enforcement, legal, and prison systems that attempt to deter it. In the long run, our country and our region are going to survive in global competition and in human terms only with the realization of the potential of all its population, not just the affluent.

THE ARCHITECTURAL COSTS OF SPRAWL

There are also several architectural costs associated with sprawl. They can be divided into categories: banalization, scalelessness, commodification, and typological impoverishment. Another way of describing these costs is as losses: loss of architectural detail, loss of human/pedestrian scale, loss of local authenticity, and loss of building types. These losses apply to all contemporary architecture, but they seem more acute in suburbia.

Architectural banalization is another negative byproduct of the automobile. Designing buildings for the side of the highway, to be seen at high speed through a windshield, is a different problem from designing them for a pedestrian environment. For the former, the building must be set further back from the curb and possibly sited at an angle to it, so as to present a wider face to the faster-moving viewer. Also, the building won't be detailed as richly or as authentically, because few people will get close enough to it to scrutinize or appreciate any virtuosity at the small scale. Compared to traditional architecture, which rewards approach and inspection, the architecture of the commercial strip is a cartoon. Sometimes exaggerating but always simplifying the imagery, it tends to flatten, cheapen, and trivialize the building. The architecture of the strip tends to be two-dimensional—like the signboard that sits out in front of the obligatory parking lot and is often grander, more carefully designed, and crafted with better materials than the building it advertises.

Another architectural byproduct of the automobile is the loss of human scale. The suburban strip is a place where buildings are often very large in footprint and surrounded by parking lots even larger. The parking lots are oceanic, designed to a formula of 400 square feet of parking outside for every 250 square feet inside. Along the highway strip of offices and stores, horizontal distances between buildings are vast. There is a corresponding lack of vertical dimension in these one-story buildings of big, simple footprints. The dearth of human-scaled, outdoor space enclosed by humane architecture can make for bleak, wind-swept wastelands piled high with dirty snow in winter and hot, hazy wastelands sweltering with asphaltic fumes in summer.

In the parking lot, the human body is no longer the basic measure of architecture, just as the pedestrian is no longer the design determinant of the street. Scalelessness can also be a problem in the inner city, where the erosion of fabric has been social as well as spatial. To quote a recent HUD document: "In its most concrete expression, human scale is the stoop of a rowhouse or the front porch of a home rather than the stairwell of a high-rise; it is a cop walking a beat rather than the helicopter overhead. Human scale in housing means creating homes with individualized detail, identity, and a sense of place."[20]

Like much of contemporary culture, architectural design has been commodified for the marketplace. The gift wrapping of Postmodern buildings, nowhere more obvious than in a suburban shopping mall or office park, is indicative of how commercialized and trivialized the role of the architect has become. The design of retail architecture is usually formulaic, superficial, and divorced from place, however sophisticated its imagery and packaging may be. It is also repetitive, with many buildings identically designed except for their signs and facades. Many retail buildings are chain stores or franchises, often with national or regional affiliation. Nor are arterial strip stores constructed very well or very permanently, because they are seen by their owners as quick investments. Wal-Mart expects and sometimes gets a pay-back period of less than two years for some of its big box stores.

The residential architecture of the subdivision is no better than its commercial counterpart. Houses are often designed by builders or their engineers, who are looking for ways to offer inexpensive homes with a splash of variety. While this is a predictable even commendable intention, it results in cosmetic differences. The stylistic variations in speculative development tend to cater to the least common denominator. "Greige" becomes the standard color and hodgepodges of colonial, modern, rustic, French provincial, or Mediterranean become the architectural norm. Such is the nature, quite understandable given the risks, of speculative building. The commodification of taste cannot be blamed on the developer, although some clearly take design less seriously than others. The speculative real estate system and the consumer mentality themselves are to blame.

Finally, suburban architecture tends to be more typologically impoverished than urban architecture. Although, typology will be discussed at length in chapter 3, mention of it must be made now. An architectural type is, to employ a tautology, a typical or standard building configuration. Commercial types in the suburbs include the corner gas station, the single-story strip retail or office building, the tilt-up warehouse or factory, the fast-food restaurant, the big-box discount or "category-killer" store, the shopping mall, and the drive-through bank. Residential types include the ranch, split-level, bi-level, mini-chateau, and center-hall colonial, as well as the garden apartment. The architectural expression and style of these and other housing types usually vary more than commercial types, although genuine regional differences in domestic architecture are continually being veiled and blunted.

Although quite a few suburban architectural types have been mentioned, the range is less than in a traditional city, where a city hall is typologically distinguished from a church, school, library, or concert hall, which in turn is different from a jail, train station, post office, office building, department store, shop, apartment house, townhouse, bungalow, etc. Nor are different functions always housed in different building forms in the contemporary

"Just as this printed page, if it is legible, can be visually grasped as related patterns of recognizable symbols, so a legible city would be one whose works districts or landmarks or pathways are easily identifiable and are easily grouped into an overall pattern."

—Kevin Lynch

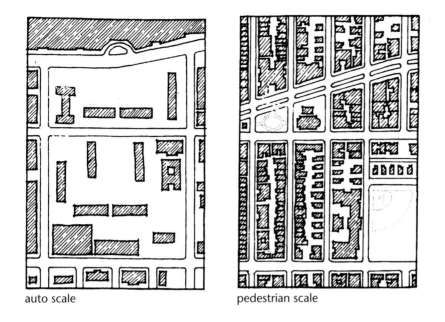

auto scale   pedestrian scale

The automobile and our growing dependence on it have slowly changed our built environment to a completely different scale and pattern than prevailed in the American city before World War II. Not only are building footprints bigger and farther apart, elevations are less detailed and less crafted in our high-speed, throw-away culture. (Calthorpe Associates)

city. Indeed the fit between function and form is far from exact in either the suburb or the city, but there is often enough consistency to establish a recognizable hierarchy and some common legibility and meaning in the city. Suburban architectural types are fewer, since different functions are housed in the same forms. A Modernist glass box on a suburban street could be a gas station, an insurance office, a church, or a house.

The looser fit between function and form, to be discussed in greater detail in chapter 3, has resulted in a less articulate and more confusing built environment. Not only is the function of a building not legible, but the distinction between public and private buildings is lost. While this vagueness is true throughout the contemporary metropolis, it is especially true in sprawl. If the public post office looks like a medical office building, the public school like a factory, and the public motor vehicle inspection station like a gas station or drugstore, suburbia is a less intelligible and intelligent place. People who are born and raised in suburbia no doubt develop new sensibilities and antennae that can better read subtleties in their environment. Even so, they are reading a less architecturally thoughtful and less rich text than dwellers in a traditional city.

OTHER COSTS

Ideally, the psychological and health costs of sprawl would be included in this critique. These are the personal tolls that living in a disaggregated community takes on us individually, whether it be in suburban, rural, or urban conditions. They are, alas, bottomless and beyond the scope of this book.

However, some things are clear, such as the obvious health hazards of pollution. The impact of traffic on the conviviality of neighborhoods has been measured, as shown in the diagram below. It is also clear that endless chauffeuring of children is a heavy burden on parents. What is less obvious is the developmental toll on the kids themselves, for whom healthy autonomy and maturity is postponed. This toll is especially high on children living in suburban nuclear families: "The urban child sees the harshness of the street; the rural child witnesses the frightening operations of nature. Both have contact with an eternal reality denied the suburban middle class child who is cushioned from risk and fear."[21]

The psychological effects of such things as ennui and privatization are impossible to measure. Nor can we know what long-term impact perpetual driving or TV watching might have. When the weekly "Ozzie and Harriet Show" broadcast a happy picture of suburbia to suburbanites in the 1950s, there were two lanes on the arterials and three channels on television. We cannot feel too sanguine about children averaging twenty-six hours of television per week on dozens of channels, while their parents scoot out for seventy automobile trips per week. Unfortunately, many of these conditions and problems are experienced by city dwellers as well. In fact, city residents are more heavily assaulted by some environmental irritants and pollutants. Noise is especially invasive, both in the street and through the less massive walls of cheaply constructed apartment buildings now being built. Any call to greater densities and more urban lifestyles must address issues such as acoustic privacy and noise abatement.

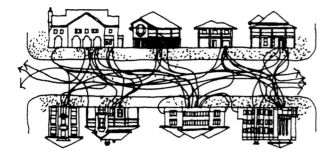

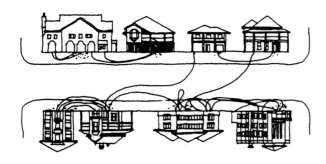

Traffic Volume vs. Community
This diagram illustrates social interaction along and across streets. The top street experiences 2000 vehicles per day and the bottom street 16,000 per day. Heavy traffic takes its toll on neighborliness and friendships. (Donald Appleyard, *Livable Streets*, University of California Press, Berkeley, 1991, p. 21.)

Sociologists, social pundits, screenwriters, and novelists have addressed the psychosocial dysfunctions and cultural deficits of sprawl. But musicians, poets, and artists have been slower to respond. Unlike the city and the country, few songs have been written about suburbs. No body of memorable or distinctive music has come out of suburbia, unless grunge can be indirectly attributed to the boredom and alienation of suburban teen-agers, and the Beach Boys to the automobile lifestyle of Southern California youth. The jet lag blues, Ralph Lauren ballads, or fast food musicals may perhaps emerge. Nor has there been much strong visual art, with the exception of David Hockney's swimming pool paintings. Tellingly, there are few postcards of suburban scenes.

THE SHORTFALLS OF THE MARKETPLACE

Traditionally, the distribution of goods and services has been left to the market in our economy. This market economy has proven better at creating wealth than any other system known. It has been extremely efficient and fruitful, lifting the average American household to a standard of living that ranks among the highest in the world. While this chapter does not question the general validity or efficiency of a market economy, it does challenge the notion that all durable goods are commodities in the same sense as a pork belly or tennis racquet. Housing is a big exception. Because shelter is a necessity, it requires government interventions in its supply and demand. Indeed, the federal, state, and local governments have been regulating housing for generations in recognition of the fact that shelter is not a straightforward commodity. In many cases the accumulation of these regulations has had a negative effect on housing affordability and density, despite their good intentions as individual policies and laws. Zoning and housing regulations have been conflicting and duplicative. Some regulations need to be modified or eliminated.

We still treat housing too much like a commodity and not enough like a right. Its price is determined almost exclusively by supply and demand, as are its mortgage rates. It is bought and sold for financial speculation as well as for shelter. When housing is traded in the marketplace, one person's gain is another person's loss. As long as this is the case, there will be citizens—decent citizens, playing within the rules of our moral and economic system—in whose interest it will be to make housing *less* affordable. As long as people see their homes as the major investment of their lives, as hedges against inflation, and as their financial nest eggs, there will be economic and social forces in favor of increasing the price of housing. While this may be fiscally understandable and sound behavior for individuals, it is devastating to that segment of society who cannot afford to buy or rent their first home.

When housing is traded in the marketplace, one person's gain is another person's loss. As long as this is the case, there will be citizens—decent citizens playing within the rules of our moral and economic system—in whose interest it will be to make housing less affordable.

An additional exception to simple supply-and-demand economics has to do with transportation, another sector of the economy that is not pure commodity or service. Vehicle travel has long been subsidized by government and paid for by people other than the user, including future generations who must shoulder government debt. It has been estimated that auto commuters in major cities directly pay for only about one-quarter of the total costs of their commute. The other three-quarters is jointly carried by their employers (free parking), other users (in reduced safety and increased congestion), fellow workers and residents (air and noise pollution), and governments, who pass some of the cost on to future taxpayers.[22] Public transit has been subsidized, although at token levels compared to the automobile.

ECONOMIC COSTS TO THE HOUSEHOLD

If society cannot afford low-density sprawl, can the individual home buyer or renter afford it? Does our economy still allow the average household to accumulate the downpayment and to carry the monthly costs of owning a new home? Clearly low-income households can't afford to buy new homes, but does the average household have the economic wherewithal to purchase or rent the average new home? The answer across most of the region and much of the country is no.

A quick look at the monthly carrying capacity of a low-income household is instructive. Housing that is affordable to a low-income family is shelter than can be occupied for 30 percent or less of their income (anything more than that, although commonplace, is judged by government and banks to be a prohibitively high burden on the household budget). If the 1994 U.S. median household income was $32,000, then a low-income household earned between $12,000 and $20,000 per year. If a household earns 50 percent of the median, or $16,000 per year, it can afford $4,800 for rent, which is $400 per month. It is difficult to find decent quality or sufficiently large rental units at that price in most parts of our country, hence, low-income households often settle for substandard units or pay more than 30 percent of their income.

Housing affordability for a first-time, average-income home buyer is now a national problem. If that household spends 30 percent of its $32,000 annual income, it has at its disposal $800 per month. Assuming $200 per month for utilities, taxes, and insurance, there is $600 available for monthly mortgage payment. Such payments would support a thirty-year, 8 percent mortgage of about $82,000, which is 80 percent of a home price of $103,000. A house at that price might normally require a down payment of 20 percent or $20,600. Assuming such a down payment could be amassed and interest rates are available at this favorable rate, housing units would have to be priced under

$105,000 to be affordable. It is very difficult if not impossible in many parts of the U.S.A. to find new housing units priced in this range. The situation is not as dire for the average family as for the average household. U.S. median income for all families in 1994 was $38,782, and for married-couple families was almost $45,000.

The fiscal gap that many households face when trying to buy a house is exacerbated by automobile ownership and usage. Many families spend as much money on their cars as on housing. In contemporary suburbia, the average household drives about 30,000 miles per year, while its counterpart in urban centers drives only 8,000 miles, and 15,000 miles in traditional mixed-use neighborhoods. Many suburban households spend $6,000 per car per year for insurance, maintenance, car payments or depreciation, fuel, and parking. If a household could get by with one less car by walking, carpooling, and using transit, they would have another $500 per month to apply towards housing. This money could amortize a mortgage of an additional $50,000 or so. Banks should liberalize their mortgage lending policies to acknowledge home buyers who live in neighborhoods well served by transit—just as they sometimes discount for design that reduces the consumption of energy, the other major operating cost of the American household.

Many families spend as much money on their cars as on housing.

The reasons that the average home price has risen dramatically are many and complicated. Some of them are regulatory impediments and code requirements. The accumulation of these well-intentioned regulations has created a litany of problems: innovative developers struggle with variances, financing, and concerns of "not-in-my-backyard" (NIMBY) neighbors; median-income households have mortgage loans rejected because of the gap between income and mortgage payments; low-income households are not even considered because banks have red-lined their neighborhoods; many households have to devote an increasing percentage of their budget to owning and operating two or three vehicles; banks fail because of bad risks; the FDIC has to bail banks out at huge taxpayer expense; speculators and immigrants from wealthier states help drive up the price of real estate; developers build ever larger and more expensive houses for ever smaller and less affluent households; communities fail to provide their fair share of low- and moderate-income housing; building officials try to enforce complicated and sometimes contradictory codes; state government struggles to subsidize and finance housing without federal assistance; the federal government has trouble providing housing aid to state and local governments because it, too, is plagued by deficits. In short, the whole housing delivery system is troubled.

Nonetheless, housing costs on a square-foot basis remain lower than most industrialized countries and much lower than Japan or Europe. The affordability gap in the United States pales before Japan's, which requires 100-year mortgages to bridge. In the welfare economies of Europe, government programs often make up the difference. Americans have always opted for larger houses than Europeans—not only because more space and building materials have been available here but also because the New World considered itself bigger in every way. Americans were able to maintain generous standards because land and natural resources remained plentiful and environmental controls lax. Now these factors have tightened and the middle class is having trouble mustering down payments and mortgage payments, especially for first houses. Housing is reaching crisis proportions in some areas, but the real crisis is not economic. It is a *crisis of expectations*. Americans have simply come to expect—because of good luck, favorable economic conditions, hard work, regulations, and bountiful land and natural resources—large houses. By any other standards, including those of richer countries, these expectations are unrealistically high. They need to be downsized.

GOOD INTENTIONS

Automobiles are too basic to our culture and economy to be eliminated, but suburban Americans are more than ready to take fewer and shorter trips.

Architectural and urban design can play an important role in kindling a new vision. During this century in the western world, there have been many heroic visions presented by designers, including Frank Lloyd Wright, Le Corbusier, Ebenezer Howard, Patrick Geddes, John Nolen, Tony Garnier, Antonio Sant'Elia, and Leon Krier. C.I.A.M. (Congrès Internationale d'Architecture Moderne) attempted to codify and promote modernist notions of city making. Less idealistic but no less profound visions, such as company towns and Levittowns, are scattered around our country, some with a well-developed sense of community. Many turned out to be unsuccessful when implemented. This is because city making is among the most complex and difficult human undertakings—as complex as life itself. It is beyond the powers of rational analysis and synthesis. Like civilization or language, cities cannot be invented in one generation. They must be designed and built incrementally, evolving slowly and laboriously—the sum of many acts, some large, some small. And, like any self-regulating system, they must correct and recorrect themselves continuously.

During the last decade, there has been a surge in design charrettes, competitions, essays, books, and projects that attempt to reform or preempt contemporary and modernist models of urbanism. Central to these efforts is the New Urbanism, or "Neotraditionalism," which will be discussed in greater detail in chapter 4. It is less intent on reinventing the design of community than previous movements have been and can be seen as a revival of earlier models and patterns. It addresses head-on the economic, environmental, and social costs of sprawl. As for affordability, the New Urbanism is predicated on the notion that the most promising and cost-effective strategy for affordable housing is the development of affordable communities. Among other things, the new model better accommodates smaller households. It also sub-dues the automobile. Automobiles are too basic to our culture and economy to be eliminated, but suburban Americans are more than ready to take fewer and shorter trips, as well as to be freed from excessive fuel and insurance expenditures. The oil companies in Houston and the insurance companies in Hartford need to take heed as much as the automakers in Detroit.

This quiet revolution has been going on in town planning and architec-tural circles over the last decade. Established zoning and urban design ideas are being questioned and reversed. There is less of the modernist mandate to be inventive and heroic. Designers are remembering, reviving, and re-inter-preting ideas that prevailed before the automobile spread our cities apart, before television kept us inside our houses, and before telephones and home computers reduced face-to-face interaction. Although these technologies have increased the convenience and efficiency of daily life, they have precipitated a widescale privatization of our lives that is deleterious to community. These revived models are to be distinguished from most Master Planned Commu-nities, Planned Unit Developments, and cluster housing—all of which were important steps in their day toward reestablishing community but remained too auto-dependent and too low in density to redress the costs of sprawl.

REDREAMING THE AMERICAN DREAM: A QUIET MANIFESTO

The new paradigm might be reduced to the following principles and ideals:

1. Denser, more compact and clearly bounded communities that preserve sacred places, places of beauty, open space, agriculture, natural systems, and natural habitats need to replace continuous, undifferentiated subur-ban development.
2. A fairer sharing and finer-grained mixing of diverse land uses, household types, building types, age groups, and socioeconomic groups need to replace the single-use zoning that has sponsored the all too ubiquitous housing subdivision, the shopping mall, and the office park, as well as excessive dependence on the automobile.
3. Walking, bicycling, and public transit on an interconnected network of streets, alleys, paths, greenways, and waterways that enhances convenient and healthy mobility, connectivity, and efficiency need to replace the auto-mobile for routine trips.
4. Because their social, physical, and institutional infrastructure is in place, conserving, restoring, revitalizing, and infilling existing urban centers and towns need to be given higher priority than building new communities on greenfield sites.

5. A spatially coherent and cohesive sense of place, of neighborhood, and of community that builds on what is locally unique and enduring needs to replace the monoculture, anonymity, and placelessness of sprawl.

6. The strengthening of the public realm, with face-to-face interaction, citizen participation and public/community art in dignified, physically defined places, needs to be given higher priority than electronically mediated reality (TV, video, computer, fax, virtual reality) and life spent primarily in privatized spaces (the home, mall, car).

7. Environmental, economic, and cultural practices, traditions, and mythologies need to become more sustainable and energy-efficient to reduce the commodification and consumption of land and natural resources. (The lone-riding Marlboro man needs to be overtaken by a bus-riding urban hero; Paul Bunyan needs to give way to Johnny Appleseed; and the detached house with three-car garage needs to move over for the solar townhouse with bicycles and walking sticks.)

. . . employment, health care, education, crime, energy, pollution, growth management, etc. There is neither the time nor money to solve these problems one at a time.

Town making and city making should become our central mission, within which other issues facing society are confronted: employment, health care, education, crime, energy, pollution, growth management, etc. There is neither the time nor the money to solve these problems one at a time. We need comprehensive, place-specific solutions for these chronic and interdependent problems. This strategy is not a 180-degree turnabout. It is a 90-degree shift that addresses problems vertically (i.e., co-locating resources and services in one place) rather than horizontally (i.e., relying on agencies and initiatives that address a single problem throughout a city, county, state, or country.) At present, there is an utter lack of connection between housing, health, social, welfare, education, law enforcement, and environmental and energy conservation programs—both to each other and to physical infrastructure and place. Even infrastructure—highways, streets, bridges, waterways, parks, and utilities—is often ill-coordinated.

Under this scheme a city would have, like Seattle, a Department of Neighborhoods with reasonably autonomous budgets, offices, and agendas for different neighborhoods rather than a general Department of Housing and Social Services. Neighborhoods, in turn, could focus on place making and place management, appointing place managers to look after specific blocks, streets, centers, and parks. To maintain regional differences, the federal government might have a Department of Appalachia or of New England, for instance. Rather than the Department of Housing and Urban Development, there should be a Department of Neighborhood and Urban Development.[23] Federal and state grants to local government could be orchestrated to focus on particular places and neighborhoods rather than remain a shotgun of separate programs, which now number in the hundreds. This sea change from a problem-specific to a place-specific approach would result in more holistic governments and communities.

Suburbia may be paved with good intentions, but mainly it is paved. A new paradigm and a new movement to promote these ideas have emerged to fill the vacuum. Like all visions, the new paradigm is idealistic. Is it another road paved with good intentions that simply leads to a New Urbanist hell?—with "hundreds perhaps thousands of attractive Charleston, Nantucket and Seaside look-alikes springing up across the American landscape wherever large landowners and developers happen to own a suitable piece of land."[24] There are tradeoffs with any vision, and this one has its dangers and penalties to be sure. Not everyone will benefit. However, on balance, it offers a much more promising future than business as usual. Many of the following chapters illustrate and apply this new vision, and demonstrate its applicability to the Seattle region.

CHAPTER 2

Critical Regionalism
An Architecture of Place

"I didn't like Europe as much as I liked Disney World. At Disney World all the countries are much closer together, and they show you just the best of each country. Europe is boring. People talk strange languages and things are dirty. Sometimes you don't see anything interesting in Europe for days, but at Disney World something different happens all the time and people are happy. It's much more fun. It's well designed."—A college graduate just back from her first trip to Europe

Regionalism is an ambiguous term. To an urban planner it means thinking bigger—planning at the scale of a region rather than at the scale of the subdivision or municipality. To an architect, regionalism means thinking smaller—resisting the forces that tend to homogenize buildings across the country and around the globe in favor of forces that are local. Critical Regionalism is a term invented by architects that means thinking regionally in ways that are wary and nonsentimental. It guards against the mindless nostalgia for traditional architecture to which regionalism has been prone in the past.

Although most of this book is about planning and designing a region, this chapter is about the flip side: regional design. Specifically, it's about the theory of regionalist architecture. It theorizes about what kind of architecture is appropriate for regionalism in general rather than for one region in particular. Although there are many characteristic traits of our region's architecture —such as the prevalence of wood, large windows and overhangs, attention to views, lush and natural landscaping, a soft and impure color palette, and Japanese influence—this chapter is not a treatise on Pacific Northwest architecture or its history. That analysis is left to architectural historians.

Critical Regionalism is actually more of an attitude than a theory. It is an attitude that celebrates and delights in what is different about a place. What makes a local architecture local and unique is valued more than what makes it typical and universal. In that sense it is a reaction to the standardization that Modernism promoted. It is also an attitude of resistance, sometimes an angry response to many of the changes made in the name of progress that are blanching geographic differences in place and culture.

Architecture is in a rare position to embody and express regional differences—more so than manufactured products like cars, chairs, shoes, or even clothing. Perhaps only food is as local, although regional food products are now shipped far and wide. Because architecture is one of the few remaining items in modern life that is not mass produced and mass marketed, it can resist the commodification of culture. Because it is a site-specific and one-of-a-kind production, it can resist the banalization of place. And because it is one of the few handbuilt items left in the industrialized world, it can resist standardization. Architecture can still be rooted in local climate, topography, flora, building materials, building practices, architectural types, cultures, history, and mythology.

THE PACIFIC NORTHWEST: REGIONAL SUPERLATIVES

Seattle is set near the middle of the bioregion that is referred to by Americans as the Pacific Northwest (although this name unnecessarily tips its hat to places south and east, i.e., to California and to the East Coast. It is a large and remarkably beautiful piece of the planet. Spanning 20 degrees of latitude from northern California to the Alaskan panhandle and stretching 30 degrees of longitude from the Pacific Ocean to the Continental Divide, it is roughly ten times as big as New England (or England). Despite its incredible spectrum of flora, fauna, and geography, it is bound together by common geology and climate into a single biological whole. More precisely, the region is defined by the watersheds that are drained by the Columbia, Fraser, Skagit, Skeena, Stikine, and myriad other smaller rivers. They flow through the only coastal temperate rain forests in North America. The land is dominated by three young mountain ranges—the volcanic Cascades, the verdant Coast range, and the rugged Rocky Mountains. Its weather is defined by ocean and land. Wet air masses from the Pacific encounter the deeply folded landscape, drenching the western slopes of the mountain ranges with some of our continent's heaviest rainfall. Purged of moisture, this eastern-moving air has little rain to offer the desertlike interior of the region.[1] Sometimes this contrast is vividly juxtaposed, such as on the Olympic Peninsula, where America's heaviest annual precipitation (240+ inches) in the Olympic Mountains is only a day's hike from its driest coastal spot (15+ inches) on Dungeness Spit.

Windows tend to be numerous and generously sized to let in the soft light of the Pacific Northwest, as well as take advantage of its magnificent views. (Doug Kelbaugh, Architect)

The world's largest conifer forests grow in this region, including the biggest and oldest spruces, firs, and hemlocks found anywhere on earth. Offshore lie some of the planet's most productive waters, with the largest octopuses and marine invertebrates, as well as the greatest salmon runs, once so plentiful that they supported the densest and possibly wealthiest Native culture in North America. Strong tides push large volumes of water in and out of the region's estuaries, making them some of the richest living systems on earth. Willapa Bay is one of the least degraded large estuaries in the lower-48 states. The Fraser River Delta is the largest river estuary on the West Coast, habitat for millions of migrating birds and British Columbia's most valuable farming area. And the mighty grizzly bear roams and the majestic bald eagle soars in the world's densest concentrations in Southeast Alaska.[2]

This public rest facility at Washington Pass on the Cascade Scenic Highway uses local and natural materials to reinterpret the muscular National Parks architecture of the 1930s. The building defers to the magnificent setting by keeping a long, low profile and to its remoteness by utilizing composting toilets, photovoltaic power, and low-maintenance landscaping. (Kelbaugh, Calthorpe & Associates

A natural environment of this magnificence and grandeur has had a humbling impact on the region's architecture. Nature's setting can be overwhelming and intimidating. Buildings sometimes try to get out of the way of nature, rather than compete with it. As a consequence, they are often built of natural wood, stone, and other matte materials of low chromatic value (e.g., gray, green, gray-green, etc.). The shapes and finishes of their roofs are not usually strident and the architecture could be described for the most part as nonstriving. The deep, continuous carpet of evergreens often swallows up buildings, masking sore thumbs that codes have not already mitigated. The wooded shores of the San Juan Islands, for instance, appear untouched despite countless homes hiding under the trees. Even in the cities, where design is often more outspoken and self-conscious, the architecture has been relatively quiet and low profile, at least until the 1980s. This modesty is probably a manifestation of the drizzly rain, the soft "oyster" light, and mild temperatures—and, remarkable to flatlanders, very little lightning and thunder. This is not the climate for loud and glamorous architecture.

Light *is* distinctive in our region. There's not much of it in winter, when days are short, cloudy, and rainy. Although the weather can be somber when rainy, reflections in puddles add some sparkle and glistening. This is especially true at night or when the sun comes out after the rain. When the sun

A natural environment of this magnificence and grandeur has had a humbling impact on the region's architecture. . . .This is not the climate for loud and glamorous architecture.

At latitude 48° N, the light in Seattle penetrates deeply into interior spaces while it makes its long arc from east to west. Shadows can be startling in their length and the speed with which their long arms move across the floor and walls. (Miller Hull Partnership)

It is a region that respects competence and craft, whether it be Boeing engineering or fine woodworking or the elegant hardware of sailboats, bicycles, and mountain climbing.

is out, light slices deeply into our building interiors in winter and makes a dramatically wide sweep from east to west in summer. Because of frequent and heavy cloud cover, windows are large—like the huge windows of Dutch townhouses rather than the widely spaced windows of Italian palazzos or the tiny apertures of New Mexican pueblos. Tall trees and hills make these glazed areas all the more necessary—either because they block light or open onto dramatic views. The short winter days are conducive to indoor work and a Scandinavian taciturnity; the long summer days beg a life out-of-doors, often on large porches and expansive decks. Sunshine is more cherished here than in sunny places. The hours of daylight, which range widely here over the year, are closely watched and appreciated, especially around the two equinoxes when change is fastest.

Another distinguishing regional characteristic is the industrial quality of the infrastructure. There is a great array of civil engineering scale: bridges, docks, trestles, causeways, cranes, tunnels, and dams. Because of the topography and the prevalence of water, there is a particularly broad array of bridges—arched, trussed, wood, high, low, floating, lift, and draw. There is also a long tradition of piers, docks, and warehouses in a region with a history of maritime trade. These structures tend to be no-nonsense, straightforward buildings, much like the simple barns and sheds that grace the Skagit Valley. This functional architecture has been slowly honed to minimal and economical shapes over the generations, and constitutes a rich heritage within the built environment.

The regional history of Architecture with a capital A is too long and complicated to present even a personal view. Like other regions and cultures, styles and paradigms have constantly changed. Although off to a late start in the mid-nineteenth century, the architecture of the Pacific Northwest followed the normal American chronology from Victorian, Richardsonian, Arts and Crafts or Craftsman, Art Deco, neo-Georgian, neo-Tudor, International style, Brutalism, and Postmodernism, in roughly that order. There are some periods that went undernourished in Seattle; for instance, the Beaux-Arts or Neoclassical style was never particularly well developed[3]; hi-tech architecture was tame; Postmodern was toned down. In general and not surprisingly, this succession of styles was played out in Seattle in quieter and less excessive ways than in bigger, more cosmopolitan cities such as New York, Los Angeles, or Paris. This modesty is probably the result of more factors than size and sophistication. It is a reflection of the modesty, honesty, and humility of the populace, who have historically been generally undemonstrative, pragmatic, and uncorrupt and who like their streets and government clean.

It is a region that respects competence and craft, whether it be Boeing engineering, fine woodworking, or the elegant hardware of sailboats, bicycles, and mountain climbing. Native Northwesterners have been generally skep-

Shingle siding and shingle roofs, horizontal overhangs and brackets, and the lush landscaping of the Pacific Northwest seem to resonate with the wood architecture of Japan, which many local architects have admired and emulated. (Nakata House designed by Smith Nakata, Seattle)

tical of gloss and pomp and like their buildings more reasonable and straightforward. As the population becomes more diverse and cosmopolitan, these generalizations are becoming less true. Nonetheless, Seattle remains a place of high averages more than superlatives. Typical houses, restaurants, arts and crafts, performing arts, etc., are high in quality, rather than a few that are spectacularly so—yielding a more livable, balanced, and sustainable urban culture than cities of equal size and age, such as Dallas or Denver. Passions are quieter and gentler. Perhaps this is so because of the steady, mild, and muffled climate. If there is little thunder or lightning, there is little macho chest-beating or high-strutting glitz. But the moderation can be fanatical and tenacious. It is the moderation of conviction, not of indifference or of paralysis. If the region were to adopt a motto for itself, what would it be? Extremism of the middle? Passionate moderation? The vehement center?

The region, despite its low profile, has a few architectural conceits: the Craftsman style bungalow is as highly developed and as widely built as in any American city, because Seattle boomed during the heyday of that style. (During the first decade of this century Seattle's population trebled from 80,000 to 240,000. This is a far greater rate of growth than presently has the region worried.) The Tudor and Swiss chalet styles are also well represented. Seattle and Portland's interpretation of the International style in wood and glass, rather than steel and glass, developed a national reputation as Northwest Contemporary at mid-century. This was a time when regionalism was a subject under discussion in the profession and the national architectural press. This architecture, with its dark stained wood siding, wood shingle roofs, and window walls of plate glass, was sometimes a painful compromise between the Craftsman and the International styles, with traces of Japanese influence.

There are some notable and curious exceptions to the Northwest's lack of superlatives and firsts. Its plentiful gardens, despite the gray dampness, can be intensely colorful—although their blooms are spread out over a long, cool spring as opposed to a single explosion of blossoms in April or May. The Seattle park system boasts one of the most complete realizations of a city-wide park system by The Olmsted Brothers (who also designed park networks for Tacoma, Spokane, and Portland, which must be a record in and of itself). Reputedly, the world's first gas station opened in Seattle, in 1907. Seattle was the first city in America to offer free downtown bus service. On the other hand, the nation's first suburban shopping center organized around a pedestrian mall was built in the late 1940s at Northgate—a dubious distinction given malls' subsequent destruction of the public realm and neighborhood retail. A more illustrious distinction in marketplaces would be the Pike Place Public Market, the oldest continuously operating farmers' market in the country. The Seattle skyline has long claimed the tallest building west of the Mississippi River, first the Smith Tower and now the Columbia Seafirst Building. (The Smith Tower was the tallest building outside of New York City and the fourth tallest in the world when construction was completed in 1914). The biggest building in the world, the Boeing Assembly plant in Everett, is in the region. It is big enough to envelop eleven Kingdomes, which itself has the largest single-span concrete roof in the world. The Tacoma Dome is the largest wood dome ever built.

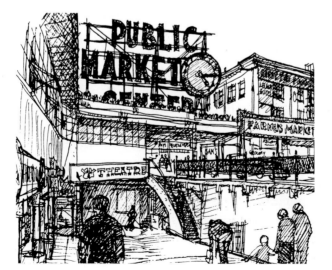

A public development authority owns and operates Seattle's Pike Place Market, a farmer's market that has been in longer continuous operation than any in the U.S.A. It was lovingly but not overly refurbished in the 1970s, after being saved by a 1960s community movement led by Victor Steinbrueck, who did this sketch.

As already noted, the infrastructure of the region can be exceptional. The neighboring mountain ranges are dotted with ambitious dams that are part of the largest hydroelectric system in the world. The world's longest floating bridge is in the region, as is one of its longest railroad tunnels. The nation's busiest drawbridge (Fremont) crosses the ship canal, which boasted its largest locks when built in 1911–1916. Although the region's rugged topography and wide waterways have called forth many great feats of engineering, the region has also had its share of spectacular structural failures. The Tacoma Narrows bridge, a.k.a. "Galloping Gertie," shook itself to ruin. The collapse of the north stands of the University of Washington's Husky Stadium during construction and the sinking of the Interstate 90 floating bridge across Lake Washington were recent engineering catastrophes that drew national attention.

A more systematic and thorough review of the architecture of the Seattle region can be found in *Shaping Seattle Architecture*, edited by Jeffrey Ochsner, who here generalizes about Seattle's architects:

> First is a concern for the particular characteristics that have given Seattle its individuality. Although local designers may disagree on what these characteristics are, most seem to be attempting to respond through design to their own understanding of the city and region as a specific place. There is also a recognition of the importance of the natural environment and a concern that it be respected and conserved, both at the level of individual project design and in relation to regional resources. Simultaneously, the profession can probably be said to share a commitment to the city and to the values inherent in urban living. And many in the profession likely share a concern for social equity and could be considered supporters of recent Seattle efforts to provide low-income housing and social services. Finally, while there may be disagreements regarding individual buildings, most in the profession share a concern for the architectural heritage of the city and the preservation of its essential resources.[4]

Before exploring Critical Regionalism's general principles—ones that could be applied anywhere—it is necessary to take a relatively lengthy and admittedly subjective look at recent architectural history. First, a few words about the twentieth-century chronology of architectural history in this country might be helpful. Roughly speaking, the century started during an architecture of Neoclassical or Beaux-Arts style. In America, Neoclassicism—sometimes simply called Classicism—was given a big boost by the Columbian Exposition in Chicago in 1893. Beaux-Arts refers to the Parisian academy where leading architects of the era studied the axial formality and monumentality that often characterized civic architecture during the City Beautiful Movement around the turn of the century. Modernism started as an avant-garde movement in Europe after World War I. It was brought to America in the 1930s, debuting as the International Style in a show at the Museum of Modern Art. It slowly became accepted by American corporations, institutions, and individual clients and was the prevalent architectural mode after World War II. Postmodernism emerged in the 1970s, about the time solar and environmental architecture were a movement. Deconstruction replaced Postmodernism in the late 1980s and still has momentum in some areas of the country. Critical Regionalism started to gain a following in the 1980s.

The pioneers of Modernism had heroic visions of a new society served by new technologies. LeCorbusier's proposal (top) in the 1920s and 1930s for high-rise office towers and high-speed transportation was a precursor to modern downtowns. Frank Lloyd Wright's Broadacre City with its one-acre lot for every citizen was prophetic of today's sprawling suburbs. Both visions celebrated mobility, including family helicopters in the latter—an idea whose future has passed.

MODERNISM AS A MOVEMENT AND A PERIOD

In architecture, Modernism started out in the 1920s as a polemical and radical rupture with hundreds of years of tradition. There were bold manifestoes and a messianic avant-garde. Its pioneers had a heroic vision of a new society served by a new technology. It was to be an international movement that would erase national differences. Walter Gropius, Mies van der Rohe, Le Corbusier—to mention a few of its most famous pioneers—preached a complete break with Neoclassicism and the lassitude of fin de siecle art and architecture, which they attacked as corrupt, inefficient, and outmoded. They and their colleagues bravely fought and won many ideological, technical, and aesthetic battles. Their architecture, at first scorned or ignored, eventually served as the basis for an international design orthodoxy and what amounted to a doctrinaire religion for many designers. The Modernist building was, as the eminent architectural historian Colin Rowe put it, "an icon of change, an icon of technology, an icon of good society, an icon of the future."[5] Functionalist philosophies and designs ultimately prevailed over the Beaux-Arts establishment. Le Corbusier, Mies, and Aalto were finally accorded the stature of masters and their influence was broad and deep in both the academy and the profession.

Although the public was slower than academia to accept Modernism, after World War II corporations and government began to embrace the International style as their official architectural language. Its stripped forms and no-frills functionalism appealed to their sense of efficiency and economy. It was cheaper to build and represented technical modernization as well as cultural modernity. More recently this style and certain of its more conspicuous building types, such as the high-rise office building and airport, have become economic status symbols in emerging nations. For most of the industrialized world, however, Modernist buildings have run the inevitable course from prototype to type to stereotype, and Modernism as a movement has lost its intellectual and moral clout.

After the public finally warmed up to modern architecture, it was forsaken by academicians, critics, and professionals, who began to embrace Postmodernity. In architecture and urban design, the term Modernism no longer refers to a movement but to a period, not unlike the terms Gothic, Renaissance, and Baroque, although these periods were of longer duration. It refers to that half-century from the First World War to the Vietnam War. There was no unitary style adopted by the Modern Movement. With the exception of the International style, stylistic consistency was rarely achieved, even within the *oeuvre* of an individual master. There were, however, consistent attitudes about architectural and urban space and form, as well as an abiding faith in technological progress and rationalist methodology.

These two toilets—one historicist and the other functionalist—vividly illustrate the difference between the neo-classicism that Modernists rejected and the industrial rationalism they embraced.

MODERNIST METHODOLOGY: LOOKING INSIDE THE PROBLEM

From the outset, Modernism put great stock in the ability of rational analysis to provide both functional and aesthetic designs. A clear statement and rational analysis of the problem, the site, relevant technology, and user were to produce a new, superior architecture that was scraped clean of the encrustations of historical styles. At early Modernist design schools such as the Bauhaus, it was believed that by looking hard and deep enough inside a problem, the designer could unlock solutions that were a rational and inevitable outcome, uncontaminated by preconception, precedent, or tradition. Looking inward—into physical materials, processes, and production and into social and psychological needs—was necessary and sufficient to design good products and buildings. In fact it was believed that probity and aesthetic integrity could come only out of this rational and empirical methodology.

The study of design methodology, which peaked as a discrete movement in the 1960s, brought a rigorous new look at the process of designing, just as "whole systems" were bringing a similar rigor to large building design and urban planning. The question of technique was paramount. This focus was possible only because the question of direction was rendered less important by a prevailing orthodoxy and broad consensus in the schools and profession. This agreement allowed the pursuit and refinement of technique: more scientific programming, systems engineering, better drafting tools, better simulation devices, earlier involvement of the building contractor, construction management, critical path scheduling, value engineering, more prefabrication, kit-of-parts construction, post-occupancy evaluation, etc. It was all part of the positivistic attitude that a definite, correct solution would become transparent for every problem if only the method or system was rational enough.

This overly optimistic paradigm harkens back to the Enlightenment and the scientific and industrial revolutions of the seventeenth and eighteenth centuries. Science and technology have had us in their clutch ever since. Geology was the most popular science of the first half of the nineteenth century, while botany and zoology seemed most to intrigue the second half. The first half of our century was excited by atomic physics and relativity theory; the latter half has been more in the thrall of ecology, biotechnology, cybernetics, and genetic engineering. If Modernist architects had "physics envy," regionalists are jealous of the life sciences.

Modernist methodology made a sharp turn in the late 1960s when advocacy planning and citizen-participation took hold. Coupled as it was with political issues, especially civil rights, the movement attempted to replace technical methodology with a social and ideological one. Rather than entrusting professional experts and specialists to program and design buildings, advocacy planners tried to enfranchise local groups with more control

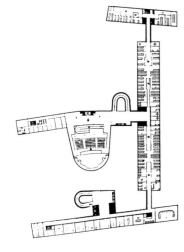

The Modernist expression of discrete functional areas and the circulation systems of a building were the result of looking inside the problem for a solution, in this case inside the building's program. In many cases, Modernist buildings were functional diagrams writ large—efficient, but harsh on the occupants and neighbors. (Centrosoyus Building, Le Corbusier)

of design and planning within their community. Community design centers sprang up where free or low-cost design services were given to disadvantaged and grass roots organizations. It was not just a question of helping a sector of the population that could not otherwise afford professional services, but also of reforming the delivery system for architecture and planning services in society as a whole. The more militant advocates wanted a radical redistribution of power and capital. Advocacy planning was primarily concerned with what was being designed for whom, by whom, rather than what it looked like or how it was constructed. Ironically, it paralleled a period of professional and governmental interest in prefabricated housing systems—a methodologically driven idea somewhat at odds with the activists' do-it-yourself ethic but consistent with the commitment to make new housing affordable to all.

The advocacy movement petered out, except for scattered pockets of activity, by the mid 1970s when radical and liberal sentiment shifted to other issues such as energy, ecology, self realization, feminism, and gay rights. It also lost momentum because of the broad, simultaneous swing toward conservative politics and religion. But it left a legacy of citizen participation in architecture and planning that is still with us today, in fact on the upswing again. Some architecture schools have continuously maintained community design centers and others are reinvesting in community outreach, including design centers, design charrettes, and involvement in primary and secondary education.

The Modernist search for standardized solutions has since devolved into the Postmodernist search for variety, made possible by contemporary modes of production and transportation. Standardized building components are reverting again to customized components, helped along by both the flexibility of computerized manufacturing and the speedy international distribution of goods and services. It is now possible for designers to specify any product in any color from anywhere in the world. This freedom has not necessarily resulted in better design. Indeed, it can be argued that modern buildings, towns, and cities have developed too much visual variety, that they are a riot of different building materials, colors, and shapes. *Sweet's General Building and Renovation Catalogue,* the eighteen-volume library found in every architect's office, contains 21,000 pages of products offered by 2,300 manufacturers. When products are vended in this variety and at this rate, it is impossible for users to evaluate them and for knowledge to accumulate in meaningful ways. Is it any wonder our buildings and cities are such visual circuses?

Perhaps this visual chaos is why a traditional English town where every roof is covered in slate or an old New England town in which buildings are clad only in wood is so appealing to today's sensibilities. Tourists spend a lot of money visiting preindustrial settings. The lack of material limits coupled with pluralist design attitudes have given too much discretion to designers and builders. This lack of constraint and restraint has tended to blot out regional distinctions, as well as to add to the clutter and chaos of the environment.

POSTMODERNIST METHODOLOGY: LOOKING OUTSIDE THE PROBLEM

As recently as the 1970s, Modernism was still a true movement with its polemic intact and its protagonists still vocal. Modernism still has its staunch loyalists, zealots, and diehards. These old warriors continue to teach in the academy and maintain aging practices. Recently, there has been a Neo-modernism afoot. But Modernism has clearly lost the moral and formal potency it had when it prevailed as the norm during the middle half of the twentieth century. To be fair, this loss of influence and exhaustion of forms are not entirely due to its internal shortcomings. There are "global economic and cultural forces that turn all architecture—modern, traditional and post-modern—into a commodity that merely adorns an increasingly degraded environment."[6]

After the decline of both Modernism and advocacy planning in the 1970s, a new design paradigm emerged to fill the vacuum. Rather than a single orthodoxy, it was a pluralist array of attitudes—the historicism, contextualism, neoclassicism, and neotraditionalism of Postmodernism. Instead of an inward examination of the plan, the outside of the building—its elevation—often became the point of departure for the designer. How the exterior relates to the immediate visual context and to historical precedent became major design questions.

Relating to physical context literally and sympathetically is not surprising in an approach that respects the traditional street and square above the individual building. Postmodernism tended to view program as secondary to historical continuity and architectural context. It used the public faces of the building to mediate between the interior and exterior forces that push and pull on every building. Composing the elements of a facade in an expressive and artful way became more important than directly revealing the structure, materials, and functions of the building. Indeed, the very ideas of composition and expression ran counter to the tenets of Modernism, which wanted to *reveal* rather than *express* a phenomenon. The transparent and unadorned presentation of physical fact was a canon of the Modern Movement. Postmodernism rejected this austere ethic for a freer representational mode. It used figural and representational form to symbolize or signify ideas, rather than the abstract forms of Modernism, which were intended to embody ideas or simply be themselves.

PHENOMENOLOGY

Phenomenology, especially in the Pacific Northwest where it seems to be more widely if unconsciously valued than in other parts of the country, is worth a little digression. This philosophical term refers to a way of knowing and being in the world through the senses rather than through the mind. It is based on sensory experience, ranging from everyday kinesthetic experience to sublime aesthetic experience. In architecture, phenomenology is used to refer to the experiential or perceptual rather than the abstract or conceptual dimension of buildings. It is about direct and active aesthetic perception of the physical environment with all the senses. Aesthetic experience, according to philosophers of art such as Suzanne Langer, is only possible through direct and total sensory connection to an object, image, or scene. In her theory, aesthetic experience bypasses all conscious mental interference. At its quietest, it is Zen meditation. At its most active, it is dancing.

Grounded in the physical world, phenomenological architecture is very different from conceptual architecture, which springs from the mind and is more abstract. Conceptual architecture is more autonomous, based on ideas and mental constructs such as geometry and logic. It is not associated with any particular instance or place. At its purest and most Platonic, it is conceived apart from application to a particular use or site. In some quarters conceptual design is considered more sophisticated than phenomenological design, presumably because it is more idealized, intellectual, and cerebral.

A phenomenological architecture is rooted in its place, its material being. As such, it is more akin to Critical Regionalism than to Modernism. It seems sympathetic to the designers of this region, who tend to reject the mind games of East Coast and European architects and to respect work that comes more from the stomach than the head. It is not surprising that Steven Holl, a practitioner and protagonist of perceptual architecture that is simultaneously palpable and transcendent, grew up and was educated in the Seattle region. It is also not surprising that some members of the University of Washington architecture faculty, most notably Folke Nyberg, are fans of the philosopher Martin Heidegger, the great exponent of phenomenology who believed being in the world is revealed through active involvement rather than detached observation and reflection.

. . . designers of our region . . . tend to respect work that comes from the stomach more than the head.

HISTORIC PRESERVATION

The nation's historic preservation movement was a major challenge to modernity. It put the Modernist axiom "form follows function" to a test it would continually fail. An old building often became more interesting and potent when a new function replaced the original one—a bakery in a firehouse, an apartment in a stable, a restaurant in a factory. The best buildings frequently turned out to be the ones where new function and old form were not a tight fit.

Vincent Scully has called historic preservation "the only mass movement to affect critically the course of architecture in our century."[7] Although the environmentalists may challenge this assertion, it was a remarkably swift and successful revolution that happened everywhere, without as much hoopla or as many high profile leaders as the environmental movement.[8] This movement was an extremely broad one nationally and locally. Historic structures and areas were passionately championed by a loud chorus of enthusiasts from all walks of life.

Many deserving buildings were saved and restored, sometimes to mint conditions that might be described as overly precious and slavishly archaeological. Compared to Europe, historic preservation in this country was very literal, correct, and zealous—perhaps because Americans have a shorter architectural history and a smaller inventory of distinguished structures with which to work. (Europeans, on the other hand, seem more zealous about technology, something we take for granted as much as they tend to take history for granted.) In European cities adaptive reuse of buildings, rather than historically exact restoration, is prevalent. This attitude allows life in the city to respect history while accommodating new technology and functions. Nonetheless, American historic preservation has recuperated scale, character, and authenticity to American cities and permanently stopped the foolish demolition of significant building stock.

The preservation movement remains particularly successful and lively in Seattle and Tacoma. In Seattle, the Pike Place Public Market could never be called overly precious. When Victor Steinbrueck started the Friends of the Market in 1964, little did he know it would result in a popular civic movement that would ultimately bring $60 million in funding. These funds would turn the dying farmers' market into the city's greatest attraction. Nor did those responsible for demolishing the Seattle Hotel at Pioneer Square know they would trigger the creation of King County's first official historic district. The Pioneer Square Historic District, designated in 1970, is one of the most intact late-nineteenth-century commercial areas in the country. Significantly, this historical milieu has been achieved without over-gentrifying the neighborhood. Homeless shelters and missions sit side by side with professional offices and cafes. In Tacoma, the old Union Depot has been restored to its glorious past and acts as a centerpiece to a recovering urban district of great character. The permanent installation of Dale Chihuly glass bespeaks the cultural confidence to adapt historic structures in new and creative ways.

ENVIRONMENTAL AND SOLAR ARCHITECTURE

The energy crisis in the 1970s promoted an architecture more sympathetic to the environment. Petroleum and other natural resources were seen as finite, as was the planet's capacity to absorb our wastes and support our consumption. The search for sustainability and the belief in global limits were first imprinted on the psyche of America during that period. This ecological view encouraged architects to employ design strategies of active and passive solar heating and cooling, as well as natural lighting and ventilation. (Unfortunately, these energy-saving techniques often were used to compensate for rather than to correct low-density, gas-guzzling land use patterns.) More importantly perhaps, it compelled many designers and builders to make buildings more site-specific, that is, crafted to the local climate, solar radiation, terrain, building materials, and construction practices. It was not only a question of saving BTU's but also of assuming a more humble view of humanity's place in the natural world and accepting a more modest planetary allotment for our national and individual needs. It was also about holistic design, especially passive solar, which rejected the single-mindedness of engineering solutions in favor of designs that addressed social, environmental, and aesthetic issues simultaneously.

The connection between modernity, or the modern "project" (as Europeans like to refer to it), and the exploitation of natural resources and the environment became more and more evident in the 1970s. Modernist architecture seemed to be the vehicle of quick and dirty growth, increasingly devoid

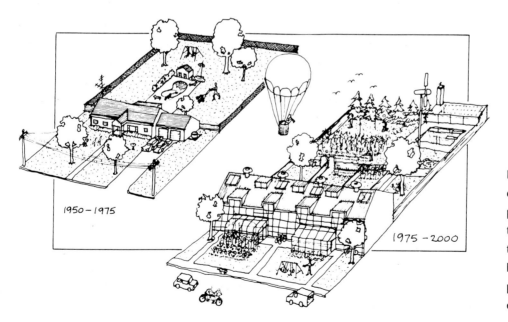

1950–1975

1975–2000

New models for suburban development were promoted by solar architects—ones that replaced the large single-family home on a large lot with passive solar townhouses on more productive land.

of its original social agenda. Its freestanding, horizontal buildings seemed to go hand and in hand with low-density suburban sprawl, its vertical skyscrapers sprouted higher and higher in downtowns. As awesome and beautiful as these high-rise skylines appear from several miles out—especially at night—they can dehumanize life at street level and on the countless floors of offices or apartments. (If these sixty-story buildings told sixty slightly different stories rather than repeating the exact same tale, they might be more humane. At the least they should tell three stories: one at the base, another in the shaft, and something quite different at the top.) These tall, vertical glass boxes and their long, horizontal counterparts in suburbia were invariably designed with four equal sides, indifferent to climate and site.

Site specificity was the passive solar movement's greatest architectural legacy. It expanded for some design professionals and academics into an interest in regional specificity in the 1980s. Regionalism elevated local culture, history, and mythology, as well as environmental factors, to be prime determinants of form. This more complete set of concerns attempted to inform an authentic, local, rooted architecture that resisted mass culture. A minority position, it necessarily operated on the margins of the corporate world, which continued to commodify and co-opt regional and cultural differences.

POSTMODERNISM

While energy buffs and environmentalists were struggling for the attention of the academy and design professionals in the 1970s, Postmodernism emerged with greater force and a larger following. It was particularly strong in the schools of architecture, where there was an increasing intellectualization of the discipline and a search for new theoretical legitimacy in other scholarly fields, like linguistics, philosophy, and history. Questions of architectural meaning and interpretation or hermeneutics overtook more practical issues. The discourse, which was both heated and rarefied, came to dominate academic conferences and journals. In the meantime, an elite group of star architects came to dominate the professional magazines and awards programs, both of which seemed to multiply in this age of media hype and glamour. Several economic recessions during this period hit the profession very hard, as did the gradual erosion of the architect's power in the construction process. The new-found fame for a few stars did "not compensate for the profession's weakness or its strategic withdrawal into discourse. . . . The freedom to imagine and conceive appears to have been paid with irrelevance and exacerbated professional segmentation."[9] In retrospect, giving up power on the construction site and in the corporate boardroom for a higher profile in the media and more design freedom was not a good trade for most members of the profession.

"Architects since the outset of Modern architecture have been anti-ecological . . . the International Style proclaimed that modern buildings are all coequally suitable for all people, all places and all times."

—Ian McHarg

Postmodernism let loose the reservoir of architectural tradition that Modernism had dammed up (and damned) for half a century. This quickly eroded the moral force, technological prowess, and social vision of Modernism. It licensed designers again to employ ornament, symbolism, wit, irony, color, and history, much of which seemed welcome relief after the severity of Modernism. The single-minded orthodoxy of Modernism was undermined by pluralism and diversity. If Modernism represented the dominance of western rationalism, Postmodernism held out the possibility of multicultural architecture. It also called for the suspension of experimentation and bringing design and planning back into the bosom of the community. But, instead, it tended to degenerate into an empty formalism.

Postmodernism tended to deaden social conscience and ignore technical advancements. It revived eclecticism, historicism, and pluralism that often proved superficial and banal in the hands of less skillful practitioners. In talented hands it proved more successful, as exemplified locally in the Seattle Art Museum and the Washington Mutual Tower, both of which were composed by a sophisticated eye and talented hand. In general, buildings of the 1980s overflowed with an excess of architectural forms and materials. With the floodgates open, Postmodernism ran the course from prototype to type to stereotype with record haste. It failed to capture the lasting and popular support that historic preservation had gained a decade earlier.

The style also seemed to aggravate the already precipitous decline in quality of contemporary building construction. The sheetrocking of America happened in a single lifetime. Ersatz and fake materials that imitate nobler

The sheetrocking of America happened in a single lifetime.

The Seattle Art Museum uses its public faces to mediate between interior and exterior forces rather than to express only its internal spaces and structure. Figural forms, including inscriptions, are used as ornament, as opposed to the abstract and stripped forms of Modernism. (Venturi, Scott-Brown and Associates; photo by John Stamets.)

Postmodernism brought figuration, including the human figure, back to architecture and urban design, but the materials and construction were not up to their neo-classical antecedents.
(The Portland Building by Michael Graves)

materials have been a fact of life throughout the history of building and architecture. But tectonic impersonation and cheap construction have worsened with the commercial image-making and shorter life spans of late-twentieth-century buildings. There are Postmodern walls that cannot take a kick or even a punch from a wanton vandal. As a result, some Americans have developed an especially hearty appetite for more permanent materials and better craftsmanship during the last generation.

To be fair, cities are the richer for Postmodernism. It championed better urban design and planning than Modernism, although suburbia continued its cul-de-sac sprawl throughout the period. Very importantly, it revived more positive and figural public space, often treating private space as secondary and residual. This represented a dramatic shift from the object-making of Modernism, which tended to treat buildings as sculptures in the round. The Postmodernists' respect for traditional street, building types, and context— so often looked down upon as ordinary and even contemptible by Modernists—brought renewed interest in public spaces and in the urban fabric.

The Postmodern interest in architectural typology and urban design was its greatest legacy, although often realized on paper rather than on the ground. Its revival of typology as a design methodology helped heal the rift between architecture and urban planning. Its revival of traditional urban and town planning lives on in the New Urbanism. As Alex Krieger has observed, "for many, the most important mission of Post Modernism became the reform of Modern planning: to strip away its abstractions, universalisms and apparent disregard for the places which the modern world inherited. . . . The greatest sin of Modernism, its most problematic abstraction, may have been its insistence that the city was fundamentally . . . an amalgam of systems rather than as a collection of places."[10]

DECONSTRUCTIVISM

In the late 1980s, there was a quiet, almost embarrassed shift in the academy away from Postmodern architecture toward Deconstructivism. Still in fashion in the 1990s, it is likely to prove to be another brief chapter in the architectural history of the twentieth century. Like Postmodernism, it is heavily based on theory, but literary rather than linguistic theory. Its theoretical construct (if such a word can be applied to poststructuralist theory) has its foundations in the philosophy of Jacques Derrida, a latter-day Nietzsche. Essentially nihilist, it accepts and even celebrates the fragmentation, dislocation, acuteness, and impermanence of contemporary life.

Deconstructivists have embraced fractal geometry, a new branch of mathematics that has discovered shapes that repeat themselves in nature at all scales, from snowflakes to mountain ranges. Unlike humanist architecture, Deconstructivism has adopted a mathematical system that has nothing to do with the human body or human scale. Its proponents often try to express the complex crosscurrents of the city in a single building, rather than in a larger accumulation of urban fabric. But they never incorporate familiar bits of context, say a conventional shed, roof monitor, balcony, doorway, or window. They seem to have little faith in the acts of other buildings to help make an urbanism that is sufficiently fractured to be an accurate reflection of the contemporary social condition. In this sense, Deconstructivism is a less orderly version of Modernism, which was equally solipsistic and distrustful of context. Both have produced self-centered buildings, the former ones of pure, Euclidean geometry and the latter ones of shattered, fractal geometry.

"Decon" architecture, as practiced by Frank Gehry, Peter Eisenman, et al., uses a formal vocabulary that is Modernist in its abstraction and minimalism. There is an ironic consistency of shapes and materials for an architecture that celebrates complexity and violation. The shapes and facets are all

Some contemporary Deconstructivists slice and break their building forms into slivers and shards; others twist and contort them into warped and disheveled buildings. In celebrating decentered and fragmented contemporary reality, Deconstruction has given up hope of urban clarity, coherence, and civility—even of the possibility of urbanism itself. (Frank O. Gehry & Associates)

abstract, clean, fragmented fractals, whether pure or "degenerative." Perfection has not so much been deconstructed and violated as it has been artfully sliced and diced into a carefully random, carefully collaged collection of forms.

Its drawings and models can be elegant and its built examples can be powerful, beautiful sculpture. It can, however, often be second-rate sculpture, compromised by both function and budget. In Southern California, it can slip into angry and perverse architecture—convincing neither tectonically nor sculpturally, however earnest its angst may be. Not surprisingly, Deconstructivist designs, produced by collisions, splinterings, and fragmentations of form, are often impractical or even impossible to construct and maintain. Because its designs are difficult to build, Deconstructivism needs the media more than previous episodes in architecture. Its slivers and shards are another architectural dead-end, first kindled only to be later dropped by the media in its endless search for newness and novelty.

GREEN ARCHITECTURE

Also emerging in the 1990s is "green" architecture. It is not so much a revival as a survival of energy-conscious design started twenty years earlier. It seriously addresses the energy embodied in building materials and practices, as well as energy consumed by buildings. It also tackles the issues of toxicity and pollution much more aggressively than the passive solar or "smart building" movements of the 1970s and 1980s, respectively. It also revives the idea of reusing and recycling building materials, a regular practice in earlier eras. (In medieval construction, heavy timbers were unpegged and reused in new structures.)

Although increasingly international in following, green design is ultimately dedicated to local acts of design and construction and therefore sympathetic to regionalism. It is a welcome, if sometimes too single-minded, force in environmental design. It is paralleled in landscape architecture by such ecological practices as xeriscaping, i.e., using native plant materials that need less water, fertilizer, and pesticides. This movement promises to be both more politically sophisticated and more internationally coordinated than earlier environmental movements, as evidenced by the Earth Summit and International Habitat conferences in Rio de Janeiro and Istanbul, respectively. An excellent book on green design is Sim Van der Ryn and Stuart Cowan's *Ecological Design,* which outlines five insightful principles of sustainable design.

REGIONALISM WITH AN EDGE

If Modernism as it was once known is dead, Postmodernism in decline, and Deconstructivism suspect, there is an existential dilemma for architects. On the one hand, the social and technological agenda of Modernism still seems correct. But the Modernist commitment to place, context, history, craftsmanship, and resource and energy conservation seems distinctly lacking. On the other hand, the urban agenda of Postmodernism still seems right-minded, but its Neoclassical ornament and tectonics seem pasty and superficial when attempted today. There is something spiritually as well as physically hollow about most Postmodern structures. And Deconstructivism gives in too easily to the dehumanizing and alienating forces of the millennium at hand.

On another axis altogether is a third position that breaks this existential bind and "that distances itself equally from the Enlightenment Myth of Progress and from a reactionary, unrealistic impulse to return to architectonic forms of the pre-industrial past."[11] This alternative way of looking at things is Critical Regionalism, a term popularized and given gravity by Kenneth Frampton. To further quote his seminal text, it resists the contempo-

The urban agenda of Postmodernism still seems right-minded, but its Neo-classical ornament and tectonics seem pasty and superficial when attempted today.

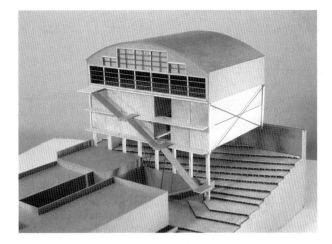

This studio and warehouse building designed (but not built) for Dale Chihuly attempts to be regionalist without resorting to nostalgic local references. For its underbelly of storage rooms, it uses recycled cargo containers, a by-product of Puget Sound's shipping industry. (Doug Kelbaugh, Architect)

rary practice of architecture that is "increasingly polarized between, on the one hand, a so-called 'high-tech' approach predicated exclusively upon production and, on the other, the provision of a 'compensatory facade' to cover up the harsh realities of this universal system."[12]

Critical Regionalism is two-handed. On the one hand is the mark of a particular region: each region determining its own architectural fate and shaping its built environment without mimicking other places. On the other hand are characteristics common to regionalist architecture in any region in the country, perhaps the world. These regional characteristics are most easily expressed at the scale of small buildings, especially residential architecture, where designs and builders are often most sensitive to site, climate, and tradition. Large buildings, particularly high-rise and long-span structures, have design determinants that are more universal, such as gravity, wind, and, to a lesser extent, seismic loads. Climate affects large buildings less, because their heating and cooling needs are driven by the internal loads of lights and people, rather than ambient solar radiation and temperature. Accordingly, they are less likely to develop regional idiosyncrasies or variations.

FIVE POINTS OF A CRITICAL REGIONALISM

These five characteristics or attitudes are proposed as a common basis of Critical Regionalism, wherever it manages to take root:

1. Sense of Place
Critical Regionalism first and foremost starts out with a love of place. This topophilia seeks to liberate the *genius loci*. It is critical of simple-minded or excessive importation of culture from other places. It honors local climate, topography, vegetation, building materials, and building practices. It prefers

CRITICAL REGIONALISM

local authenticity to sophisticated imitation. That which makes a place unique is worth celebrating and protecting with architecture. This act of protection is also an act of resistance. Critical Regionalism says no to outside influence and hot new ideas more than it says yes. It must be picky and stubborn in this age of aggressive hype and universal civilization. It realizes that the more well-defined and highly evolved a place is, the less likely it is to be improved by random imports, experimentation, or change for change's sake. It resists the kind of cultural homogenization and commodification that makes the Puget Sound Basin like the Bay Area, Kirkland like Sausalito, Poulsbo like Scandinavia, and that makes one of its suburbs like the next.

Critical Regionalism must, on the other hand, be careful not to be too sensitive or resistive to change, lest it turn into a sour cynicism or saccharin sentimentality. It also has the potential to degenerate into a scared or snobbish xenophobia. It must walk that thin line between conservation and reactionaryism. It can't afford to be bitter about lost battles for former good causes or it will risk becoming too negative about today's challenges. As Jacques Barzun ends *The Columbia History of the World*: "The building or rebuilding of states and cultures, now or at any time, is more becoming to our nature than longings and lamentations."[13]

Critical Regionalism is not provincialism, a myopic cousin of regionalism. Provincials don't know what they don't know. Critical Regionalists know the limits of their world, which can be cosmopolitan without being elitist. Travel

Vernacular buildings, like this Skagit Valley hay barn, can be as beautiful and inspiring as high style architecture. They are unconsciously regional.

This house on Bainbridge Island reinterprets traditional architectural elements of the Pacific Northwest in modern materials and construction practices. (Miller Hull Partnership)

can build an understanding of what is worthy of both bringing home and returning home for. Indeed, the revolution during the 1960s in air travel, which made it possible for the middle class to see the world, accelerated the awareness of regional differences. As much as they respect place, Critical Regionalists are not sentimental about it. They resist indulging in nostalgia and literally recapturing how sweet it was in the old days or old country. (Leavenworth, to name but one regional example, is not a very convincing imitation of either.) It may at times be too self-conscious about what is worth preserving about a place, but cannot be afraid when it is necessary to be bold and visionary about the future.

2. Sense of Nature

Nature is a good model for design because it holds the key to vitality and sustainability. Designers can learn from the incredible sophistication of biological and ecological systems. Diversity, symbiosis, synergy, balance—these are profound and inspiring messages for all designers. Working together, architects, industrial designers, landscape architects, urban designers, and urban planners can fulfill an ecological role, namely to protect and preserve ecosystems, natural cycles and chains, and the symbiosis between organisms and their environment. Their role, as mentioned in the Introduction, is also to reverse entropy, which is done by creating order and meaning. The most meaningful and highly evolved order is to be found in nature.

Nature has inspired designers and artists in different ways. The word "natural" has been used over the years to describe and defend varying positions, such as romantic, picturesque, and organic. Nature per se does not demand

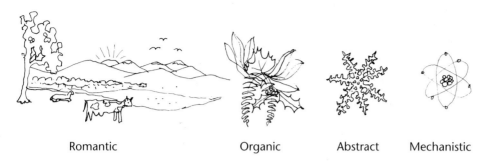

| Romantic | Organic | Abstract | Mechanistic |

any one interpretation. In fact, all phenomena can be called natural in the final analysis. Many positions, some opposing, can be taken from or based on nature and natural phenomena. It depends on the scale at which the artist or architect views nature. It can be called romantic at the landscape scale, humanistic at the anatomical level, organic at the vegetable level, abstract at the microscopic level, and mechanistic at the atomic level. Nature seems most understandable and accessible at the scale of fauna and flora. These scales, although ruled by natural laws that can be expressed as abstract mathematical formulae and Euclidean and fractal geometries, are less abstract to the human eye. The animal and plant kingdoms are full of figural, ornate form.

Nature has provided a bottomless source of forms and images. The Romantic Age looked to nature at the scale of the bucolic landscape. The Art Nouveau period looked to nature at the vegetative scale—the palm frond and sinuous vine—much as the Victorians had admired the giant lily pads they imported into their hothouses from distant continents. The Arts and Crafts movement had its love affair with wisteria, dripping from wooden arbors. Modernist architects and theorists have also extolled the virtues of nature, looking for underlying formal principles there rather than in history or culture. One scale at which nature seemed to inspire them was atomic physics. This subvisual scale represents nature at its most abstract, which is not a surprising preference given the Modernist mania for abstract form. Natural forms at a visual scale, like the symmetrical snowflake or the Nautilus shell that grows in a pure spiral, were also an inspiration to modernists.

Critical Regionalists and green architects are enthusiastic about a water hyacinth or sea manatee, which can cleanse sewage treatment wastes of heavy metals. They might also be attracted to fuzzy theory and chaos theory, which deal with natural phenomenon that are too complex to be described or even understood by linear analysis and conventional geometry. A sense of nature for them is messier, more organic, and not as visual as the precise, dry, Euclidean geometry of Modernism. While Modernism looked to physics and engineering for lessons and inspiration, regionalism looks to the environmental sciences and ecology, which have enjoyed great attention and breakthroughs in recent decades.

Nature has been viewed and copied at different scales by different epochs. Critical Regionalists, like environmentalists, particularly admire and are inspired by nature at the organic level. Modernists preferred the abstract mechanics of atomic physics, just as Romanticists took great strength from pastoral landscapes. Deconstructivists have mimicked fractal geometry, which attempts to describe nature's irregular shapes that repeat themselves at any scale. Architectural thinkers have also been inspired by chaos theory, an attempt to describe nature's uncertainties.

The cabin in the San Juan Islands by the Miller Hull Partnership incorporates elements associated with Pacific Northwest architecture, such as wide roof eaves and rakes supported by brackets, board and batten siding, generously-sized wood windows, and natural landscaping. (Miller Hull Partnership)

Buildings and cities, like plants and animals, can be viewed as vital rather than as inert and denatured. They can be treated as organisms which are conceived, grow, flex, adapt, interact, age, die and decay—always rooted in their habitat. Site-specific design—with its sensitivity to the living environment—is fundamental to a sense of nature.

We must occasionally remind ourselves that human culture and its artifacts are young and immature compared to nature. A trip to the mountains or the forests is a sobering if pleasant reminder of nature's power. Architects who cavalierly dip into the history of architecture for pleasing and familiar forms rather than into nature for enduring patterns and types must beware: history's gene pool is smaller, its process of natural selection far briefer. A Gothic cathedral, as refined as it is, pales before the overwhelming complexity and four-dimensional order of a rain forest or salt marsh, perhaps even a cubic yard of rich topsoil. A modern metropolis might match the complexity of an ecosystem but not its order or sustainability. The history of architecture, replete as it is with impressive and wonderful achievements, is nowhere near as amazing or as sublime as nature.

CRITICAL REGIONALISM

3. Sense of History

No one can deny that the best buildings, gardens, and cities of the past are overwhelming in the awe and joy they can elicit. But they yield more than beauty and pleasure. They offer lasting lessons—ones that are more easily applied than the lessons of nature. History should be respectfully studied for design principles rather than used as a grab bag of forms. Time-tested architectural types are more valuable antecedents than specific historical styles, however beautiful they may still appear. An architectural type that has stood the test of time, like the basilica or courtyard house, must be doing something right in terms of responding to climate, social and cultural needs, tradition, and economy. The best buildings from the past—whether vernacular or Architecture with a capital A—continue to set the high standard of excellence for today's designers.

Architectural history is also a deep and rich archive for designers. Whether by a vernacular farmhouse or classical temple, architects have always been inspired by the past. Historical precedents are a good point of departure when designing buildings. Their design vocabulary and syntax can be creatively transformed to express and to accommodate new technical and programmatic forces. Traditional architectural language can evolve, much as spoken language does in multilingual dialects and much as new words are coined to name new scientific and technological developments. This incremental evolution applies to both vernacular and high-style architecture. Conventional architectural language can be converted, subverted, inverted, or perverted. If it evolves too suddenly, it loses its meaning and power. Change is most successful when it is fresh but not too radical or too abrupt, so that it "rhymes" with a familiar imagery. Rhyme—likeness tempered by slight variation—is naturally pleasing to the human eye, as it is to the ear.

To paraphrase psychologist Nicholas Humphrey, aesthetic pleasure must convey some biological advantage, as nature gives away nothing for free.[14] His thesis shines a different light on the role of history in aesthetics. If aesthetic pleasure, like sexual and appetite gratification, has played an important role in our biological survival and evolution, it is because it provokes and encourages human beings to classify the sensory world visually. Subtle variations on a shape are more visually stimulating than exact repetitions of a shape. Unstimulating patterns are inherently less interesting to the viewer and therefore less likely to be viewed attentively. Sorting out and correctly reading the sensory world were critical to survival and evolution. To put it simply: the more pleasurable the task, the greater the attention, the greater the understanding, and the greater the biological advantage. Humphrey postulates that what is both stimulating and legible is imagery that "rhymes" with other familiar images, whether across space or over time. To "rhyme," images must be neither too similar nor too dissimilar. In the former case, the

History is replete with exemplary architecture and urbanism that set a very high standard. Basic building types—like the basilica, campanile, palazzo, and galleria—were brought together over many centuries in Piazza San Marco. The world-famous composition was not planned by anyone but was the result of each Venetian doge making a careful addition that respected what came before—a sense of history tempered by a sense of place.

human tends to lose interest too easily and in the latter case to become confused and discouraged too easily. Thus, the happy medium between these two extremes has over millions of years, Humphrey hypothesizes, come to be seen as beauty. The aesthetic pleasure it affords is functional as much as titillating. When design rhymes across time it demonstrates a sense of history, and when it rhymes across space, it reinforces a sense of place.

4. Sense of Craft

Suffice it to say that the construction of buildings has become junkier. Stewart Brand, who has studied the evolution of building technology since founding *The Whole Earth Catalogue* a generation ago agrees. "The trend in construction during this century has been toward ever lighter framing with the result that buildings look and feel increasingly like movie sets: impressive to the eye, flimsy to the touch, and incapable of aging well."[15] They are usually built with less human care and of less natural and less substantial materials. Copper has given way to aluminum, brass to brass plate, slate to asphalt, marble to plastic laminate, wood to particle board, tongue and groove siding to Texture-111 plywood, and plaster to sheetrock. It's the last of these, gypsum drywall, which epitomizes the deterioration of quality in our buildings and the slippage from tectonic toward scenographic design. The sheetrocking of every new house in America has brought a slow and subtle loss of precision and substantiality in construction. The ubiquitous aluminum sliding glass door and T-111 plywood, which mimics vertical board and batten siding, have had an equally widescale and regrettable effect.

The loss of craft is part of a bigger economic web that is unfortunately beyond the control of the designer, or for that matter, the region. Basically, architectural craft and detail are getting relatively more expensive than manufactured items—especially products that take advantage of miniaturization and of mass production. Because the construction of architecture is labor-intensive, it is doomed in the foreseeable future to fall further and further behind more mechanized and industrialized production. Unlike the performing and visual arts, which suffer economically from a similar labor intensity, there are no government subsidies for architecture. For the public's dollars architecture also has to compete with ever-cheaper consumer items, such as televisions, cars, clothes, travel—all of which continue to become cheaper in real dollars. Most Americans will choose—sadly but understandably—a $400 CD player over a solid-core oak door. In the meantime, Critical Regionalists keep ripping the fake plastic wood off their dashboards and refrigerator handles.

The love of craft need not be expressed in traditional ways, so long as it respects materials and their joints. The top photograph illustrates that hi-tech architecture can be as carefully and elegantly detailed as earlier hand-crafted buildings. (Richard Rogers and Partners/Kelbaugh & Lee)

Handcraft, however, still survives in contemporary architecture as exemplified at the Bill Gates residence. (James Cutler Architects and Bohlin Cywinski Jackson; photo by Art Grice.)

5. Sense of Limits

The sense of limits is one position on which passive solar architecture, Critical Regionalism, and Postmodernism all converged.

The Modern movement, especially the International Style, saw space as abstract, neutral, and continuous. It placed objects in a universal Cartesian grid, ignoring circumstance and place. At the regional scale this grid ultimately came to spread itself evenly across the countryside. At the architectural scale, Modernists saw space as flowing freely within open interiors and between the interior and exterior in buildings that were increasingly transparent. With Postmodernism there arose a renewed interest in discrete, static space. Human-scale rooms began to replace free-flowing spaces. The notion of a room before Modernism was positive, figural, contained, often symmetrical, and enclosed by thick walls of real mass. These are the attributes of Postmodern space, although the mass is now more apparent than real. The notion of public space as finite, contained, outdoor rooms, defined by background buildings and punctuated by foreground buildings, was also revived in the 1980s.

The room as a discrete architectural element was respectable again. Also seen as positive were other aspects of finite geometry: the axis, which establishes geometric beginning and terminus; symmetry, which creates a cen-

Modernist space was conceived of as universal, continuous, and boundless. Form is reduced to abstract rather than recognizable figures or shapes. Mies van der Rohe took Modernist reductionism to its greatest level of abstraction. Imitations of these platonic Chicago buildings can be found in any modern city.

terline; frontality, which distinguishes front layers from back layers; and fat walls, which rely or pretend to rely more on compression than tension for structural stability. These formal devices all resulted in an architecture and urban design that looked and felt more finite, more massive, and more static.

A sense of limits is about the need for finitude and for physical and temporal boundaries to frame and limit human places and activities. It is about the need for human scale in the built environment. It is also about the need for psychological boundaries—ones that make life more understandable and negotiable. As others have pointed out, spatial boundaries demarcate the beginning of the presencing of a place as much as the ending of a place and its power. Boundless architectural and urban space has less nearness, less presence. Limits are what differentiate place from raw space, whether they separate sacred from profane space or one secular space from another. The German language has the word *Raum* to describe a finite place or room. The Japanese use *ma* to denote a bounded space, although it literally translates as "interval." English is less precise about place.

The appreciation of natural resources as limited was parallel and simultaneous to the renewed perception of architectural space as finite. This sense of limits is one position on which passive solar architecture, Critical Regionalism, and Postmodernism all converged.

CRITICAL REGIONALISM CRITICIZED

There have been some negative responses to Critical Regionalism. One is that it is inherently elitist because of the low regard in which it sometimes holds popular taste. This disdain, architects like Dan Solomon claim, is as unconducive to the making of everyday neighborhoods and cities as is the Modernist preoccupation with individual buildings. This is a fair comment, as many of the architects (Utzon, Ando, Botta, Wolfe) cited in Kenneth Frampton's seminal essays on Critical Regionalism are striving for a profound architecture. This aspiration is not particularly amenable to doing quiet background buildings or to sublimating the designer's ego to the court of community opinion. This is not a problem when designing isolated buildings. But, in the urban context, architectural heroics can be problematic.

The contemporary works of Tadao Ando, Toyo Ito, and many of their fellow Japanese architects are examples of strong and exquisite design. But it is self-centered architecture that usually thumbs its nose at the context, which has admittedly declined since World War II. Fortunately, their single-minded pursuit of architectural integrity is often realized on remote sites. Also, many of their buildings infill along crowded urban streets and are not freestanding objects. This context-be-damned attitude produces fine individual buildings but a chaotic urban fabric in Tokyo and other Japanese cities. (It may be an inevitable and necessary irony in a society so driven by social consensus and conformity that it must find self-expression in architecture). Often this self-referential work, like its counterparts in Europe and America, is more interested in finding a place in glossy international journals and the annals of architectural history than in the local neighborhood.

Another criticism is that Critical Regionalism can be sociopolitically reactionary—a step back into the brutal national and regional ethnocentrism and racism of the past. Alan Balfour, former chair of the AA School of Architecture in London, makes these observations:

> The emergence of a European economic union is coupled, in paradox, by aggressive assertions of nationalism. Consider, for example, what is already underway in those nations lately released from the grip of Russia—Hungary, Poland, Romania—where architecture is seen as the most potent means of restoring and representing the national identity. Students are encouraged to resurrect ancient mysteries, that is, to imagine objects that may unwittingly reinforce racial and tribal differences. In spite of good intentions, the monsters may return. Critical Regionalism seemed at first a benign proposition but is now proving to have a sinister subtext. Such forms may bring with them all the wrath of unresolved injustices. Architecture must hold its place in this maelstrom of mediated reality that will increasingly try to dislocate the future. It cannot all be left to television. . . . to construct the present only from the past is to condone the death of the future.[16]

The ideal region may in fact be the metropolis.

This eloquent statement has some truth to it. Architectural regionalism and nationalism have been invoked by fascist movements. Critical Regionalism can look darkly conservative. However, it's a question of scale. First, Critical Regionalism is not nationalism. Regions are smaller than most nation states. The ideal region may in fact be the metropolis. Secondly, International Modernism, however liberal or radical, wasn't able to banish "ancient mysteries" or "racial and tribal differences." It simply repackaged these questions at increasingly larger scales. It has consorted with corporate and governmental giganticism, whether capitalist or socialist, and been party to this century's trade-up from national to global commerce and world war. Multinational and supranational corporations, international finance, continental trading groups, and universal culture can be as brutal as national and regional rivalries—only cooler and more insidious. Wars can now be very impersonal, fought at great physical distance on cool video screens with push buttons and electronic mice—without in-your-face screams and blood.

The "wrath of unresolved injustices" is less sinister and more likely to be understood and resolved at the more personal and humane scale of the city and region than at the numbing scale of the universal civilization to which Modernism tends. To be sure, the bad ghosts and negative karma that haunt local, internecine conflict are hot and ugly. But visceral conflicts are less likely to be fought than war with distant enemies who are faceless abstractions and objects of manufactured hatred. Balfour is absolutely right, however, about the need for architecture to hold its place in a reality that is more and more electronically mediated. But contemporary reality is least mediated at the regional and local scale that Critical Regionalism attempts to revive. That is precisely where it hopes to establish and find an existential foothold—not against the future but against placeless internationalism.

A third critique is that regionalism, whether good or bad, no longer makes technological or economic sense. Modern industrial production and transport make regional building practices and materials a romantic anachronism. Regionalism is wishful thinking and indulgent longing for a past that is lost forever. This argument is based on a straight-line projection of technological revolution-without-end. It fails to take into account that the march of technology and mass culture will not continue indefinitely if enough people no longer believe that it is delivering a better life. Progress may not always be measured in economic terms, at least not as we presently understand progress and economics. We need not be slavish technological drones, committed to every new breakthrough. Technology has been so spectacularly successful for so long that we've been blinded by its light and are only now fully realizing the tradeoffs and total cost—whether it be in economic, social, environmental, or moral currency. Just because there is the technological know-how and the money to dress every new Asian hotel lobby and restroom in marble from Italy doesn't mean it's sensible to ship the Cararra Mountains halfway round the planet (a tectonic shift that would make geologists blush). It may appear economical with today's market pricing, but this pricing system must and will change to better reflect the costs. As prices and costs are more accurately aligned (they will never be exactly because external costs are continually being created or discovered), regionalism and localism may be not only more possible but inevitable.

Progress may not always be measured in economic terms, at least not as we presently understand progress and economics.

A final criticism is that a singular attitude to architectural design is no longer possible, given the realities of global electronic communication. Peter Eisenman argues that it is impossible to operate with a single Zeitgeist or spirit of the times—the unitary organizing world view that animated the work of past eras:

> What characterizes the Rome of Sixtus V, Haussman's Paris or the work of Le Corbusier . . . is that their plans derived from a singular body politic. Now, ironically, at a time when the entire world can be seen as part of a single operating network, such a singular world view is no longer possible. Today, the

world can be explained not by a single zeitgeist, but by two divisions. The first division is a traditional one based on land, industry and people. The other division is based on information, which links technologically and culturally sophisticated world centers. . . . A Berliner of today probably has more in common with a New Yorker than with a resident of another German city, so similar are Berlin and New York as cultural and information centers. When physical proximity is no longer a part of the zeitgeist of a place, the traditional notions of city and architecture are thrown into question."[17]

These are accurate and perceptive comments on contemporary circumstances. Eisenman acknowledges that places such as Serbia and Slovakia are still brought together primarily by shared characteristics, land, and language. However, places that have shifted from the mechanical to the electronic age are problematic for architecture. They must, he argues, confront the possibility of a placeless, electronic reality. It is a truism that modern telecommunications—infinitely light and almost infinitely fast electrons—are transforming our world. Computers, phone, facsimile, e-mail, internet, video, virtual reality, etc., are subversive of traditional life and culture. They will be superseded by even faster, more powerful and more convenient mediations of reality and modes of communication. But none of these developments makes traditional architecture, urbanism, and regionalism less necessary and meaningful. Indeed, it can and already has been argued that the fleeting world of electronic information increases the human appetite for real, palpable place. This is especially true in residential and neighborhood design. It's one thing for Eisenman to design a decentered convention center in Columbus, Ohio, or a deconstructed office building in Tokyo; quite another for him to play with a residential quarter. He is mistaken to suggest that electronic media might kill the human need for the physical proximity of the traditional city. Like Marshall McLuhan's prediction in the 1960s that new electronic media would kill the book and unlike Victor Hugo's prediction that books would supplant the cathedral, his prognostication will prove more wrong than right.

. . . the fleeting world of electronic information increases the human appetite for real place.

The human desire and need for the commodity, firmness, and delight, as well as the meaning that architecture can provide will not be erased by information technology. Architecture *is* information. Moreover, it embodies knowledge. Architecture is a unique and irreplaceable way of knowing the world. Typing into a monitor or talking into a telephone all day makes face-to-face human interaction in well-designed buildings and outdoor spaces all the more necessary, satisfying, and worthwhile. Regional differences are relished and appreciated all the more. Authenticity and materiality command a higher not a lower premium in this increasingly mediated world. In the end, architecture is not words or paper but buildings. "Formidable or modest, they occupy a place, they transform a landscape, they loom in front of our eyes, they can be inhabited. They are the stage of power, commerce, worship, toil, love, life. . . . This is the art that does not represent and does not signify but *is*."[18]

If a region keeps seriously at it, with enough thoughtful designing and building, something critically regionalist will emerge. This is especially true for small scale residential and institutional construction, which are most subject to local climate and building practices, as well as local tradition and tastes. Careful and critical work can develop regional integrity and character any time or any place, urban or rural. It is not a question of size or wealth or age. Charleston, Savannah, and Siena achieve their greatness despite their small size, Delhi and Naples despite their poverty, Sydney and San Francisco despite their newness. It is a question of cultural confidence and fortitude, as well as critical intelligence, discrimination, and sensitivity. In the end, respect for place, nature, history, craft, and limits will precipitate a critical regionalism. These five tenets contribute to an architecture of place—not an abstract and cerebral architecture but a real, palpable one. However, for all its power to satisfy the basic human need for particular place and for home, Critical Regionalism gives us little help in connecting to universal or global patterns or meaning in the built environment or in our lives. For that we turn to typology.

CHAPTER 3

Typology
An Architecture of Limits

"To the universal plan which inspires, governs and tirelessly reconstructs the great universe, man was able to add a few pleasant footnotes. Particular cities and particular buildings can always be but imperfect realizations of these quasi-divine addenda. The house, the temple, the campanile, the roof, the column, the architrave, the frieze, the window, the door, the atrium, the street, the square and the city are inventions of man's genius, enriching nature's typological family. They are his proudest achievements, exceeding by far the discoveries of the wheel and fire, because for them he found no models but mere hints and analogues in nature."—Leon Krier

Limits are essential to freedom. Physical limits can liberate and constrain us at the same time: traveling on skis or bicycle frees us to move with much greater speed than on foot but it severely limits the ability to turn sharply, not to mention the ability to operate, say, a lawn mower. Other examples are not so obvious: being trapped in a snow-bound airport may at first seem imprisoning. If there is the slightest hope of flying, the situation can be one of high anxiety. But if there is absolutely no chance of flying, there can be a reassuring calm and free camaraderie that settles in. This irony also applies to mental activities, especially cognitive ones such as sorting sensory data and classifying information. Epistemological limits, i.e., ones that limit our ways of knowing the world, are essential. Likewise, site and programmatic constraints actually make the design process easier. Unconstrained freedom is anathema to designers, who need limits as much as civilization itself needs rules, traditions, and conventions. A blank piece of paper may be welcome to an artist but it can be intimidating to a designer.

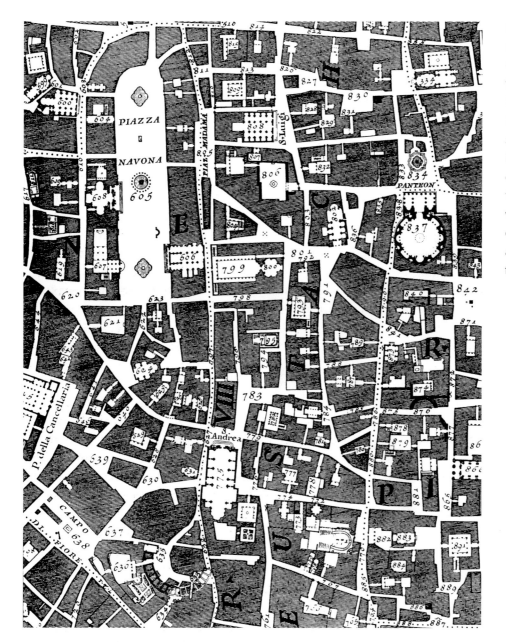

Rome—the classical city as a hierarchy and collage of outdoor rooms that are figural or at least particular, finite, and contained. Seattle lacks this sort of spatial definition and still is without a good piazza or public livingroom. On the other hand, it has well-defined edges that offer a sense of place along its many salt and freshwater shorelines.

The deeper question is whether these limits are little more than intellectual fences that we erect as boundaries to make cognition in a complex world manageable. Do they simply act as navigational devices as we negotiate reality? Or do limits in themselves embody essential truths about the world? Although the point may be unprovable, this chapter contends that limits are more than pragmatic necessities and do embody basic truths about life and offer lasting insights into the world. They are fundamental to the human condition in general and to design in particular. The categories vary from time to time and culture to culture, but limits per se are more than transitory and superficial constructs. Like our sensory screens and mental templates through which the world rushes in every day, they help make the complexities of life understandable.

Limits are part of a classical, zero-sum conception of reality. This is a world view in which we can't have it all, in which there is tragedy as well as happiness, in which there are finite resources and a limited number of times to get it right. It acknowledges that we all have within us the capacity to be cruel, perverse, and stupid, as well as kind, generous, and wise. This limited view of the human condition, with its full recognition of the dark as well as the bright side of human nature, is fundamentally different from the progressive and open-ended optimism of Modernism. The classical point of view favors harmony and balance, rather than originality and freedom. Convention takes on as much or more importance as invention. Tradition is valued as much or more than innovation.

Classicism, which has seen balance and harmony as an ideal since early Antiquity, recognizes that it is possible to take an idea too far. It would argue that many modernist buildings are too single-minded and some are monomaniacal. They sometimes pursue a single concept to exhaustion in the name of internal consistency and purity. High-tech architects, for example, are driven to make structures ever more lightweight and articulated. They can lose their sense of balance in their drive to defy physical forces. It is only a matter of time before one of their tensile roofs, trussed walls, or delicate handrails dramatically collapses, just as Beauvais Cathedral failed when its late medieval builders pushed its nave too high. The failure will not come as a result of misunderstanding gravity, wind, or seismic forces. It will come as a result of the relentless, blind push to perfect one idea at the expense of all others. Because it will be correctable with modern computational engineering, such a failure will be more symbolic than terminal. However, it will represent the same kind of dead end. Beauvais should serve as a reminder to us about single-minded architectural excess.

Every life experience is not a growth experience, as some contemporary pundits would have it. Nor is life foolproof, fail-safe, or no-fault. We make mistakes, some of which are irrevocable, even fatal. This is not to say there is no room in the classical view for optimism and growth. Classicism is not so much pessimistic about human nature and perfectibility as it is realistic and balanced. It acknowledges and tries to reconcile the conflicted, dualistic nature of the human condition, something contemporary American culture has trouble recognizing. As Allan Bloom points out: "The images cast helter-skelter on the wall of our cave . . . present high and low, serious and frivolous, without distinction or concern for harmonizing contrary charms."[1]

LIMITED SPACE, LIMITED FORM

There was a noticeable shift in the 1970s and 1980s from treating both architectural space and natural resources as unlimited and open-ended to treating them as finite and bounded. As mentioned at the end of the last chapter, a sense of finitude was perhaps the one and only convergence of environmentalist, regionalist, and Postmodernist design—a happy and significant conjunction given the divergence and pluralism of contemporary architectural thought. The Modernist conception of architectural space—Cartesian, universal, and continuous—gave way during those two decades to a static and finite conception, which was sometimes also specific to site and region. This non-Modernist or Postmodernist (it could also be called anti-Modernist) conception was a more hierarchical and classical representation of the world. It was more than a knee-jerk reaction to Modernism and was based on a realistic and balanced understanding of human and ecological forces. Balance and harmony may be too bland for today's media, but they have been of vital importance to environmentalists, Neotraditionalists, and Postmodernists.

During this same period, there was also a shift from treating architectural form and space as abstract and asymmetrical toward treating them as figural and symmetrical. Figural forms are finite by definition and natural forms are often symmetrical. The residual space often left over around Modernist "object" buildings (e.g., Seattle's Seafirst Tower, Rainier Tower, or the Kingdome) has been rejected in favor of background buildings that enclose positive outdoor space (e.g., the buildings next to Nordstrom that define the eastern edge of Westlake Square). This figure/ground reversal represents a profound paradigm shift in urban design. The outdoor "rooms" of urban streets and squares have become more valued than freestanding buildings surrounded by the empty windswept plazas of downtown office towers or the grass perimeters and parking lots of suburban office buildings.

Background or collateral buildings gain their strength from the public space they define. They also get strength from figural composition and detailing of the facades rather than from the bold footprints, gymnastic sections, and minimalist elevations that often characterize Modernist build-

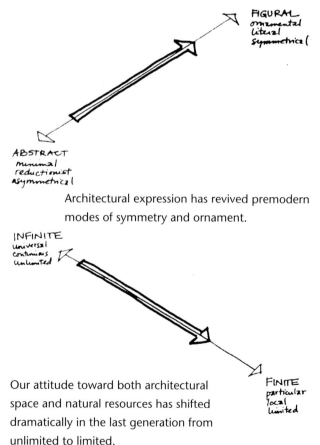

FIGURAL
ornamental
literal
symmetrical

ABSTRACT
minimal
reductionist
asymmetrical

Architectural expression has revived premodern modes of symmetry and ornament.

INFINITE
universal
continuous
unlimited

FINITE
particular
local
limited

Our attitude toward both architectural space and natural resources has shifted dramatically in the last generation from unlimited to limited.

ings. The quintessential Modernist building was like Modernist sculpture—a freestanding, abstract, minimalist object in unbounded universal space. The stand-alone building has given way to the infill building, where more design attention is lavished by the architect on the composition of facade than on the logic of the plan or the bravado of the section.

Like avant-garde artists, modern architects were not above indulging in original forms simply for their shock value. As Jacques Barzun has pointed out: "The cult of originality, the growing need of artists to singularize themselves within the growing mass of the talented, has encouraged the strong and the arrogant to administer ever more brutal shock treatments to the public."[2] Aesthetic brutality is the chronic problem with avant-gardism and compulsive originality: the shock or surprise must be continually increased in dosage to keep up with inflated expectation and higher threshold of aesthetic stimulation. Media coverage exacerbates the problem by fanning the flames of expectation and excitement even higher. At its worst, the media have turned art and architecture into a thrill ride.

By opposing the two axes on which there have been these diametric shifts, a map is created on which the work of influential twentieth-century architects can be plotted. The contemporary celebrities have staked out extremist positions that get media attention. The "Modern Masters" who have stood the test of time occupied a more balanced, centrist position. Or so it seems after the passage of time, which has exalted their position in history but also covered up some of their architectural sins. No one working in any contemporary mode—whether it be Postmodernist, Regionalist, or Deconstructivist—seems to have achieved a comparable maturity and wholeness. It is yet to be seen whether they can resist the temptation and media pressure to flee the more difficult and balanced center for the exciting and shocking edges. The media merry-go-round flings star architects to the edge, and slowly and surely erodes the credibility and relevance of the rest of the profession.

Was there also a shift in design methods that corresponded to the movement on these two axes? Or is this movement simply a measure of changing style and sensibilities? Although less heralded, there has been an equally dramatic change in design methods. The most notable methodological change has been the decline of functionalism and the rise of interest in precedent, context, and typology.

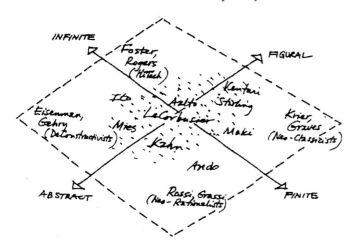

Modern orthodoxy has been scattered into Postmodern pluralism in the last quarter of the 20th century. The pendulum swung the other way earlier in the century. This oscillation sometimes seems generational, other times epochral.

FUNCTIONALISM

Functionalism, in this context, means a design mode that not only strives rationally to accommodate the programmatic needs and aspirations of a building's users, but also to express and embody those needs and aspirations architecturally. It has been one of the hallmarks of modernity and the most recent step in the philosophical march that started in the late seventeenth century with the Enlightenment and continued into this century as Logical Positivism, which sought to eliminate subjectivity in its quest for the precision and predictability of science. This philosophical tradition has given little credence to anything that cannot be measured. Metaphysics has little if any place in functionalism. "No doubt the Logical Positivists had sought to show that the classical metaphysical problem had either to be dismissed entirely, since no solution to it could be verifiable, or else transposed it into problems in the logic of science."[3] With this embrace of metrics, the spiritual and cultural sterility of functionalist buildings is not surprising.

For the functionalist, the design process starts with analysis of the problem at hand—looking inside it, as discussed in chapter 2. Before attempting any synthesis, the designer must first dissect and analyze the user, the user's program, the building systems and technics, the climate, and the site. Functionalist architects start with an empty piece of paper—literally, a *carte blanche*—and license to do just about anything formally. They commence with diagrams of uses and their adjacencies. If they are true to the tenets of the Modern Movement, they only look forward, never back to historical examples—free of any preconceptions about how a building might be configured or what it might look like. No books on architectural history would be found on the drafting table, unless it was perhaps Le Corbusier's *Oeuvre complet*. The functionalist ideal would have the program and technology design the building by itself, driven by its own transparent logic. Each building program is addressed as unique, requiring fresh learning and a new start. "Following their functionalist theory, they believe[d] every new design problem to consist of unprecedented requirements of various kinds, including a unique site, a unique set of functional demands, and a unique architectural form which would precisely solve this set of requirements and no others."[4]

Since functional requirements change quickly in modern society, buildings are often designed to be adaptable over the years and flexible during the daily or weekly cycle. Therefore, functionalists argue that architectural composition should visually express as well as physically accommodate these temporal changes. Thus, buildings should be designed not only to anticipate change but to read as incomplete or adaptable when first built. Building additions have always occurred incrementally, but the additions, like the host buildings, were usually treated before the Modern Movement as discrete

Modernism celebrated building as freestanding objects. These sculptures were often wonderfully composed but were difficult to work into existing urban fabric. When the same principles of composition were applied to cities, they proved equally problematic, as illustrated in these early Modernist proposals by Le Corbusier.

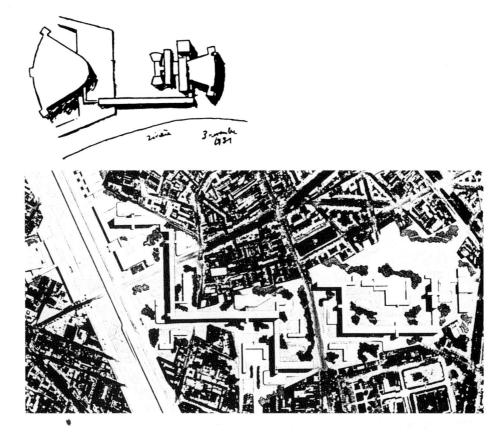

compositions; additions were used to further unify or reinforce an already complete composition or start a new one. Think of the myriad wings of the Louvre or the many additions to the U.S. Capitol (as opposed, for instance, to the University of Washington Health Sciences megastructure, which does not add up to a whole greater than the sum of its parts). Buildings tried to be compositionally complete at all times—before and after the intervention. Modernists, however, would sometimes intentionally leave a building's composition open-ended, almost as if construction had been interrupted and was waiting expectantly for the next phase to relieve the tension. The Pompidou Center in Paris is an example of a building that is intended to feel unfinished. Because these open-ended and adaptable buildings or complexes are not fully able to anticipate the future, they often end up being developed in unpredictable ways. The typical hospital complex suffers from such disjointed development. As Stewart Brand says in *How Buildings Learn*, "All buildings are predictions. All predictions are wrong."

This orientation to the future rather than the past seemed particularly acute among institutions that were experiencing rapid growth after World War II—such as colleges and universities. What American campus was not seriously marred by brutal, functionalist buildings in the 1950s and 1960s? Not only did Modernist architecture ruthlessly and blindly ignore the vocabulary and syntax of previous buildings, new academic units and complexes were started in a way that made completing them awkward in anything but the same idiom. Modernism jumped so far out of the stream of architectural history, it made it difficult for future generations to jump back in.

After more than a half-century of Modernism, its buildings are standing all over the globe and can be broadly judged. As individual buildings the best ones are, to be sure, magnificent and powerful, some of the most creative designs of all time. One has only to visit works by Wright, Le Corbusier, Kahn, Aalto, Mies, and many of their disciples to realize the strengths of Modernism. Although these masters did not work in the Seattle region, they influenced local practitioners to a great extent. The Seattle, Tacoma, and Bellevue skylines are a testimony to both the strength and pervasiveness of Modernism.

Although Modernism produced some of the greatest individual buildings of all time, it failed outright to produce good streets or good cities. Its buildings, because of their obligatory originality and direct expression of the interior, weren't likely to speak the language of neighboring buildings, especially traditional ones. (Seattle's Pike and Virginia Building by Olson and Walker is a local Modernist building that is an exception: it's a building that completely fills the site; its concrete frame honors Western Avenue precedents and it enhances the streetscape of Pike Place.) If not by demolition, they related to their context by contrast and counterpoint—a simplistic defense frequently used by Modernists. Along with the upheaval of neighborhoods and cities by urban renewal, the automobile, and zoning, the Modern Movement produced buildings that ignored each other and their older neighbors. To be fair to American Modernists, U.S. cities are by no means the least unified. They are not as chaotic or fragmented as Pacific Rim cities such as Tokyo or Seoul, where every commercial owner and architect tries to outdo the neighbors with an architectural statement. Nonetheless, American cities have too many self-centered buildings.

Functionalism sought to be internally consistent and coherent. Concerned with the unity and integrity of the individual building, which it saw as the inalienable building block of the city, Modernism's primary canon was to express clearly and honestly the internal logic of the building's program as well as its materials and structural systems. Style, per se, was forbidden— whether invented or copied. (Ultimately, it proved inescapable even to the most die-hard Modernists.) Functionalism reserved new forms to express new technical or programmatic developments and did not permit willful and arbitrary formalism. But even its best examples had trouble relating to the surrounding fabric of the city, not only in its historic districts but also in new districts. In the latter cases, the problem was uniformity and scalelessness

Although Modernism produced some of the greatest individual buildings of all time, it failed outright to produce good streets or good cities.

rather than discord with the context, because there was no traditional urban fabric with which to contrast. This inability to achieve consistency or even sympathy with neighbors was perhaps Modernism's biggest shortcoming.

As functionalism strove to be a "styleless" aesthetic, it did not typically produce buildings of a scale and richness around which popular affection and memories could easily develop. Instead it often produced cold and faceless buildings. As a consequence our cities lost much of their ability to nurture and transmit values of place, nature, history, and craft. In the hands of genius, it could reach the sublime, but in the hands of everyday practitioners Modernism fell short of what everyday architects have done in other periods. "For modernism had not produced a style which could simply be drawn upon by lesser practitioners, as had classical or Gothic architecture. Instead it had produced too much freedom—almost anything could be attempted. . . . Such freedom could constitute a breathtaking release in the hands of the masters—in the hands of followers it could easily become a new imprisonment."[5]

The average building was more urbanistically responsive and responsible in the nineteenth century, when architecture was more normative (e.g., Seattle's Pioneer Square or Capitol Hill, where single buildings don't stand out but the overall character is architecturally superior to, say, downtown Bellevue). Modernism's best solo performances may have been more virtuoso, but the typical fabric and its overall orchestration were better in previous eras. This past harmony was to a large extent the result of designers and builders being guided by a tacit understanding of convention and precedent. Among the most important conventions was architectural typology.

TYPOLOGY?

Typology is an idea that the Modern Movement intentionally abandoned. As Rafael Moneo writes:

> When, at the beginning of the twentieth century, a new sensibility sought the renovation of architecture, its first point of attack was the academic theory of architecture established in the nineteenth century. The theoreticians of the Modern Movement rejected the idea of type as it had been understood in the nineteenth century, for to them it meant immobility, a set of restrictions imposed on the creator who must, they posited, be able to act with complete freedom on the object. Thus when Gropius dispensed with history, claiming that it was possible to undertake both the process of design and positive construction without reference to prior examples, he was standing against an architecture structured on typology. The nature of the architectural object thus changed once again. Architects now looked to the example of scientists in their

. . . in the hands of everyday practitioners, Modernism fell short of what everyday architects have done in other periods. The average building was better in the 19th century.

attempt to describe the world in a new way. A new architecture must offer a new language, they believed, a new description of the physical space in which man lives. In this new field the concept of type was something quite alien and unessential.[6]

Typology—the study and theory of architectural types—revived a traditional way of looking at function in the 1970s and 1980s. Theorists asserted that it was a better point of departure than modernist functionalism when designing a building. Typologists like Leon Krier argued that almost any spatial problem at hand has been solved in the past. They defended enduring and commonplace architectural types that have evolved over time rather than following the mandate of the Modern Movement to discover new forms latent in program, site, or technology. In architectural education, typology brought academics to see their discipline more and more as a traditional language and not as a scientific/technical field in which invention is valued more than convention. Although the center of gravity of architectural theory later moved on to Deconstructivism and to social and environmental concerns, the idea of type remains alive as a result of Postmodernism.

Typologists may admit that a design problem can present unprecedented social issues and new technical opportunities, but they also know that human nature, human needs, and the human body haven't changed; nor has climate (yet) or geography (much). They also believe that cultural continuity is more desirable than constant change. Because types represent origins, a return to typology is an attempt to recover purity and continuance. As such, it privileges enduring tradition over endless progress.

Typologists look at how the design problem at hand has been solved in

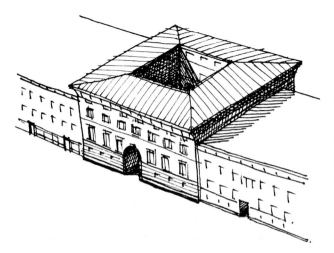

The Italian palazzo or urban seat for a wealthy family of the Renaissance has been successfully adapted and copied over the centuries by different cultures to house many different functions.

the past, especially in similar physical and cultural milieus. They visit built examples in the field. They visit the library, unashamed of learning from the history books that were not allowed any influence in the functionalist's office. They ask if there is a normative or standard architectural type that has evolved over time to solve the problem. If, for instance, the problem is a house, there are many types to draw on. Some types are ancient: the country villa and the atrium house. Some are high Architecture: the palazzo and the Palladian villa. Some are low: the sharecroppers' cabin and the garage apartment. Some are prehistoric and universal: the yurt, the thatched hut, and the house on stilts. Some are national: center hall colonial, bungalow, cottage, row house, ranch house, split level. Some are regional: the New England "salt box," the Charleston "single," New Orleans "shotgun," Philadelphia "trinity," Seattle "box," Florida "cracker," and so on. Some are from other countries: the Dublin "Georgian townhouse," the Sydney "terrace," the New Zealand "villa," and the Russian "dacha," to name a few.

TYPE

An architectural type is not an easy thing to explain. It is like a three-dimensional template that is copied over and over in endless variations. It is a norm, an abstraction, not an actual building. It is not usually the kind of abstraction that is ordained from on high or that springs whole from a single designer or builder. A type is rooted in the commonplace, the unselfconscious, even the unconscious. It is idealized in its archetype, which is its purest or most exemplary expression. A type devolves as a characteristic and typical representation of the archetype. It can be vernacular or high-style architecture. Even in the latter case, its origin cannot usually be traced to a single architect.

An architectural type is morphological, although it can also be characterized by specific materials (e.g., a Georgian townhouse is brick). It is to be distinguished from building type, which refers to function rather than form. The distinction between architectural types and building types is as important as it is confusing. The word "type" is sometimes employed loosely to refer to a functional building type with no standard morphology or configuration, such as an office building or apartment house. Other times it is used to refer to an architectural type with a standard morphology, such as the Italian palazzo.

In its ideal or archetypal configuration, the palazzo is a four-sided, three-story urban domicile with other buildings abutting on either side and with a squarish courtyard, which is reached through a front portal and which provides light and air to a rusticated ground floor, a piano nobile (second floor), top floor, and possible attic. There are many variations: the footprint might be rectangular or trapezoidal, the courtyard circular, skewed, or multiple, the

The "Seattle box" is a clear residential type, with predictable floor plan and massing, but a long and rich run of details.

site might be a corner or midblock, and the piano nobile may be doubled (as is the rare case at the UW's facility in the Palazzo Pio in Rome.) More to the point, the function can change and has changed over time. This basic configuration has been adapted or built anew to house offices, institutions, or apartments, among other things. Another example of an enduring type is the ancient Greek temple, a configuration that has also been revived for originally unintended purposes, from churches to banks to picnic shelters. A third enduring example is the Georgian townhouse, variations of which are still being adapted or built today to house a myriad of functions.

An example of a modern architectural type is the American gas station—with the cantilevered canopy, pump islands, cashier room, and service bays. Although it has increasingly been adapted to fruit stand, video store, or adult book store, it is not a type likely to be built anew to house these or other new functions. This is because its archetype is a very specific configuration designed for the all-weather vending of fuel and the indoor servicing of automobiles. Form and function are not so loosely matched as in the palazzo, temple, or townhouse, which have proven such versatile and lasting types. At the rate at which gas stations are changing to convenience stores—vending sugar as well as gasoline as fuel and without maintenance or repair services—the classic version may soon be on the historic register. The airport terminal and the parking garage are other modern architectural types. Also highly specific in configuration, they will not be easily adapted to or reincarnated for new uses.

When a type is realized as individual built form, it is called a model. A model has inflections and idiosyncrasies that accommodate and express its

The Seattle region is replete with examples of one- and two-story shops in neighborhood commercial centers. The wide and high bay storefront with clerestory windows and often a sidewalk awning or overhang is a successful and long-lived architectural type.

particular site and crafting. It is not a clone, which has no individuality and is the mechanical product of a prototype. Prototypes are part of an industrial paradigm, wherein standardized design and mass production crank out clones that are exactly identical or in which the differences are too random, too superficial, or too small to constitute true models. In speculative housing, changing the color of the cladding or brick, flipping the garage from one side to the other, or adding shutters to the front facade are usually too artificial to make a type into a model. The model is a thoughtful accommodation of a building type to a specific site and a personal expression of its designer, builder, or owner—not just a marketing ploy.

An example of type and model is the bungalow. The bungalow was originally a horizontal, one-story, detached house in seventeenth-century India, especially Bengal. The type was adapted by the British, North Americans, Australians, and South Africans as a vehicle for the early suburbanization of their cities. In the Seattle region, where it was built in the Craftsman style, it was widely and sensitively adapted by a generation of builders to fit different sites and household sizes. In other regions of the United States, it took on other architectural styles, including Spanish Colonial and American Colonial. It proved to be an extremely successful type. Among other virtues, it was within the financial reach of the carpenters who built them. It was the first housing type to intentionally accommodate the family automobile. It was also one of the first types to have a relatively spacious living room and efficiently designed kitchen. The bungalow is a good example of typology, but it is not a good example of Critical Regionalism. Although its origins in rural Hindu culture are genuinely regionalist, it could be considered one of the first and

TYPOLOGY

most widespread examples of the global system of production and consumption, as well as suburbanization.[7] For such a lovable little house type, the bungalow has an ironic and not so lovely pedigree of mass production, mass consumption, and urban sprawl.

If architectural types keep working well, they remain alive and are reproduced in new models. But if no longer functional or meaningful, they lose their vitality and degenerate into hollow or sentimental stereotypes. This has been the fate, for example, of the contemporary ranch house or split-level, which is now built with superficial variations all over the country in countless suburban subdivisions. Although the bungalow was also built around the country, there were more genuine differences from region to region. At least it seems that way today. Perhaps their differences now seem more genuine (and appealing) simply because of better and more substantial craftsmanship. They didn't all suffer, for instance, standard aluminum windows with snap-in plastic muntins or sliding glass doors, so cheap and oblivious to climate and culture.

Perhaps a more easily understood example of type and model is the human body. The human being is a single biological species, but it keeps reproducing in miraculous variety. There are two sexes and three basic body types, but no two models of the type are exactly the same. Differences of millimeters in facial structure are immediately recognizable; friends can be spotted at once in a crowd. Not only are subtle differences appreciable, humans do not tire of looking at each other. Indeed, we look at thousands of faces every year and are never bored by the next one that comes into our cone of vision. We are intrigued not just by visual differences and superficial details. We are interested in and drawn to the person behind the face, just as authentic differences in a building's facade promise differences inside. The ability of variations on a single theme to hold our interest is remarkable. Those

Typical Seattle bungalows, consistent in massing and floor plan, modest in size but dignified in their presence. The builder probably took the plan from *Bungalow* magazine (published early this century in Seattle) and added or subtracted a few details. Built two or three houses at a time, the plan added up to a neighborhood with more architectural interest than the contemporary subdivision which may consist of scores or hundreds of houses constructed by one builder with fewer and more artificial variations.

that argue that typology makes architecture inherently less interesting fail to recognize this immense human capacity to appreciate subtle differences and minute details.

THE BEHAVIORIST TRAP

Typological design, like Critical Regionalism, tends to shy away from the term methodology and its shop talk that were popular in the 1960s. At the architecture schools on such campuses as Berkeley, MIT, and the University of Washington, it was thought that the process of design could be linearly analyzed and demystified. Some proponents felt the act of design could actually be codified. Environmental psychology or person-environment relations, based on the detached observation and study of human behavior in the built environment, borrowed heavily from psychology and sociology. This design methodology illuminated some valuable insights into human factors as design determinants but failed to come up with a body of knowledge or information that could be easily applied by designers. Although it has uncovered unquestionable truths about human interaction within and with the built environment, applying the scientific method in general and behavioral science in particular to design has often produced a low yield for the time and effort expended.

Design methodologists pursued a scientific approach in order to predict human behavior and thereby accommodate it in the design of buildings and communities. However, precise prediction of human behavior is impossible, because the human being is a self-defining animal and because society and its physical props are continually changing. Attempts to quantify and predict psychological and social phenomena are usually doomed to chase but never catch up with what they are attempting to measure—like a dog chasing its tail. Or like a physicist measuring subatomic particles that are forever too small and too fast to track both weight and location simultaneously. Psychosocial issues may be subject to a sort of Heisenberg Principle of their own. They may be too slippery to be quantified in a timely enough and useful enough way to be readily applied by designers.

THE LIMITS OF ORIGINALITY

Although Modernists eschewed the concept and tradition of typology, they might admit to three morphological types: centroidal, linear, and field or scattered. These basic categories were abstract diagrams, devoid of function or history. They would also admit to functional types, but not in a way that prefigures a building's form. They tended to reinvent architecture with every new program. Architects lost the decorum and discipline to do straightfor-

Because society and its physical props are changing quickly, attempts to quantify social phenomena are usually doomed to chase but never catch up with what they are attempting to measure.

ward, nonheroic buildings when the program was ordinary and modest. To refrain from conspicuously creative statements when they were not needed became an act of architectural courage in our media-saturated society. Originality and creativity became the curse rather than the blessing of Modernism.

The time and the place for idiosyncrasy and originality are when the program or site or both are unusual. Designers need not feel compelled to be constantly innovative with every commission, at least not at the scale of the whole building, where invention was most valued for the Modernist. This does not mean that typologists are not creative. It means their creativity is exercised at a smaller or larger scale than the individual building, such as at the scale of the room or street. Nor does it mean that all building types are equally conducive to originality. Housing, because it is a place of rest and retreat, tends to be more conservative and less inventive than other building types. It also numerically compromises the bulk of the urban fabric and consequently must play a more subdued role in the city.

The types with which to be most architecturally inventive and expressive are places of work, recreation, and entertainment, where people extend themselves. Architects who radically innovate or experiment with individual homes or second homes are acting within a long and fertile design tradition. But those that take similar liberties with multifamily housing and residential neighborhoods forget that home and community are about haven and familiarity, not ambition and striving. When a talented architect like Rem Koolhaas conducts exciting and creative experiments like the Congrexpo at Euralille, it's a reasonable and exciting proposition. But when he experiments in Fukuoka, Japan, with housing that looks like a mortuary or night club, it's not. Residential communities are more socially fragile than business centers— or, for that matter, airports, convention centers, entertainment centers, and sports arenas. Architects must know the right type and place to thumb their noses at convention. Not all parts of the city are appropriate for experimentation. Most neighborhoods need stability, not innovation.

Typology can also be an act of efficiency and economy for the designer. It is considerably easier to start with a time-tested architectural type and modify it into a suitable model than to start anew with every architectural commission. A typological point of departure is quicker in that it draws on types that are finite in number. It does not start out with the near-infinite architectural possibilities that a functional analysis or "bubble diagram" of the building's program permits. The Modernist insistence on starting from scratch is very expensive. It often overtakes the architectural fee and exhausts the design team and client. As much as anything else, economy has encouraged architects to embrace typological design.

"Form follows function" was the rallying cry of Modernism. Although it may have achieved this correspondence at the building scale, it ignored the

To be always innovative is as tyrannical as to be always traditional. . . . Designers need not feel compelled to be constantly innovative with every commission.

connection between form and function at the urban scale. Because many Modernist buildings are creative translations of one-of-a-kind programs into unforeseen and never-before-seen forms, materials, and structural systems, they are often unrecognizable as urban elements. Most people would not recognize Frank Lloyd Wright's Guggenheim as a museum, for example. Nor would most people recognize Le Corbusier's Ronchamp Chapel as a church.

On the other extreme, commercial Modernism has recently put complex or mixed programs under one roof, sometimes in a single large volume. These inexpensive sheds, Butler buildings, tilt-up boxes, and megastructures tend to be so unarticulated and generic as to be mute lumps in the cityscape. They lack the tectonic quality of traditional market halls and sheds. These warehouses offer the same potential for adaptability for which palazzos and townhouses have been praised, but they are built of much lower quality construction and are more loosely configured. Space is not made for particular uses but is simply made available. The huge metal and concrete boxes could house a discount mart, tennis courts, or dairy cows. As pointed out in chapter 1, this reduction in the number of architectural types is more acute in suburbia, where building is even more expedient and repetitive.

Typological design is also less likely to produce visual chaos in the built environment than Modernism. Buildings of the same type naturally tend to rhyme more with each other over time and space. Cities are once again more legible and therefore more understandable to their inhabitants and guests. They are vital not because they are a breathless collection of novel and exciting buildings, but because they are an understandable hierarchy of buildings that are big and small, important and unimportant, vernacular and monumental, background and foreground. When understandable to their citizens, cities can again help record, legitimize, and transmit the values of culture and community.

Does typology dull architectural creativity? No, but it does put limits on it and shifts its scale. Like many ordering systems, it can actually liberate and unleash more coherent creativity. The type offers a known framework in which creative change can take place—either during the initial design process, during construction, or after occupancy. It frees the designer to concentrate on changes that truly make a difference rather than on the superficial or arbitrary invention of form. It limits originality for its own sake—the kind of novelty into which commodification, marketing, and avant-gardism can degenerate. The Modernist imperative to innovate ultimately became just as tyrannical as the former imperative to follow tradition. Typologists can be original and go beyond the ordinary, but only at the appropriate scale and when extraordinary circumstances warrant it. They do not feel that they must be original with every design problem. On the other hand, they must guard against being too slavish in their replication of a given type.

Typology has a different attitude toward change over time than Modernism. High-style Modernist buildings tend to be unique responses to specific programs for particular users. They start out specialized, with interiors and exteriors that are hard to adapt to the subsequent uses that will be invariably asked of the building. Types are not overspecialized and are usually more adaptive. The palazzo, the basilica, the Georgian townhouse, the Cape Cod cottage, and the loft warehouse are examples of versatile architectural types. Not all types are this adaptable, but most buildings based on types are general enough to be customized over time. In a sense, they start out conservative, conventional, and traditional and become radicalized over their life. High-style Modernist buildings, on the other hand, often start out as radical and are made to become more normal over time as they are changed by their users.

A QUESTION OF SCALE

Typology has also shifted the scale at which invention occurs. Instead of sculpting a creative statement at the building scale, a hallmark of the Modern Movement, a typological design is often concerned with the scale of the room. Rooms take on the importance that Modernism tended to lavish on the circulation system. (Such elements as stair towers, corridors, and elevator shafts were often expressed as bold and conspicuous elements.) Related to this reemerging interest in discrete rooms is a renewed emphasis on components such as the door, the column, and the window, which no longer are thought of as standardized. At the other end of the spectrum—the scale of public space—typology also disciplines creativity. Spatial variety is encouraged at the urban scale, because public spaces are treated as particularized outdoor rooms that are site specific. They are not treated as generic streets and plazas. In a sense, typology trades creativity at the scale of the building for creativity at the scale of the detail and of the city.

The scale at which architectural expression and creativity take place on these two Seattle residential streets is radically different. The traditional street consists of similar housing types of consistent bulk and footprint but with great variety in their detailing. The Modernist street has wild variations in bulk and foot-print, but standardized windows, trim, and hardware. The former streetscape offers a more coherent and cohesive sense of place than the latter.

Modernist functional zoning has segregated the city into zones of single uses, greatly reducing the number of types with which to shape urban form and space. Bulk requirements, especially set-back regulations, have often resulted in empty, windswept streets and plazas—residual rather than positive public space. As stated earlier, urban typology reverses this figure/ground relationship, trading figural object buildings for figural public spaces. The reversals are remarkably consistent across the board.

	DETAILING	ROOM	BUILDING	STREET
MODERNISM	Generic	Generic	Particular	Generic
TYPOLOGY	Particular	Particular	Generic	Particular

Modernism was creative primarily at one scale. It put all its fertile eggs in one basket, the individual building, preferably freestanding. Common building types help us appreciate the typical and generic aspects of a city, while variations of details, rooms, and streets satisfy our need for the particular. Modernism has tended to predictable and anonymous detailing, rooms, and urban design, but often to wildly different buildings. Typology is only predictable and anonymous at the scale of the building.

With a typological approach, the architect is more concerned with the smaller, more private compositions of architecture—the facade, the room, and the details, all of which are less prescribed than overall configuration by the type. At the scale of the city, the uniformity of zoning yields to mixed-use neighborhoods and districts. Like the architectural detail and the room, the city becomes a rich array of different architectural types and public spaces, while the individual building becomes more predictable and well-behaved.

A QUESTION OF HIERARCHY

If Modernism bleached variety out of architectural detailing and urban space, Postmodernism artificially restored it. It started dressing a single architectural type in different garbs, often trying to pump up the importance of a building or trying to be contextual where there was no distinctive context. This dress code often inflated the visual importance of a building beyond its programmatic importance in the city- or townscape, adding further confusion to the built environment. Like signing an unimportant document with a grand flourish, it overembellished everyday buildings. Indeed, architects were hired to put their signatures on mundane, commercial buildings. Postmodernism overreacted to functionalism. To quote Leon Krier:

Whatever the pretensions of its forms, a supermarket is no less or more significant, whether wrapped in architectural, nautical or commercial dressing. Its very typological and social status will forever prevent it from becoming culturally significant. The reverse is also true: however beautiful and dignified an historical city center may be, it cannot survive for long its transformation into a shopping, business or leisure zone. In the same way even the largest housing scheme cannot become a city or public monument. . . . its functional monotony and uniformity simply do not provide the typological materials for significant monumental and urban gestures.[8]

BACKGROUND AND FOREGROUND BUILDINGS

This is another way of linking architectural expression to function. Here the function is urban coherence rather than the internal accommodation of a building's program and its honest expression on the exterior. Putting private and commercial functions in foreground, monumental buildings is inappropriate. Putting important public functions in background, vernacular buildings is equally wrong. As stated in chapter 1, the local post office often looks like it could be a warehouse, and conversely the branch bank or medical office building looks like it might be a post office or a branch library. A local mismatch was relocating Seattle's municipal offices into existing office buildings. Office blocks may sometimes be appropriate for a city's bureaucracy, and the strategy may in this case have saved several historic structures, but it missed a crucial opportunity. Building a new City Hall is a chance—one of the city's few remaining ones—to make a monumental civic building. There is still the possibility of housing its more ceremonial parts in an

With a clear distinction between residential and public buildings, Seaside, Florida, is zoned more typologically than functionally. This Neotraditional resort community trades uniformity of function within a zone for a variety of building types within a neighborhood. A common architectural language is also prescribed in its codes, which reinforce a hierarchy of building and street types. For instance, only public buildings can be white; all houses must be colored, have picket fences, etc. Public buildings are far less constrained by the code. They are treated as figural monuments and foreground buildings set off against the background residential buildings. (Duany and Plater-Zyberk)

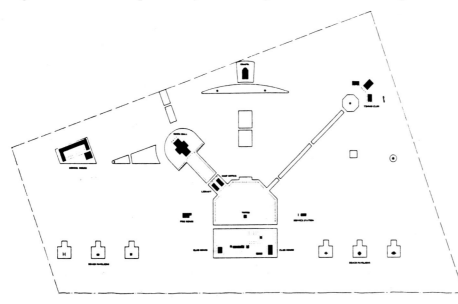

honorific, foreground building on or near the present site of the Municipal Building—that latter-day Holiday Inn as City Hall.

Monumental buildings need not be large in size. They need only be civic in their presence. Sometimes stature is enhanced by miniaturization and refinement rather than grand size. A well-designed, low-rise city hall can tame surrounding private high-rise buildings into the backdrop roles they should have been playing in the first place. The temples at Japan's Ise Shrine are but one famous example of the power of smallness and refinement. Teahouses are another example from this country that values modesty. In Philadelphia, Independence Hall makes civic dwarfs of much larger surrounding buildings, as do gemlike colonial buildings in Boston. In Seattle, the Pioneer Square canopy evokes a power well beyond its size. So does Tacoma's Union Station. Seattle's neighborhood libraries and firehouses are small, but they command a strong public presence.

The appropriate expression of a building's importance is a critical part of restoring meaning and clarity to both architecture and the city. The hierarchy of importance as well as the distinction of public and private realm have become confused. As development mixes public and private uses again, the city becomes even more confused, making a clear typology all the more necessary. Indeed, the relaxation of single-use zoning makes a typological approach to urbanism essential. (Look at the Port of Seattle's Bell Street Pier, where a rich and positive mix of public and private functions is jumbled together without distinguishing between commercial, industrial, and institutional.) It is good to mix uses, including public and private ones, but not to confuse architectural types or their hierarchy of importance.

Like the loss of biological species, there has been a decrease in the number of architectural types, especially in suburbia. As a growing range of functions is housed in generic tilt-up warehouses, glass boxes, and preengineered metal sheds, there are fewer and fewer types with which to shape and articulate the built environment. This makes a smaller, dumber palette for architects, engineers, and urban designers. Ultimately, it makes for a physical monoculture.

There are other problems that grow out of the functionalist paradigm that are beyond the scope of this book. Specialization of labor is one—the splitting of the act of design from the act of construction in the Renaissance and later the division of architecture into separate professions (engineers, planners, landscape architects, interior designers, industrial designers, and urban designers, in approximately that order). While construction was divorced from design well before the rise of functionalism, the proliferation of design professions and the corresponding fragmentation of architecture schools into colleges with multiple departments have happened in the second half of this century (with the exception of civil engineering, which has been separate

Those who think typology and endless variations on a theme are boring should listen to Bach (or rock-and-roll), or better yet take a stroll in Dublin, where the front doors of identical Georgian town-houses are a rich array of the same type. The high quality of design and craftsmanship makes these superficial changes more convincing than variations found in a contemporary subdivision.

for centuries). This multiplication of professions and specialized expertise has diluted the power of all the design professions to know and re-present the world as holistic.

Architects and other design professionals are well served to recognize the limits of functionalism and embrace the benefits of typology. This does not mean the end of functionalism per se. Obviously, buildings must continue to function efficiently and economically. But not at all costs and not at the loss of urban decorum and coherence. In recent decades, function as a design methodology and as the sole organizing device for building plans and sections has given up much of its preeminence to contextualism and typology. Typology, after all, functions very well in urbanistic terms by flexibly addressing the needs of the city and sustaining a degree of continuity and contiguity in architecture. It is, in fact, the link between architecture and urbanism that was missing in Modernism.

Architectural types are to urban designers what building components are to architects. Typology is the language of urban design. Getting the types right for a given street, neighborhood, or community is usually more important than the architectural brilliance of individual buildings. A collection of beautifully designed buildings does not a city make. Witness a World's Fair with many pavilions designed by their country's star architects. They don't necessarily add up to a sense of place or community. Columbus, Indiana, has individual masterpieces by many of the nation's most distinguished and talented architects. But this trophy collection does not guarantee a coherent, well-designed town or city. At the moment, most American cities suffer more from typological confusion than architectural mediocrity. However, the right typology alone cannot provide for a good built environment. It takes both good architecture *and* the right types to imbue the built environment with the magic and coherence that design can give it.

Our individualistic architecture of function is abating in favor of the architecture of urbanism. For no other reason than the arithmetic of population, the fulcrum has slowly but inexorably shifted from rugged individualism to urbanity. We have reassessed the scales at which we should be bold and innovative. We have started to downsize our expectations and to realize—as players in a classical tragedy realize—that the physical world is finite and must be fashioned out of limited resources, energy, space, forms, and architectural types. There is not the luxury of endless time or bottomless resources to pursue cavalierly our architectural and urban agenda.

TYPOLOGY VERSUS CRITICAL REGIONALISM

If Critical Regionalism celebrates and reinforces what is unique and enduring, typology provides us with a connection to something bigger and more universal. It furnishes us with a connection of our buildings to our city and region as well as to architecture and urbanism around the world. It also provides us with the building blocks—the DNA, if you will—to coherently shape a city that is more than a collection of its pieces. In a secular culture, the city may be the biggest and most long-lived thing to which most people can hope to connect. The city is made for us by people who preceded us, and we make it for people who follow us. It is both unique and great. Both needs—to be unique and to be part of some great idea or large group—seem to be a major part of the modern Western psyche. It could be argued that typology alone answers both of these needs, because it speaks about both the singleness and the commonality of building and city. But it no longer speaks loudly enough about the regional differences that are quickly becoming extinct around the globe. Nor does it satisfy our need for a phenomenology of place. Typology is not strong enough alone to withstand mass culture and resist the commodification of architecture. For this, we need a rooted and judicious regionalism.

The tension and friction between these two proclivities can be fertile.

Because Critical Regionalism is critical, even disdainful, of popular culture, it is not always conducive to city making. More concerned about place than community, it is very compelling at the architectural scale, but its critical stance can be counterproductive when trying to make a street or neighborhood. In making its critiques of popular culture, Critical Regionalism perpetuates the avant-garde attitude toward culture, with its endless overturning of tradition by an artistic elite. In striving to be authentic, pure, and timeless, Critical Regionalism sets itself apart from the norm. This stance may produce good, even profound, architecture but not necessarily good neighborhoods, towns, or cities. A townperson knows the importance of a collective framework or covenant that brings people together in less critical and more tolerant ways. This means many background buildings that behave in predictable, normal ways and that honor their context for every foreground architectural/artistic statement. In short, we must beware of architectural snobbery when designing whole communities. And we must remember that typology can help us make our communities whole.

Complex, self-defining systems like society and culture need competing ideas and contradictory forces to invigorate and regulate themselves. Other periods and cultures have put the human ego to higher purposes and fostered a greater sense of a community. Contemporary Americans seem saddled for better or worse with this equally strong need both to individuate and to be part of a group. Rebelliousness and egotism are joined against connectedness and community. If we are to design for both the individual and the group, if we are to express what is local and what is universal in our built environment, regionalism and typology must engage in continuous dialogue.

CHAPTER 4

The New Urbanism

Urban Villages, Pedestrian Pockets, Transit-oriented Development, and Traditional Neighborhood Design

"Perhaps architects of the first half of the 20th Century, compelled by the prospect of a modern age, too easily shed the conventions of city building. We, who experienced the consequences of this abdication of precedent, have reciprocated: redeploying time-honored civic traditions has become increasingly tempting. Estranged from the new city, we seek comfort in convention. When conventions fail to solve contemporary needs, we place faith once more in radical innovation. The strokes of this pendulum have shortened considerably as we approach the end of this century."—Alex Krieger

What can truly and effectively be planned and designed? Certainly not civilization, as F. A. Hayek and others have persuasively argued.[1] Nor the economy, as Eastern Europe's failed experiments in centrally planned socialist economies have dramatized. These "extended orders" are too complex to be rationally or scientifically understood, much less planned or designed. Like culture, they must slowly evolve through endless self-correction, inflection, trial and error. Culture embodies a sort of meta-intelligence which is far greater than individual genius, just as the Gaia Hypothesis contends that our whole planet acts as an organism with a collective intelligence greater than any single species. Human culture allows rationality and intelligence to develop; it is not the other way around. Culture is far too complex to be figured out and orchestrated by human ingenuity, however effective our rationality may be for getting to the moon or however brilliant our imagination may be in the arts. It will never be fully understood.

History has shown, however, that we can make some headway in planning the city. Every continent, save Antarctica (the saving of which is not a bad idea in and of itself), has successful examples of planned cities. Some are the results of grand plans, others more piecemeal interventions, but the best always have a vision and sense of themselves. They have clear centers and edges, healthy neighborhoods, exciting districts, and strong corridors. Indeed, cities that are not planned in some manner end up as illegible and confused as Houston or Tokyo. This book contends that we can envision and plan the metropolitan region—even though its fringe is increasingly amorphous. It's not that suburbs are without order; in many ways their order is too predictable. But their whole is an incoherent, gelatinous sum of the parts. Designing a region need not be a single grand plan or vision. It can be a series of interventions in key locations at critical times. These interventions of various scope and intensity at local pressure points are what Part II of this book is all about.

PRIVATE PILLAGE

Before the automobile, streetcar suburbs (Capitol Hill, Madison Park, Leschi, etc.) made eminent sense. At their outset, automobile suburbs made sense too. Living on a shady, quiet lane with a stream out back and a half-empty school bus to pick up the kids was a tempting alternative to noisy, messy city neighborhoods. These inner city neighborhoods were beginning to be cut up anyway, as freeways slashed their way through them on their way to the suburbs. What ensued is all too familiar: empty downtowns at night; decline of the neighborhood school, church, and store; urban renewal; lots of vacancies and vacant lots; traffic congestion; cul-de-sac subdivisions; wider arterials and longer red lights; regional malls and office parks; fewer truck farms; increasing crime; more parking lots and less green space; smog and air pollution; gridlock downtown; gridlock in suburbia. . . .

Seattle has been spared the full measure of some of these nightmares. It still has a strong middle and upper middle class that has not fled to the suburbs. Nonetheless, we are Los Angelizing the Seattle region more quickly than we think. It's as long and often as congested a drive from Puyallup to Everett as from Santa Monica to San Bernadino. And our basin of potentially buildable land is much bigger than the Los Angeles basin. Potentially, we could carpet it from mountain to sound. If you drive western Snohomish County, you know that the strip 'n mall are already the norm rather than the exception and that traffic is getting as bad as in downtown Seattle. The sheer amount of retail boggles the mind. Just who is buying all that merchandise? And do they really need it?

Many of our region's suburbanites commute forty-five minutes to work,

It's not that suburbs are without order; in many ways their order is too predictable. But their whole is an incoherent, gelatinous sum of the parts.

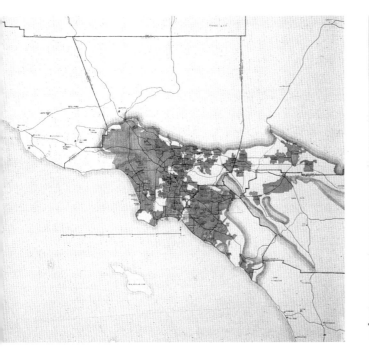 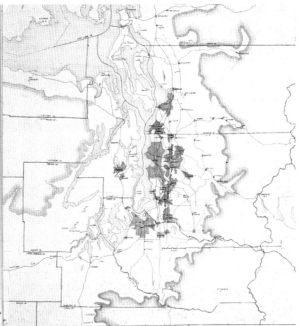

These maps of the Los Angeles and Seattle regions are at the same scale. The buildable land and the potential for sprawl is much larger in the Puget Sound region because the mountains, shown with the wide grey line, form a larger basin. (Personal communication from a Seattle citizen)

which adds up to 2.4 years of eight-hour days over the first eighteen years of their children's life. They are unlikely to have kids, however, as couples with children now account for less than one in four of the new households formed in the U.S.A. Most new households are single parents, seniors, and unrelated adults—not the flesh and blood of the original American Dream, much less the clientele for our annual Street of Dreams.

So how have we ended up in this predicament? Contrary to what conspiracy-minded critics would assert, it is not a particularly conscious or well-orchestrated plot. Like the rise of urban civilization, the advent of suburban culture and society is far too complicated a phenomenon to mastermind or control. Of course, people and institutions continually try to control the course of events, but no cartel has all the cards in its hand. As stated earlier, the oil companies and automobile manufacturers have done their big share in promoting automobile suburbia, as have government highway and sewer programs and tax deductions for home mortgages. The building-products industry, including the timber companies, have certainly known that their bread is buttered on the suburban more than urban side. And environmental laxity has helped underwrite the whole project. But it can't all be blamed on the greed of big business and the power of big government. As individuals we've been covetous consumers, too easily stimulated to artificial consumption by Madison Avenue and Sunset Boulevard. As Wendell Berry has put it:

However destructive may be the policies of the government and the methods and products of the corporation, the root of the problem is to be found in private life. We must learn to see that every problem that concerns us . . . always leads straight to the question of how we live. The world is being destroyed—no doubt about it—by the greed of the rich and powerful. It is also being destroyed by popular demand. There are not enough rich and powerful people to consume the whole world; for that the rich and powerful need the help of countless everyday people.[2]

We've been quick to exchange the more raw and uncomfortable sidewalk life of the inner city neighborhood for the easy and banal TV life of the suburban family room. We have been too quick to give up the public life that American cities have slowly mustered in spite of a long legacy of Jeffersonian anti-urbanism. It has been our good fortune that immigrants from countries with strong public realms (and cities where the wealthy citizens live

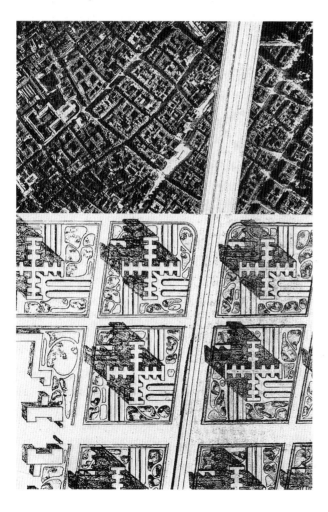

Le Corbusier's Plan Voisin (1925) for the demolition of central Paris and the building of a Modernist skyscraper and highway city. It literally killed the street and the very idea of street life. It is also a blatant example of starting over again, although this time in a European context. (Le Corbusier, *The City of Tomorrow*, 1928)

"The width of streets is inadequate. . . . The distances between street intersections are too short. . . . The city block, a direct by-product of the street system . . . has long ceased to correspond to any need. . . . The pedestrian must be able to follow other paths than the automobile network. This would constitute a fundamental reform in the pattern of city traffic. None would be more judicious, and none would open a fresher and more fertile era in urbanism."—The Athens Charter of CIAM, 1933 downtown rather than at the periphery) have imported urban and ethnic values for which we are much the richer. But many European immigrants have wanted to leave the public life behind. Indeed, the pioneers of Modernism in Europe came out against traditional urban streets and the messy complexity they contain. The Athens Charter of C.I.A.M., led by the most mythical of all twentieth-century European architects, Le Corbusier, joined the battle for a more rational separation of vehicles and pedestrians in a new urban vision that spread to America.

African Americans—the group brought to America most forcibly and most unfairly—have maintained a strong and rich street life, as have Latinos. But European Americans have continued to flee the public realm—most recently from public city streets to the privatized cul-de-sacs of suburbia. They have taken the money with them, and the best schools. Our cities' public parks cannot match the lushness and opulence of suburban golf courses. Now half of all Americans live in suburbia, where incomes average 60 percent more than those of city-dwellers. The good life is associated with the private rather than the public realm in America. The coffers of the private sector overflow, while public treasuries dwindle.

Despite our inevitable inability to micro-manage all the forces that have resulted in sprawl, we can do better at managing some of them. First and foremost, we must eliminate the two principal causes of sprawl: artificially cheap land and artificially cheap energy. Like a supertanker that takes ten miles to stop, the American economy will be slow to change, even if we throw ourselves into reverse immediately. However, if we don't reverse these twin propellers, many of our other urban reforms will be in vain. In the meantime, we must stop smearing a monoculture across the countryside, where the biggest cash crop now is houses sprouting up like so many acres of wheat. We've traded the growing season for the construction season. The two most far-reaching corrections would be to make gasoline and rural land more expensive, so that their market prices more closely reflect their true cost.

In absolute terms, urban infill is cheaper in both capital and operating costs than low-density development of rural land. The capital costs of sprawl are high: new highways, roads, sewers, utilities, water system; new schools and school bus fleets; new stores and jobs that require the private transit of automobiles with the attendant air pollution, congestion, and lost time. Yet, we continue to develop the urban fringe like Topsy despite the high costs of improvement. Why? Because it's so profitable. The capital cost of land is still cheap and the burden of infrastructure, despite the trend toward concurrency mentioned in chapter 1, can often still be shifted to the public sector. And subsidized energy masks the high operating costs of suburbia—fueling and maintaining all the cars and yellow schoolbuses, as well as heating and cooling all the freestanding houses.

The capital cost of urban infill development is less, because much of the physical, commercial, and institutional infrastructure is already in place. Operating costs are also less, because urban compactness makes for more energy-efficient buildings and for less transportation. The cost is also easier to bear because it is more incremental than huge new suburban developments. Unfortunately—very unfortunately—the pricing mechanism of our not-so-pure market system puts a *much* lower price tag on suburban than urban land. The attempt to shift some of the public sector's costs to the developer and in turn to the homebuyer helps compensate for some of these market oversights. But not all of them: institutional costs, such as zoos, aquariums, city parks, art museums, arboretums, and symphony halls, continue to be more heavily borne by city taxpayers, with little help from suburban tax revenues. Revenue sharing at the metropolitan scale is as essential as land reform.

Another approach to dealing with the underpricing of rural land and the windfall profits of land speculators would be to let the public sector itself speculate in the market. In this scenario, the local government would buy land on the urban fringe at agricultural prices, rezone it, and then sell it to developers. Impoverished local governments could thereby realize the huge profits that often accrue to the developer. The value added by up-zoning is captured by the public sector, which can then use it for infrastructure development, with a considerable balance left over for other public purposes. Moreover, it can guide, require, even plat development to conform to a preferred pattern. Quite common in Europe, this idea is not an un-American one; no less a patriot than George Washington did it. As president, he condemned much of the private landholdings in the District of Columbia and had L'Enfant lay out and plat a beautiful national capital, some of which was sold back to the private sector to be developed.

This scheme has more benefits than concurrency to recommend itself in fiscal terms, especially at a time when American cities are struggling for funds. However, it has one large potential flaw: it puts the government into commercial business. As Jane Jacobs points out brilliantly in *Systems of Survival*,[3] government does not do well when it engages in commerce. Nor does business do well in government. When these two fundamental worlds—commerce and guardianship—get reversed, confusion and problems ensue. In short, government bureaucracies may be too slow, too inefficient, and too mired in the values of guardianship and fairness to do a credible job at buying and selling, something at which the commercial marketplace is so adept. Land development may also be too great a temptation for corruption, because the dollar amounts involved in appreciated land values can sometimes be incredibly large. We should approach this option cautiously, but nonetheless test its applicability to the American metropolis.

If artificially low-priced land is the biggest single reason for sprawling devel-

If artificially low-priced land is the biggest single reason for sprawling development, then cheap gasoline is the next biggest culprit.

opment, then cheap gasoline is the next biggest culprit. Gasoline prices have actually dropped in real dollars over the years. Pump prices would be a lot higher if we paid the full cost of fossil fuels. As mentioned in chapter 1, the externalities include the environmental costs of drilling deeper in more remote parts of the planet and the clean-up costs of air pollution, oil spills, and the greenhouse gases, not to mention again the military and human costs of keeping foreign oil sources secure. We need a heavy gas tax, a.s.a.p. We would only be doing what Europe and Japan had the good sense to do long ago.

These sorts of sweeping macroeconomic reform are well beyond a state's or region's capacity or jurisdiction. Nonetheless, a metropolitan region can do its local share by reforming its land use and transportation policies. To restate a central thesis: there is not enough time or enough resources to solve society's many problems one at a time; we need a comprehensive vision that solves many problems simultaneously. There is a true crisis brewing because so many of our government services and institutions are in trouble—K-12 education, university education, health care, public safety, public welfare, public transit, roads and bridges, housing for the homeless and the poor, etc. Because our solutions are piecemeal, many American cities are now bankrupt, and many state budgets are in the red. A highway cloverleaf can equal the cost of a hospital and a nuclear power plant the cost of a state university campus.

Countries that impose a higher gas tax come closer to charging the true cost of fueling their automobiles and trucks. The U.S.A. has fooled itself into automobile dependency with artificially cheap gasoline. It cavalierly burns more and more fuel in more and bigger cars driven farther and more frequently than do equally productive and prosperous countries.

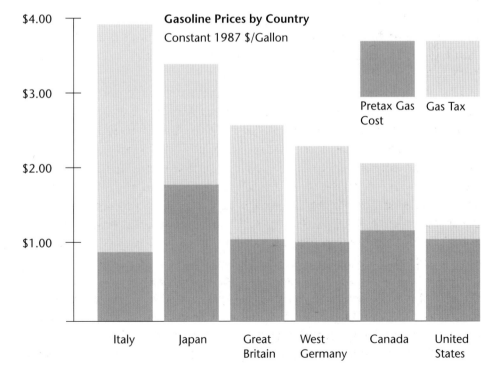

Gasoline Prices by Country
Constant 1987 $/Gallon

ZONING SPOILAGE

As well as reforming land use and transportation policy, the state and region should rethink zoning and the whole patchwork of land use laws. For generations, zoning and related laws have tried to protect the health, safety, and welfare of the urban population by segregating uses. Noxious activities were kept away from less noxious ones, with residential areas treated as a city's most protected use. (Now, for good reason, industrial zones are sometimes the most protected.) Bulk requirements, such as set-backs and height limits, were added to insure the provision of light and air and to promote fire safety. Unfortunately, these regulations have been used more and more to protect property values than to preserve life and health.

Although uses are often neatly zoned in American cities, the visual ambience can be cluttered and incoherent. Modern zoning has tended to create functional uniformity within single zones, but visual messiness. This result is not surprising when you consider that zoning was never truly intended to deal with urban design values per se. Zoning does not set out to achieve specific architecture or urban design goals. Written by lawyers, often for lawyers, its language is often quantitatively precise but qualitatively loose. It is able to produce physically segregated districts and neighborhoods with consistent building uses and maximum heights, footprints, and yards. But these zones often have incompatible architectural types. For instance, a residential street might have, on equally sized lots, a string of houses that includes single-story bungalows, two- and three-story cottages, split-level houses, and ranch houses. Although they all conform to bulk and use regulations, they

"Functional zoning is not an innocent instrument; it has been the most effective means in destroying the infinitely complex social and physical fabric of pre-industrial urban communities, of urban democracy and culture."

—Leon Krier

The shopping mall, a machine devoted entirely to consumption, is a single use monoculture surrounded by a sea of asphalt. It often masquerades as a public realm—with its exhibits and performers—but is owned by private interests whose bottom line is not community but profits.

create an incoherent street. The incoherence is a product of the different architectural types and the different architectural styles and materials characteristic of these types. What is needed is more typological consistency, which, in turn, will bring more architectural consistency.

Seattle and Tacoma's most memorable and architecturally successful neighborhoods are ones where there are many buildings of a similar architectural type (Pioneer Square, parts of Capitol Hill, Queen Anne, Ravenna, Madison Park, Wallingford, and the North End in Tacoma). It is in areas of highly diverse architectural types (parts of Denny Regrade, of downtown, and of First Hill) that urban order breaks down. Although these areas can be redeemed by good architecture and building maintenance, as on First Hill, they are successful in spite of rather than because of their highly varied building stock. On the other hand, too much typological consistency, without variations in detail, can be as negative as too much disorder. Witness the monotonous row houses and tenement houses in Philadelphia, New York, and Baltimore, as well as the repetitive rows of Neocolonial houses or ranch houses in suburban subdivisions. The goal of a good neighborhood design should be a balance between variety on the one hand and order on the other.

As noted in chapter 1, suburban land-use zoning has created large zones of single uses: the housing subdivision, the apartment complex, the shopping mall, the office park, and the school and recreation zone. Each megazone is separated from the next by open land and excruciatingly wide arterials that defy crossing by foot. Not only are all trips between zones made by auto, many trips *within* a residential or office park zone are by car. And, of course, carpooling is unpopular because commuters can't walk to a restaurant or drycleaners on the days they leave their car at home. The beautiful landscaping and picturesque ponds in office parks may look beautiful, but these horticultural ornaments can mask a social desert. Recent attempts to introduce a gas station, restaurant, and/or convenience store at the entrance are steps in the right direction, albeit feeble ones. Decorating auto-dependent office parks with lush landscaping and handsome signage is the environmental equivalent of sprinkling perfume on a toxic dump. Unless they actually reduce auto dependence, office parks are part of the problem, however pleasant their grounds may appear.

What we need now is smaller scale, more compact development that is truly mixed-use and walkable. Also, there is too much functional clarity in suburban zoning. More functional jumbling is needed, but is difficult with present-day zoning codes. Seldom does the vitality and mixture of an old fashioned town obtain. In fact, it is against the law in most suburban areas to build a traditional town. But it is possible to triumph over these outdated codes, as seminal projects around the country by such town planners as Duany and Plater-Zyberk and Calthorpe and Associates have shown. Their work has eschewed conventional zoning codes for design guidelines and design codes, often only a few pages long.

At a time when a municipality's codes are thicker than its phone book and hard for anyone but lawyers to decode, these graphic charts and diagrams are a welcome tonic. Because conventional zoning codes have been written and added to by non-designers over many decades, their physical consequences are hard to visualize. Building and zoning codes are in as much need of simplification as the IRS tax code. In Washington State, the four-volume Uniform Building Code of over 1,000 pages is now supplemented by more than a dozen other codes. Zoning codes come on top of these regulations. They are all well-intentioned but their cumulative effect is staggering. Design guidelines, whether for a private development or a city or county, are drawn up by designers and planners in plain English. They have simple diagrams that developers and lay people can quickly understand.

. . . it is against the law in most suburban areas to build a traditional town.

Design guidelines represent a typological approach to regulation that is fundamentally different from functional zoning. Zoning codes are technical, verbal, and additive, whereas design guidelines are graphic, illustrative, and integrative. Seattle's present code of abstractly conceived and neutrally labeled zones, such as NC-1 or DOC-2 or R-5000, is typically more prohibitive, opaque, and conditional than it is illustrative and suggestive. In a sense, modern zoning codes are like a performance specification, that is, they require conformance with certain conditions and criteria, usually quantitative ones. As a result, the codes do not prescribe or prefigure preferred design qualities so much as they allow a range of design possibilities (a notion very consistent with Modernist architecture). This freedom amounts to architectural roulette, especially when coupled with free-range Modernism. The price of uniform land use and consistent building bulk has been visual confusion and architectural disorder—so messy that architectural guidelines have had to be adopted later to compensate for the resulting cacophony. "Design" guidelines are different from "architectural" guidelines, which are more concerned with aesthetics and consistency of architectural details, materials, and color. Because of this confusion, it is clearer to refer to design guidelines as "urban design" guidelines.

As important as urban design guidelines are to fleshing out the Comprehensive Plans now required by the state, they are not enough. The third essential element is the Neighborhood Plan, also called the Specific Area Plan or Specific Plan. It is as essential to community planning and community building as a third leg is to a stool. If the Comprehensive Plan provides an overall framework and vision for a municipality or county and the urban design guidelines illustrate the character and physical configuration of development, the Neighborhood Plan maps out the future of a particular neighborhood or district. More than a land-use map, it is an illustrative masterplan that delin-

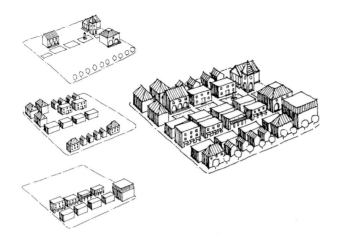

Design guidelines must prescribe a clear hierarchy of buildings—public and private, vernacular and architect-designed, foreground and background. Here, three constituent parts of the city—institutions, housing, and commercial buildings—are legible because they are regulated to be true to their typologies. (Calthorpe Associates)

eates building type as well as use. It can actually plat streets and lots, as the public sector once did in American cities. (Municipalities need to take back this important function from private developers or at least provide and enforce guidelines.) It also suggests phasing of development and may include three-dimensional drawings and scale models of critical areas. Citizens can and should play an active role in generating these plans, although professional urban designers and planners are also essential.

Part II of this book, which features the design charrettes, is essentially a presentation of Neighborhood Plans. They plot land uses, plat lots and streets, and show illustrative building types. They typically focus on underutilized areas in which there is no existing neighborhood or constituency. Just as important and more difficult in many ways is the development of Neighborhood Plans for existing neighborhoods and districts. Normally, each neighborhood in a region should initiate this process for itself and develop a plan that is consistent not only with the prevailing Comprehensive Plan but also with urban design guidelines adopted by its municipality. Indeed, inspiring and helping such local initiatives, including community charrettes, is one of the aims of this book.

URBAN VILLAGES

Why do Seattle's urban villages make sense? For starters, they are fair—in the sense that they are an effective way for the city to take its fair share of regional growth. They also go easy on the city's many existing neighborhoods that don't want increased density. This is an important political advantage that, understandably, is not lost on elected officials.

Second, they are economical, in that much of the physical and institutional infrastructure is already in place in possible locations such as Interbay, Seattle Commons, SoDo, NoDo, Rainier Avenue, Northgate, and the

Tacoma Dome area. They are more affordable in the absolute sense—that is, their total cost to both society and the individual is less than building a new neighborhood on the urban fringe.

Third, they are walkable, which is even better than being transit-oriented. Because they are small and dense and contain a diverse mix of uses, many household trips can be done on foot—the cheapest, healthiest, and most enjoyable transportation system of all. Human beings, who may have evolved as nomads, are designed to walk efficiently and comfortably. (Our big toe, for instance, evolved to give us an easy push off in our graceful gait, which is of a speed that allows us rich interaction with our social and physical world.) Walking is a permanent solution to chronic transportation problems, as it obviates the need for mechanized transport in the first place. (Goods, on the other hand, need more than handtrucks.)

Fourth, they are also transit-friendly. Walkable neighborhoods are good origins and destinations for transit trips, as a car is not needed at either end. If they are compact and dense, they aggregate enough riders near a bus, tram, or rail stop to support the investment in a transit system. It is important to note that all public transit systems, the world over, are subsidized to some extent—as will be any regional transit system in our region. But highway travel is subsidized too. It should be remembered that both are an investment in more than a transportation system; they form the infrastructure and corridors along and around which towns and cities structure themselves. They are the bones that hold the urban tissue together. But, it's hard to build a coherent neighborhood around a highway cloverleaf or at the intersection of six-lane arterials. On the other hand, light-rail transit stops are an excellent way to anchor and center a neighborhood.

Fifth, urban villages are neighborly. They can create coherent neighborhoods where none exists. It's quite possible, for instance, to create three different neighborhoods in and around the site formerly proposed for the Seattle Commons, each with its own mini-park and convenience shops. Recent studies and a millennium of experience show that an area contained within a quarter square mile with 2,500 to 5,000 residents makes for a good neighborhood—an urban quarter. One quarter can support an elementary school and two can support a supermarket, both of which are necessary and important community anchors.

Sixth, these villages are sustainable, by helping to abate environmental problems such as air pollution, the greenhouse effect, and the depletion of energy sources, natural resources, habitats, agriculture, and open space. They are also socially healthy in that they mix different age groups, socioeconomic classes, ethnicities, and household types, including the single-person and elderly households so poorly served in auto-dependent sprawl. Although this mixing may be less comfortable and genteel than gated subdivisions, social insulation slowly builds the kind of alienation that ultimately erupts in civil violence. As mentioned in chapter 1, it is better to take our legitimate differences and frustrations out on each other in small, everyday doses than in episodic racial and class upheavals. The more personal interaction certainly offers greater hope of understanding among human beings. This is not to say racial and ethnic groups should not have their own neighborhoods if they so desire. It is to say that a social mosaic at the scale of urban villages is better than vast urban ghettos. (A neighborhood has a balance of housing, shops, and recreation, whereas a district is unbalanced, often intentionally, to specialize in a single use, such as entertainment or industry.) For instance, each of the three neighborhoods or urban villages originally proposed around the Seattle Commons could develop different socioeconomic and/or ethnic character. There is at least the possibility that distinctively different neighborhoods could maintain their identity but come together in the large central park. The harmonious coexistence of a broad spectrum of ethnic groups occurs comfortably at such regional parks as Seward and Marymoor. Ideally, every new city neighborhood would also have its own small park and community center.

Seventh and last is that urban villages are lively and rich environments, full of services and amenities. Suburban life and environments are predictable at best, boring at their worst. With their single-use residential qualities, they are bedroom districts rather than neighborhoods. Moreover, the suburban pattern, not just content to devour the countryside, is actually invading the city. Large parking lots in front of one-story buildings have taken over Seattle's south Lake Union and Rainier Avenue, and have long dominated Aurora Avenue. Parts of Tacoma and Everett are thoroughly suburbanized. Eventually these districts will need to be reconfigured into neighborhoods or at least transit-oriented districts. More urban neighborhoods in places like the Uni-

It is better to take our legitimate differences and frustrations out on each other in small, everyday doses than in episodic racial and class upheavals.

versity District need to be intensified, and places like the north Kingdome parking lot should be infilled as illustrated in the charrettes.

Urban villages could be diverse, vital, urbane pockets, with housing and offices over retail shops that front onto wide sidewalks with street trees and cafes. Alleys could be mewslike, with small affordable apartments over parking or work spaces. Penthouses and common roof gardens could take advantage of our region's splendid views. Buildings need be no higher than six stories: four or five stories of wood construction over a one-story concrete commercial and parking plinth—an economical building type that has proven to offer many livable design possibilities in the Denny Regrade and other areas of the Seattle region. This is pre-automobile urban fabric. It is rich in its attention to pedestrian-oriented detail rather than the flashy, sculptural signage and freestanding buildings designed to be seen through a windshield at high speed.

Residences and retail shops should be background buildings, forming clearly bounded street walls on either side of the street. These street walls should be as continuous as possible, without parking lots arbitrarily interrupting them. As with Seattle's pedestrian-friendly Pioneer Square District, the street walls can be richly detailed and individually crafted. They can be incrementally built (and owned) but with building footprints that always come out to the sidewalk and with cornice lines that are reasonably similar in height. The linear space of streets should give way on occasion to public squares and plazas, as it does at nearby Occidental Mall. These pools of space punctuate the public realm and make outdoor rooms for the city. They must be thoughtfully designed because they act as a surrogate for nature left behind in the countryside. The excitement of streets and squares is at a human scale, to be enjoyed on foot—not the high-rise skyline that looks so inspiring from several miles out, but does not make for very pleasant streets, unless they have correspondingly large open spaces across the street, like New York's Central Park.

URBAN SPILLAGE

Lest you think this text is too blithely supportive of urban villages, here are several reservations. One is their potentially negative impact on industry and production. If areas like Seattle's Interbay are recycled as primarily residential urban villages, there is a concomitant dislocation or loss of industry. Accordingly, the Terminal 91/Interbay charrette attempted to retain and intensify industry while knitting in other uses. However, the Seattle Commons charrette was not able to relocate all the existing warehouse and light manufacturing uses within its reconfigured neighborhoods. Although it can be argued that industry is moving out of the city and out of the country any-

"The greater the density and number of houses, the greater the displacement of nature and the environment and thus the more important the artificial spaces become. Streets and squares are the vehicles of public life, while quiet cells in the form of courtyards are places of refuge, intimacy and retreat."—Rob Krier

way, a healthy and sustainable city needs diversity. An old-growth city needs production and manufacturing as well as the panoply of dwelling, commerce, institutions, and recreation.

Strictly service cities can slouch into the white-collar monoculture that much of suburbia has already become. Some urban children grow up never observing an airplane built, a ship unloaded, a garment sewn, a newspaper printed; some of their suburban counterparts never see a farmyard animal except at a petting zoo. While it is true that urban villages can accommodate "live-work" housing with production spaces for artisans, artists, and high- or low-tech cottage industry, they cannot as easily handle large-scale, noisy, or hard-core industry. This is, of course, also true of existing residential and mixed-use zones, but some urban villages could have the added handicap of displacing existing heavy industry and jobs from a city which already is losing its capacity for physical production. This trend must be arrested and reversed if we want economic and cultural health.

Another way to absorb population growth would be to encourage through incentives existing single-family neighborhoods to accept accessory units, which are now legal in Washington State. Many existing single-family homes could rent attached units or be subdivided into apartments. While many new houses and apartments were constructed in the last decade within the city limits, Seattle's population has risen to only about 540,000, a number which it exceeded in the 1960s, before dropping to 490,000 in the late 1970s and early 1980s. This arithmetic can only mean that there are many empty bedrooms in the large stock of bigger, older homes. It also means that many neighborhoods, including ones that complain loudest about growth, actually have lower densities than they used to. Why not bring more of these bedrooms onto the market as rental units? This would simultaneously provide housing that is more affordable for the renter and make the primary dwelling more affordable to the homeowner. The interior subdivisions of these "stealth units" do not affect the appearance of a neighborhood and, if located near public transit, need not overload street parking.

Some urban children grow up never observing an airplane built, a ship unloaded, a garment sewn, a newspaper printed; some of their suburban counterparts may never see a farmyard animal except at a petting zoo.

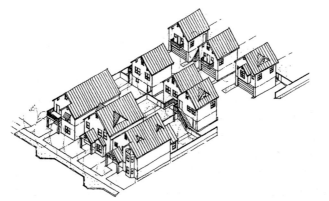

Detached homes with zero-lot lines and alley garage apartments can achieve a density suitable for public transit while maintaining the feel and scale of a single-family neighborhood. (Calthorpe Associates)

THE NEW URBANISM

A garage with apartment above in a single-family Seattle neighborhood. Accessory units above garages—a.k.a. granny flats, mother-in-law apartments, carriage houses, and garage apartments—are particularly efficient and economical ways to increase density. They make housing more affordable for singles or young families by providing starter units, and for large or extended families by providing extra space or extra income.

Our region's older cities and towns are extraordinarily blessed with alleys. They are a perfect solution to handling garbage, utilities, parking, car washing, children's play, etc. Many are lined with garages and carports. A second floor could be added to many of them to act as a rental unit or granny flat or home office, studio, workshop, or children's lair. NIMBY fears of renter's transient values and higher crime rates may prove unfounded. Unfortunately, they prevailed in Seattle's weak-kneed interpretation of the state's requirement to allow and encourage accessory units. The city ordinance fails to permit detached accessory units, a lame response from a city that should be leading the way in denser, more affordable housing. It also requires an additional off-street parking space, a regulation that ought to be waived automatically for all accessory units within a quarter-mile radius of a transit stop.

When alleys were proposed at Sacramento's first Transit-Oriented Development, the police department objected. But when garage units were added, they recanted, predicting that the increased alley surveillance would actually reduce crime. Rental units with resident landlords are usually better maintained with more responsible tenant selection than apartment houses. They also provide a more permanent supply of affordable housing units, because they are not traded up in price like many types of subsidized housing. Accessory units and garage apartments are the housing equivalent of HOV lanes. They clearly provide the biggest return on the investment dollar and should be among the first strategies to be pushed. We should pick the low-hanging fruit first.

There is also the case for some selective up-zoning in existing neighborhoods. Citizen protestations to the contrary, some of our region's neighborhood commercial areas can comfortably absorb more housing. This

Accessory units and garage apartments are the housing equivalent of HOV lanes.

growth could take the form of new apartment houses (built out to the sidewalk with courtyards and parking underneath, like some of Seattle's Anhalt apartment buildings), as well as infill townhouses, duplexes, and detached homes on smaller lots. Parking is usually cited by neighborhood antibodies as the prohibitive factor. As public transit, bicycle commuting, and walking become more feasible, the city can relax these parking requirements.

We will probably need all of the above strategies. When asked to take its proportional share of predicted regional growth, the City of Seattle originally agreed that it must absorb 80,000 new households over the next twenty years. This target was later downsized to about 60,000 households. Although this is considerably less than the estimated 140,000 new units it could physically build within existing zoning envelopes, it is still a hefty mandate. If we assume 1.2 people per new household, that's a total of some 72,000 people, which translates into twelve to twenty-four new urban villages at 2,500-5,000 residents per village. There's not room for that many new villages. Some urban villages, like the erstwhile Seattle Commons or the University District, would be larger than 5,000 residents and have multiple neighborhoods within them. A rough guess at a reasonable scenario might be:

TYPE		POPULATION INCREASE
Urban Villages	2 @ 12,500 (e.g., Seattle Commons, Interbay)	25,000
	2 @ 7,500 (e.g., Northgate, University District)	15,000
	3–6 @ 2,000–4,000 (e.g., N. Kingdome lot)	12,000
Garage Apartment Units	4,000 @ 1.25p/unit	5,000
Accessory Apartment Units	4,000 @ 1.0p/unit	4,000
Apartment Buildings	6,000 units @ 2.0p/unit	12,000
Infill Houses	1,000 @ 2.0p/unit	2,000
	Total	75,000
	Housing Loss	-3,000
	Net Population Gain	72,000

A rough cut at absorbing Seattle's fair share of predicted regional growth. This increase does not represent a proportional share. If the metropolitan area grows over the next two decades by one million, Seattle would have to grow from 540,000 to 725,000 to maintain its existing percentage of regional population. This represents a population increase of 185,000 or about 2.5 times the proposed increase.

If Seattle fails to follow through on its urban village strategy, we can't expect other cities, which are typically far more beleaguered with social, environmental, and economic problems, to take the lead. Many East Coast cities have more or less given up hope, realizing new programs and initiatives alone cannot cope with the massive shifts of wealth to their suburbs and to other parts of the country. It will take a new paradigm and tremendous political will. Urban villages could prove to be a major part of this new model.

PEDESTRIAN POCKETS, TODS, AND TNDS

If urban villages and zoning reform are good strategies for existing cities and suburbs, what strategies are needed for new suburban development? We desperately need new, compelling typologies for our suburbs—ones that take the low-density, homogenous net that has been thrown over the outskirts of our cities and gather it into finite knots that are bounded, contained, lively, and walkable communities. The old model of the single-family dwelling, large lawn, garage, swimming pool, curving cul-de-sac, and automobile commute to school, office park, shopping center, and recreation still lingers in the minds of many planners, developers, and design professionals. It also holds sway in the dreams of many home buyers.

One of the new models for suburban development to emerge in the 1980s was the Pedestrian Pocket. The idea was coined and developed by Peter Calthorpe, who came to the concept from an environmental ethic. A group of young architects who had been designing passive solar buildings came together with other environmentalists in the early 1980s for a design charrette on sustainable cities. Five years later this same group, plus a few others who had also been making contributions to passive solar architecture, coauthored *The Pedestrian Pocket Book* after the University of Washington charrette in 1988. Calthorpe and his colleagues have since applied its concepts to dozens of development projects around the country and in Australasia and lectured to numerous conferences here and abroad. This pioneering planning work is now coming to physical fruition in such projects as Laguna West in Sacramento, where the county has also adopted the principles as design guidelines for Transit-Oriented Development (TOD) in its unincorporated areas. Similar projects are on the drawing board or under construction in other states, such as Florida and Washington.

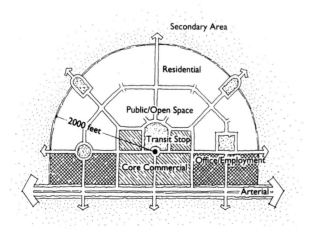

A TOD diagram. Note that the walking distance from the periphery to the center has been increased from 1/4 mile to 2000 feet. (Calthorpe Associates)

Conventional suburban development (left) separates land uses into large, single-use zones, with a treelike circulation system that has too few intersections, with too few places to turn left and a commensurate increase in friction. Traditional Neighborhood Design (TND) (right) mixes land uses in a neighborhood with a permeable street grid that provides more lane capacity and intersections for the easy circulation of vehicles and pedestrians.

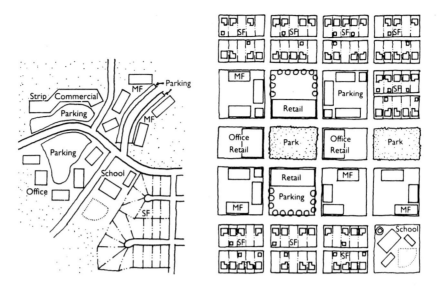

What is a Pedestrian Pocket or TOD? It is a development model for a small, walkable community that mixes low-rise, medium-density housing for a variety of household types, with retail, civic, recreational, and employment centers along a main street—all within about a one-quarter-mile radius of a central transit stop for a bus or rail system. This tight node can be surrounded by a secondary area or belt of more conventional single-family homes, separated by a natural buffer but connected by pedestrian and vehicular links. Because it is not a stand-alone community, the pocket is connected by automobile, bike, and transit to other pockets and existing towns and cities, as well as to the shopping malls and office parks that it aims to replace. The Pedestrian Pocket is small—30 to 150 acres—and, ideally, it is bounded by open space which keeps it from sprawling. Sufficient parking is provided for each dwelling unit to accommodate automobile ownership, but the number and length of trips is expected to be greatly reduced, perhaps by as much as 40 or 50 percent. Although the mix of land uses is similar from pocket to pocket, the master plan varies considerably to accept different physical constraints and citizen input, much like architectural types inflect into particular models or variations to recognize differences in local culture, climate, building materials, and practices. None of the Pedestrian Pocket precepts is new or extraordinary; taken singly they are embarrassingly obvious revivals of traditional patterns of settlement, but in concert they form a compelling new vision for urbanizing suburbia.

While Pedestrian Pockets and TODs were arising on the West Coast, the Traditional Neighborhood Design, or TND, had already taken root on the East Coast. Andres Duany and Elizabeth Plater-Zyberk were the pioneering authors of the concept and have continued to develop and apply it around the country and world. It is referred to as Neotraditionalism, a term that embraces architectural as well as town planning precepts. The two models have a great deal in common: small scale, mixed use, environmental sensitivity, internally consistent hierarchy of architectural, building, and street types, finite geometry with legible edges and a center, walkability, and alleys with accessory units and reliance on succinct graphic guidelines in lieu of traditional zoning codes. These are happy and significant convergences, especially given the fact that their respective authors come from different backgrounds and political ideologies. Pedestrian Pockets and TODs came from an energy and environmental design ethic. TNDs grew out of a more doctrinaire Euro-American urbanism. Pedestrian Pockets and TODs started with regionalism as a planning and environmental concept. TNDs originated more with traditional notions of city, town, type, and architecture, although they have a strong environmental record. Ideologically, one movement came from the left, one from the right.

While they share a great deal at the scale of the town or neighborhood, they diverge somewhat at other scales. TODs are predicated more on a regional transit and open space system, while TNDs are more rigorous about architectural typology, style, and detail. TNDs have architectural as well as urban design guidelines, regulating fence design and the color of architectural trim. Both are committed to establishing a hierarchy of known building types, but TNDs tend to be more literal in their architectural reinterpretation of historical precedent—at least at such places as the Kentlands in Maryland and Windsor in Florida. This dominance of Neotraditional architecture may lessen over time, as it has already at Seaside, Florida, the original TND and historic milestone in American town planning.

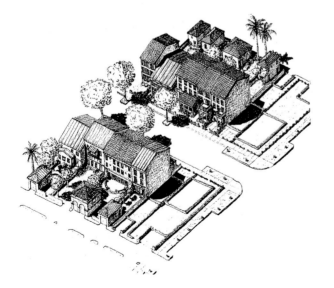

TNDs encourage incremental growth through platting land into relatively small lots. Like TODs, they emphasize alleys for parking and affordable accessory units. TNDs are often more Neotraditional in their architectural vocabulary and more rigorous typologically. (Dover, Kohl & Partners)

Despite their differences in origin and methodology, the East and West coast approaches are remarkably sympathetic and parallel in their results, spectacularly so given the myriad of design possibilities for a landscape as open as suburbia. They are both committed to environmental and social diversity, affordability, and sustainability, as well as transit and walkability. They both aim to restore a human-scaled, humane, and formally coherent sense of public and private place to American neighborhoods, towns, and cities before they dissolve further into endless, stereotypical sprawl and mindless imitations of themselves.

CONGRESS FOR THE NEW URBANISM

TODs and TNDs are so similar in intent and results that many architects and planners have embraced their principles with great fervor under the name of New Urbanism. In 1993, the first Congress for the New Urbanism (CNU) was convened in Alexandria, Virginia—called by founding members Duany, Plater-Zyberk, Calthorpe, Polyzoides, Moule, and Solomon. Since then three more congresses have been hosted, in increasing coalition with environmental and community organizations. The CNU's creed is indicative of the common polemic and concerns that have subsumed urban villages, Pedestrian Pockets, TODs, TNDs, Neotraditionalism and welded them into a single movement. Its values and goals are elaborated in the preamble to the Charter for the New Urbanism.

The Congress for the New Urbanism

views disinvestment in central cities, the spread of placeless sprawl, increasing separation by race and income, environmental deterioration, loss of agricultural lands and wilderness, and the erosion of society's built heritage as one interrelated community-building challenge.

We stand

for the restoration of existing urban centers and towns within coherent metropolitan regions, the reconfiguration of sprawling suburbs into communities of real neighborhoods and diverse districts, the conservation of natural environments, and the preservation of our built legacy.

We recognize

that physical solutions by themselves will not solve social and economic problems, but neither can economic vitality, community stability, and environmental health be sustained without a coherent and supportive physical framework.

We advocate

the restructuring of public policy and development practices to support the following principles: neighborhoods should be diverse in use and population; communities should be designed for the pedestrian and transit as well as the car; cities and towns should be shaped by physically defined and universally accessible public spaces and community institutions; urban places should be framed by architecture and landscape design that celebrate local history, climate, ecology, and building practice.

We represent

a broad-based citizenry, composed of public and private sector leaders, community activists, and multidisciplinary professionals. We are committed to reestablishing the relationship between the art of building and the making of community, through citizen-based participatory planning and design.

We dedicate

ourselves to reclaiming our homes, blocks, streets, parks, neighborhoods, districts, towns, cities, regions, and environment.[4]

NEW URBANISM CRITICIZED

As New Urbanists have stuck their chins further and further into the media stream, more and more critics have taken swipes at them. This is both natural and healthy in an open society, although it is unfortunate that much of the discourse is reduced to sound bites and short news pieces. Michael Dennis, urban designer and architecture professor at MIT, has commented that the New Urbanism is neither. Its principles and practices, he points out sympathetically and accurately, are old ones. And its primary focus, at least as reported in the press, has been suburban, not urban.

The first point is almost undeniable, but not quite. True, the New Urbanism revives many ideas about town and city planning that were mainstream before the Modern Movement. It is also true that New Urbanists believe a continued obsession with the "new" will not result in better neighborhoods, towns, cities, and regions and that there is nothing ethically or artistically wrong or weak about reviving and championing old, proven ideas. What *is* new about the New Urbanism is its totality. It attempts to promote a sort of unified design theory for an entire region—from the small scale (building block, street) through the intermediate scale (corridor, neighborhood, district) to the large scale (regional infrastructure and ecology). Although many of its ideas may seem obvious and old hat, the particular combination and orchestration of them are new. Also fresh is the New Urbanist insistence that physical placemaking must be carefully and thoroughly linked to public policy. New Urbanists have been more effective than their predecessors at reforming municipal, state, and federal policies.

The second point—that New Urbanism is not truly urban—is mistaken, although understandable given media coverage to date. The projects that have gotten the most attention are the Neotraditional towns like Seaside, Laguna West, Kentlands, and Harbor Town, most of which are located on greenfield sites in suburbia. The suburban agenda of the New Urbanists has been the most newsworthy because these new, imageable communities are built and occupied, flying in the face of conventional suburban development. But the New Urbanism is a regional strategy, with equally important ideas and proposals for downtown and inner city neighborhoods, as well as an interest in overall regional planning. (Of the seven design charrettes in Part II of this book, only one is in a classic suburban setting, and much of the CNU founders' work has been in urban areas.) Perhaps some of the confusion about the name could be cleared up by using "Neotraditional design," "Traditional Neighborhood Design," and "Pedestrian Pocket" to refer to suburban applications and "New Urbanism" as an umbrella term for the comprehensive regional strategy.

Another complaint has been about elitism within the movement. Specifically, the early Congresses for the New Urbanism were criticized for not being open to the public. This policy could be easily construed as a mark against a movement that is purportedly intended to build community. However, the conveners felt that restricting attendance to invitees was necessary to organize and focus the early events. In a sense, the early Congresses were meant to get ideas and principles on the table, clarified, ordered, and chartered before going public. Later conferences were opened up to anyone nominated by any previous attendee and ultimately to any paying registrant. This policy did step on many professional and academic toes and, in retrospect, may have resulted in more damage than operational advantage. CNU III in San Francisco in 1994 was a deliberate attempt to broaden the membership and build coalitions with other urban groups and environmental organizations. CNU IV in Charleston in 1996 invited known opponents of New Urbanism to debate openly its principles and practices. The Congresses, however, have never intended to be like the contemporary, open-ended conference or symposium, which typically asks more questions than it answers and often ends up in pluralist confusion. To design and build communities takes more than probing questions and an endless quest for all the answers. To act, we must settle on norms, standards, and specific designs, moving ahead even though all questions may not be fully resolved.

Perhaps the biggest challenge leveled at the New Urbanism is that it is another ideal vision conceived, ordained, and disseminated from above and

A California shopping center being razed to make room for high-density housing and a mixed-use transit center. Suburban renewal will become increasingly common as isolated shopping malls (and office parks) are transformed from consumption centers into more complete community centers. (Calthorpe Associates)

not rooted in specific places or local cultures. This critique contends that architects and planners have always come up with beautiful, sanitized visions that will save the world and which, although provocative and even brilliant, are too idealized, ambitious, or disconnected from place or reality. To a large extent, that has been true of twentieth-century visions (Sant' Elia, Garnier, Le Corbusier, Wright, Krier). It does apply in some measure to the New Urbanism, which, it has been argued, is a "narrow representation or framework that denies the social, physical and economic diversity of the built North American landscape."[5] True, the proposed and built projects do try to apply an ideal diagram or plan. But any development that is faithful to the principles of the New Urbanism recognizes and celebrates what is unique about a place's history, cultures, climate, and architecture. Perhaps in the early going, TND and TOD site plans have been too formulaic—a design template from on high. But it takes this sort of single-minded effort and confidence, as well as a simple, clear diagram, to launch a new movement. In today's media circus, it takes more chest-beating, ego, and bombast than when Olmsted spawned the profession of landscape architecture or Ebenezer Howard founded the Garden City movement last century.

Related to this concern is the question of whether New Urbanist projects are too stand-alone, i.e., too separate and aloof from their existing physical and social context. This is a vexing issue, because their physical context is often too flawed or frayed to respect. A congested arterial strip with a monstrously wide roadway and a sea of asphalt parking lots ebbing and flowing with a tide of cars in front of low, cheap retail boxes is not a context worth honoring. In suburbia, there is generally not much good built fabric with which or off which a designer can work. In urbanized areas, especially those

Weekday Vehicle Trip Generation for Residential Areas

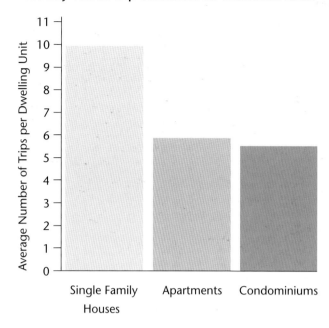

Residents of single-family houses make more auto trips than those in multi-family housing. Transit, walking, and bicycling will never completely replace the private motorized vehicle in America, but this chart shows there is hope for reducing house-hold trips.

with substantial building stock, there is a stronger argument for both infill and reuse of existing buildings and infrastructure. In either case, dealing with the existing social fabric is very challenging. It is usually easier for designers and planners to work in an empty greenfield site than to knit and nudge new development into an existing neighborhood, where social, economic, and political groups and factions are in place and in many cases entrenched. If New Urbanism is to live up to its charter, it will have to take on successfully more of the messier and compromised work of infill and repair, whether in center city, urban neighborhoods, suburbia, new towns, or small towns.

Another criticism is that, despite all the hoopla, New Urbanist developments are not living up to their transportation promises and expectations. The argument has been made that there is a weakening link between land use and transportation in an increasingly automotive world and that pedestrian-oriented communities have only a marginal effect on household vehicle miles traveled (VMT). Pedestrian trips in TNDs and TODs, it is suggested, simply add to automobile trips rather than replace them.[6] While making walking and bicycling safer and more convenient may not be enough by itself to reduce auto dependence, it *is* an essential ingredient in an overall solution to auto dependency. Also necessary is reducing the subsidy, as well as the right-of-way, priority, and authority that automobiles enjoy in our society. And more and better public transit is needed with mixed-use development at every stop, so riders can walk or bike at either end of the trip. True, transit and walking will never displace private motorized vehicles, but the New Urbanism can ultimately reduce the number of trips from about ten per household to maybe six, as well as shorten the length of those trips. Also true, transit will never eliminate traffic congestion, because if and when highways become less crowded, transit riders will tend to drive more. But transit can put a lid on congestion. We must recognize that it will not be easy to change as deep a pattern as auto-dependence. It will take *all* of the programs, policies, and development strategies outlined in the CNU charter and in this and other books on the New Urbanism.

A final critique is that New Urbanist developments are not a marketing success and that people either are not ready for them or don't like them. It's clearly too early to measure marketability. As of early 1996, there were only several thousand housing units built in a handful of TNDs or TODs across the country. New urban villages in Seattle are still in the planning stages. Consumer surveys have produced mixed but generally favorable responses from home buyers and renters, as well as from prospective residents. Laguna West outside of Sacramento got off to a rocky financial start by falling into receivership during California's worst recession, but now the original developer has bought it back and sales have improved. Until the public has had a good chance to see the New Urbanism in fuller buildout and with more mature landscaping, it is too early to pronounce a verdict. And until the economic playing field is more nearly level, biases in pricing will also distort market responses. Also, superficial imitations of TNDs and TODs will inevitably muddy the waters and skew the results. (The same problem plagued the solar movement, with many impostors and exaggerated claims.)

Even if unbiased, the market is not always able to evaluate properly something as complicated as community. Humans do not always opt for what is in their best interests, especially long term interests that are hard to comprehend, such as sustainability. Sometimes human desires and needs are two different things. Other times, subsidies and penalties have accustomed people to habits they can no longer afford or have led them inadvertently into shortsighted behavior. Yes, the marketplace must eventually accept New Urbanism if it is to succeed and endure. But only the test of elapsed time with market prices that reflect true costs will determine its true value and validity.

The New Urbanism has its flaws, to be sure. Some people want to cherry-pick the positive parts and reject the objectionable parts. Accept the walkability but reject the narrow lots; keep the overall coherence but dilute the overly symmetrical town plans; include the single-family dwelling but reduce social elitism; keep it urban but make it greener; build rapid transit but don't take away the car; etc. Unfortunately, communities come in packages. They cannot be ordered up à la carte. Community design consists of

Northwest Landing near Nisqually Delta by Weyer-haueser Real Estate Company is the first large new community in the Seattle region to be based on New Urbanist principles. Shown here is a street of narrow houses with front porches, small side and front yards, a planting strip for street trees, visitor parking at curbside, and alley garages in the rear. Two large employment centers are within walking distance.

complex tradeoffs, with a limited number of win-win solutions. For the most part it is slow, arduous, iterative, pluralist, and contested, punctuated by creative breakthroughs from time to time. It is not exact work. Community design is an approximation, community development a compromise. But that is not to say that it is casual or provisional. Once adopted—however imperfect—comprehensive plans, neighborhood plans, and design guidelines need to be implemented with consistency and conviction. (Leon Krier suggests that violations should be treated as a criminal offense.)

Why build new suburbs at all, some urbanists ask. We have no choice, because all American suburbanites and their offspring are not going to return to the urban or rural communities from which they migrated. We most need the New Urbanist models for the periphery of our cities. Flawed as it is, the New Urbanism is clearly better than the other models being purveyed in conventional suburbs. TODs, TNDs, and urban villages are far superior in economic, social, environmental, and urban design terms to the prevailing models of suburban development. In many ways they *are* a win-win proposition. Sound economics, healthy ecology, social reform, and design integrity fit happily into the New Urbanist canon. Rarely do so many moral and economic entries fall on the positive side of the ledger.

The New Urbanism is taking hold in the Pacific Northwest. LUTRAQ in Portland and urban villages in Seattle have been heavily influenced by the

New Urbanism. Peter Calthorpe's work has included projects with Weyerhaeuser Real Estate Company in DuPont and at Snoqualmie Ridge. Northwest Landing at DuPont is the first built new town in the Seattle Region to realize many of the principles of New Urbanism. Likewise, many of the University of Washington charrettes and studios have applied these same principles over the last decade to real sites in the Seattle region, in some cases, galvanizing projects that are now in the works. It is on these test cases that Part II of the book now focuses.

PART II DESIGN

"The great advantage of the charrette model is that it is the best way to get the most creative proposals for addressing the most difficult problems from the most accomplished designers in the most compressed period."

—Patrick Condon, James Taylor Professor of Landscape Architecture, University of British Columbia

CHAPTER 5

Center City
a.k.a. Downtown or CBD

The center of the American metropolis is at risk. In a few eastern cities like Boston and New York, it's as healthy as ever. But cities like Detroit and Philadelphia have been visited by rampant disinvestment. Some smaller southern cities like Charleston and Savannah continue to represent American urbanism at its best, but others are in distress. Midwestern cities are struggling, held together by their work ethic more than a love of urbanity. (Toronto, on the other hand, is the densest metropolitan area in North America and now has the most cosmopolitan population in the world.) Downtowns in western cities, never much in many cases, have gotten thinner—with the exceptions of San Francisco, Portland, and Seattle. San Francisco will always be one of the happiest and healthiest of American cities, with true neighborhoods in the center. The core of Portland is among the most walkable in North America. Seattle's downtown remains pedestrian friendly and economically robust, but the Central Business District (CBD) still lacks a mix of true neighborhoods and memorable urban plazas. Even the most vital of downtowns across the U.S.A. does not inspire any permanent confidence. With the exception of Manhattan, any American downtown could be a basket case in a generation, a casualty of technological, economic, and demographic decentralization.

The two charrettes that follow are set in center city Seattle. They attempt to translate the theory from Part I into real projects, with specific urban form.

COSTS OF SPRAWL

Both the Kingdome and Seattle Commons charrettes underscore the priority of investment at the core of our cites. They, by their location, density, and mix, directly repudiate sprawl. The costs of sprawl have been heavily exacted at the center. For every dollar we spend in developing the periphery, we forego at least one dollar downtown. Arguably, more than one dollar is lost by society, because infrastructure is more expensive per capita on the fringe than downtown. The social and environmental costs are also heavily borne at the center of a city. So many of society's dysfunctions—racial segregation, crime, joblessness, broken homes, homelessness, blight, pollution—are concentrated in the inner city. Too little tax revenue is raised in most cities to combat these chronic problems. Without metropolitan revenue sharing, these problems will rarely be corrected.

CRITICAL REGIONALISM

Downtown is perhaps the hardest place to express and celebrate regional differences architecturally. Just as long-span structures are more subject to the vertical forces of gravity, tall buildings are more subject to the horizontal forces of wind and earthquake. High rises and big buildings tend to be more generic than small, low buildings, because wind, earthquakes, and gravity behave in similar ways all over the planet. As mentioned in Part I, larger buildings are more affected by internal thermal loads (from people, lights, and equipment inside the building envelope) than by regional climate. These engineering algorithms tend to override regional distinctions.

The Kingdome charrette deals with the oldest part of central Seattle—the *centro storico*, if you will. Pioneer Square still has late-nineteenth-century building stock that to contemporary eyes looks very old and very regionalist. But, in fact, many of the brick buildings mimic the famous buildings of the era in San Francisco and New York, which is not surprising because Seattle was a young city of fewer than 40,000 people when the 1889 fire wiped the slate clean to make room for larger and more substantial buildings. Pioneer Square has preserved many buildings of character and craft that tell the story of Seattle. They were treated with great respect in the Kingdome charrette, often copied or reinterpreted. The kind of nineteenth-century urban fabric that Pioneer Square represents is hard to improve upon, many participants concluded.

The Seattle Commons charrette deals with the edge of center city, an area that is not as architecturally homogeneous as the historic center. The existing building stock is very mixed in age and quality. There has not been the spontaneous citizen movement to save historic buildings that there was in Pioneer Square. Nonetheless, there has been interest in saving buildings and businesses that are functioning well economically. And, despite the lack of historic preservation, there are some buildings of architectural merit, namely a number of bow-string-truss warehouses, brick warehouses, and light manufacturing facilities. Most of the design teams tried to preserve the scale and bulk of these buildings in their predominantly low-rise designs. This is especially true of their proposals for the Cascade neighborhood to the east of the Commons park, where a funkier, rawer mix of buildings was maintained in most schemes.

TYPOLOGY

Part I argued that there is an inverse relationship between typology, which represents the typical and the universal, and Critical Regionalism, which glorifies the particular and the local. For the same reasons that tall downtown buildings have trouble expressing regional values, they tend to be of a consistent type. There is typological consistency on many downtown streets, because of universal forces and more regulatory controls shaping the buildings and less space to build there. Additionally, there is often more building stock remaining from earlier centuries, when typology was a stronger determinant of architectural and urban form. The Pioneer Square neighborhood is perhaps Seattle's most typologically consistent. Most of the buildings are of similar footprint, section, height, and materials. The Kingdome charretters continued the scale, bulk, and configuration of the surrounding turn-of-the-century urban fabric. Some even encoded Pioneer Square types—ground floor commercial, three to six floors of offices or apartments above, with a penthouse on top and never a full-block footprint. One team declared them the only permissible new construction in the neighborhood.

The architectural types proposed for the Seattle Commons neighborhood were also consistent, although not as historical. With the exception of a few high-rise apartment buildings in one scheme, the urban fabric was designed with low-rise and mid-rise building types, mainly apartments and condominiums above storefront commerce. There were some townhouses, an architectural type that never took root in Seattle (perhaps because their party walls make them too dark for its overcast skies). There were alley garages, with live/works or accessory units above. There were few freestanding buildings. The perimeters of most blocks were continuous rows of four to six stories of light frame construction over a concrete commercial plinth and underground parking. As with most of the charrettes in this book, experimentation was not so much with architectural type as it was with block type, street type, and the hierarchy and mixing of uses.

NEW URBANISM

Both of these charrettes are quintessential New Urbanism. They are also prime examples of the Seattle Comprehensive Plan's Urban Village strategy, which exhibits many of the same characteristics—low rise, high density, mixed use, public transit, walkability, alleys, zero setback, bounded neighborhoods with an identifiable center and distinct edge. Urban villages also embody the deeper principles that underlie the New Urbanism, namely restoration, diversity, human scale, integration, and equity. Teams developed as many as three or four urban villages surrounding the Commons park, each with a different character and population. The park could then fulfill its mission of being a common place for diverse peoples from different neighborhoods. Both charrettes successfully elicited attempts to maintain and enhance existing center city neighborhoods and capitalize on their existing physical and institutional infrastructure. And they both help the city take its fair share of growth.

The Kingdome Charrette

"The task is to promote city life of city people, housed, let us hope, in concentrations both dense and diverse enough to offer them a decent chance at developing city life."—Jane Jacobs, *The Death and Life of Great American Cities*

Prospecting for developable land in the center city is not difficult, given how underprogrammed most American cities are. It is especially easy in downtowns where disinvestment has taken its toll and high-rise office buildings stand next to parking lots. This all-or-nothing checkerboard of development has made for gap-toothed streetscapes and interrupted urbanity. The life of people and buildings, the blood and bones of the city, is weak in many center cities.

The lack of mixed-use neighborhoods so notable in our suburbs also obtains in our downtowns. While many people work downtown and some of them shop there, few live there. Seattle has several downtown districts that are struggling to achieve the balance of commerce and housing that would qualify them as neighborhoods. The Denny Regrade, Pike Place Market, and Pioneer Square areas are beginning to attain a critical mass of housing. The International District has long had a commercial/residential balance and is the downtown's only true neighborhood, despite the fact that it is called a district. The other districts need all the housing they can build if they are to become true neighborhoods. This charrette attempted to jumpstart the physical expansion of the Pioneer Square District and to saturate it with more housing.

The Pioneer Square District is the city's best preserved historic area, at least for Euro-Americans. Originally part of a 15,000-acre tide flat that lay under water at high tide, it was first claimed by white settlers in 1853. Rebuilt in brick and stone after the disastrous fire of 1889, it has a nineteenth-century

The Kingdome, 250 feet high and 720 feet in diameter, is the world's largest self-supporting concrete roof. It looks convincing from the water and from Interstate 5, but is isolated in its immediate environment.

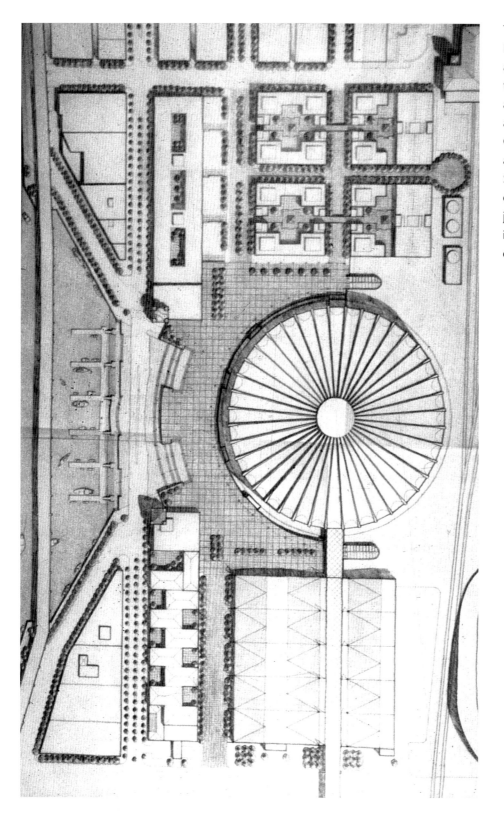

Team 2, led by Don Prowler and Dave Miller, added four full blocks in the north parking lot and an exhibit hall/basketball arena in the south lot. Offices and apartments are proposed along Main Street on the western edge of the site, which is joined to a marina. A parking structure is off the drawing to the south.

The Pioneer Square neighborhood is a fine-grain mix of uses, mainly office and/or residential above retail. Buildings with small footprints and common eave heights make for a variegated but solid street wall. The Historic District has not been over-gentrified, as these drawings by Laurie Olin illustrate. A favored sitting area for street people is the entrance to the Pioneer Building, named by the AIA in 1892 as "the finest building west of Chicago."

pedestrian scale and character. It became the first Historic District in King County, because so much of its late-nineteenth-century character was intact. "Now this district is a vital mixed-use community as well as one of the best preserved collections of late nineteenth century commercial architecture to be found in the United States."[1]

Unlike some historic districts in other American cities, it has been neither gentrified nor freeze-dried as an outdoor museum. Despite its homeless shelters and panhandlers, Pioneer Square remains popular with both tourists and locals. It has always had a spicy flavor and gritty atmosphere as home to Seattle's first sawmill, glue factory, emporiums, whorehouses, bars, gambling dens, and sweatshops. As every Seattleite knows, the term "skid road" originated here as a logging term, later to be shortened into the colloquial "skid row" to describe any central city's street for down-and-outers.[2]

THE PROBLEM AND THE OPPORTUNITY

The Pioneer Square District was selected for the 1990 charrette because it offers three opportunities: to add housing immediately adjacent to downtown Seattle, to enlarge the undersized district, and to improve and better integrate the oversized and disconnected Kingdome and its parking lot with its context. Few urban sites offer the opportunity for such sweeping solutions. In the late 1960s, the region showed the foresight and resolve not to build its major league sports facility on a suburban site, which would have guaranteed that the facility would be completely auto-oriented. The Kingdome's downtown location insured that some of the crowd would come by foot and transit. Nonetheless, the monument is surrounded by a sea of cars by day that becomes a desert of asphalt by night.

The circular structure ignores the fabric and axes of the city. At 250 feet in height and 720 feet in diameter, the Kingdome is a very large and disjunctive object. In fact, it is the largest self-supporting concrete roof in the world, anchored on thirty-six acres of landfill with piles that extend sixty feet into hardpan below. From Elliott Bay or the air, its white-ribbed dome marks the southern end of downtown, more bluntly but just as emphatically as the Space Needle marks the northern end. Sporting events, concerts, and exhibitions regularly send pulses of as many as 60,000 people through the adjoining streets. The Kingdome is a big beast to civilize, but that is exactly what the four charrette teams were asked to do. This was not the first time a group of designers had tackled the problems and opportunities presented by this kilostructure. In 1982, the Gang of Five[3] proposed ways to better join the Kingdome to its context in a four-part series published by the *Seattle Weekly*.

There were three major focal points for the charrette, all of which remain as challenges today.

1. *The Kingdome itself*, especially its overwhelming scale and lack of orientation within the immediate context. In terms of chapter 2, it lacks a sense of place, of history, of craft, and of limits (Jack Christiansen's engineering of the dome, however, demonstrates a sophisticated understanding of nature and its forces). Its circular footprint, continuous facade, and rounded profile don't recognize or inflect to the surroundings in any way. The Kingdome ignores its axial relationship to Second Avenue and its potential frontage on First Avenue. It is difficult for people attending events there to find the entrances and once inside to orient themselves to the city outside. It has inadequate exhibition area for trade and industrial shows. Its staging entrance on the north side conflicts with what is potentially a "front door." Maintaining the existing 2,200 on-site parking spaces for events while providing parking for new development is one of the major challenges and may require a parking structure or structures elsewhere. Improving traffic flow in the area is also an issue.

2. *Housing, especially market-rate housing.* There already exists a large stock of subsidized housing, low-income housing, and homeless shelters in the neighborhood, nearly 75 percent of the units in the area. In order to make for a more balanced housing mix, more middle- and upper-income housing is needed. The addition of more market-rate units will promote a greater mix and add more residents to this underpopulated area. Unlike many city and county neighborhoods, Pioneer Square enthusiastically seeks more multifamily housing. In short, the north Kingdome parking lot represents

Looking south. Three of four design teams chose to infill the north parking lot with four new city blocks of mixed-use development that is primarily market-rate housing.

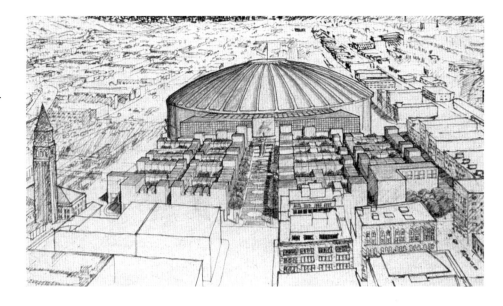

one of the largest and most eligible publicly owned open sites in downtown on which housing (and/or other functions) can be developed.

3. *The Pioneer Square Neighborhood*, especially the preservation of its scale and character. As the county's oldest urban area, it represents a significant cultural and historic asset. The density, scale, eave height, fenestration, and masonry construction of its buildings come together to make a handsome and human scaled urban environment. The fine-grain mixture of uses, mainly office and residential above retail in relatively small buildings that rarely take up more than a quarter block, makes for vibrant street life. The incremental growth and ownership of shops yields a "main street" ambience rather than the feel of a downtown shopping mall, such as Westlake.

One problem is the small size of the district. Compared to historic districts in other American cities, such as the French Quarter of New Orleans or colonial Charleston and Savannah, the Pioneer Square District is tiny. A walk of a block or two from First Avenue in any direction means leaving it. Adding four city blocks of similar size and character in the north parking lot would significantly increase the walking breadth of the district.

It was apparent to all four teams that mixed-use development is the strategy likely to solve or resolve the most issues. Determining the most effective mix of uses is a difficult and critical question. Housing above retail in increments of less than a full block would be the most desirable and appropriate building type for this area, because it would complement the existing urban grain. Some office development, including legally mandated spaces for the

Mariners and the Seahawks, is also necessary. The Pioneer Square Community Council, through the Pioneer Square Summit, had already identified the need and desire for more housing in the district. King County and the City of Seattle have in place a policy to concentrate residential development within urban centers in order to reduce sprawl, and the Downtown Land Use and Transportation Plan has identified the north Kingdome parking lot as a target area for mixed housing and commercial development. The site is well served by public transit, including the Metro bus tunnel, the waterfront trolley, and ferries. There are many advantages to mixed-use development for this site:

1. Integrating the Kingdome more gracefully with the surrounding community.
2. Enriching the experience of attending the Kingdome.
3. Adding lateral dimension to the Pioneer Square District, which is barely two blocks wide in places.
4. Providing more downtown housing alternatives, mitigating development pressure on existing single-family neighborhoods in the city, and reducing suburban sprawl.
5. Building a bridge to the International District, while replacing "missing teeth" between the two areas.
6. Increasing public safety by bringing in more residents to become caretakers of the neighborhood.
7. Recovering underutilized urban land and possible sharing of parking areas.

PROGRAM REQUIREMENTS

The charrette teams were issued a remarkably brief program:

- Ground floor retail, fronting on the streets
- Kingdome exhibition space—60,000 sf (on south side of Kingdome)
- Seattle Mariners office space—20,000 sf (to be located in the northwest corner of the north parking lot)
- Seattle Seahawks office space—20,000 sf (to be located in the southwest corner of the South parking lot)
- Housing—Provide an average 800 sf/unit in a mix of market rate for an undetermined number of apartments and condominiums (e.g., 25% studio, 50% 1-bedroom, and 25% 2-bedroom)
- Parking:
  Residential—1.2 stalls per unit
  Commercial—provide 2500 stalls for public use (approx. 1/2 on north parking lot)

Team 1, led by Mike Pyatok and Susan Boyle, terminated Second Avenue with a large, electronic scoreboard, which was flanked by a hotel built hard against the drum of the Kingdome.

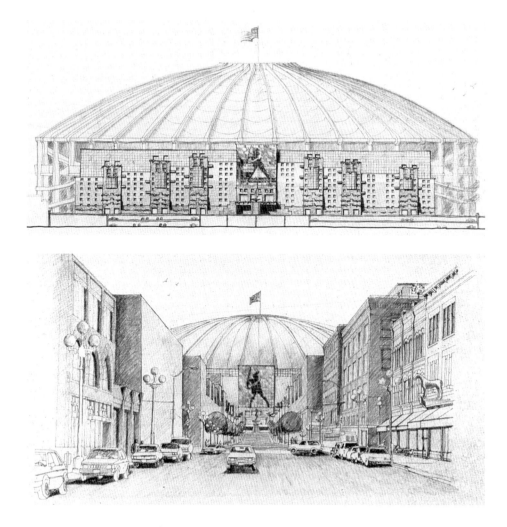

THE DESIGN PROPOSALS

Like other UW charrettes, each design team developed a separate and complete design scheme. Three of the four teams pursued remarkably similar strategies for the north parking lot. They divided it into four quarters, each a city block. This is an eminently sensible approach: it makes the Pioneer Square District both bigger and more of a neighborhood. Four additional blocks can accommodate up to a thousand new residents. They also add some needed fabric to the district, which fades quickly in most directions. Four more blocks provide the resident or visitor significantly more grid in which to stroll and explore. The additional residents would help the district become a neighborhood by improving the residential/commercial balance, which presently tilts heavily toward commerce. They would also help redress the imbalance between residents and tourists, and the imbalance between market-rate and subsidized housing.

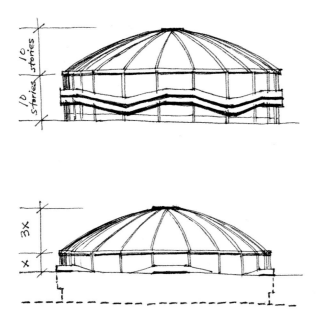

Diminishing the apparent height of the Kingdome's drum, by building 5- to 7-story structures in the surrounding parking lots, makes the dome float more buoyantly above the skyline of Pioneer Square.

There are architectural advantages to infilling four new blocks. It closes the gap between the city fabric and the Kingdome. This crowding tends to hide the drum and accentuate the dome, which then floats more gracefully above the neighboring rooftops. Perceptually, the greater the vertical rise of the dome in relation to the height of the drum, the more buoyant the appearance. At present the vertical rise of the drum is greater than that of the dome itself, which gives the building a bottom-heavy, ponderous feel. Anything that lowers the apparent height of the drum walls—such as adjoining buildings that obscure or hide the drum—will enhance the dome's proportions. Approaching the Kingdome on foot becomes more dramatic if it is surrounded by buildings. It is like encountering a cathedral in a medieval town, where tight and curving streets allow only partial and glancing views of the facades. The element of surprise would be less in this case, because the streets are wider and straighter. Nonetheless, the immediate juxtaposition of the Kingdome with smaller-scaled buildings will make the stadium more impressive than it is at present. And the pilgrimage to it would be more interesting than threading your way through parked and moving cars. If a large parking structure is built in the south parking lot, it could decrease the noisy crowds of people surging through the streets to and from the thousands of off-street and on-street parking spaces within a mile or so of the Dome.

There are also urban design advantages to adding blocks. The axis of Second Avenue runs directly through the center of the Kingdome. Extending Second Avenue farther south makes this fortuitous relationship more obvi-

Looking north up Second Avenue from the Kingdome front door affords a fine view of Smith Tower. Note that the new buildings are 5 stories of apartments or offices above ground-floor retail.

ous. It also frames a much grander entrance to the facility. A stronger axis is formed with five- or six-story buildings on both sides of Second Avenue, as opposed to its present one sided configuration between Jackson and Main streets. The street might even have a glazed roof arching over it to make an open-ended pedestrian gallery out of the final block or two. In either case, a major entrance for the Kingdome becomes clearly demarcated on the exterior of the drum, adding legibility it sorely lacks now. It is the front door in Scheme 1 and a side door in Scheme 2. The former scheme placed a large electronic signboard at the terminus of the Second Avenue axis; the latter, a large window in the drum above the entrance.

Another visual strategy for integrating the Kingdome was pursued in Scheme 3. It attempted to reduce the Kingdome's height by building two slender office towers on either side. They are higher than the dome and give it scale and contrapuntal accent, like pointed minarets next to the low, soft domes of a mosque. These towers, however, are topped, respectively, with a symbolic football and baseball, prompting one juror to compare them to olives on the end of a toothpick.

Some schemes put these four new blocks on a podium with parking below. This would provide stalls for the new residents and businesses. If parking capacity is also maintained for the Kingdome, the podium would have to be two levels. This is an unlikely cross-section given the high water table on a site that is landfill. A more feasible strategy to replace surface parking displaced by the new development would be to build a large parking structure

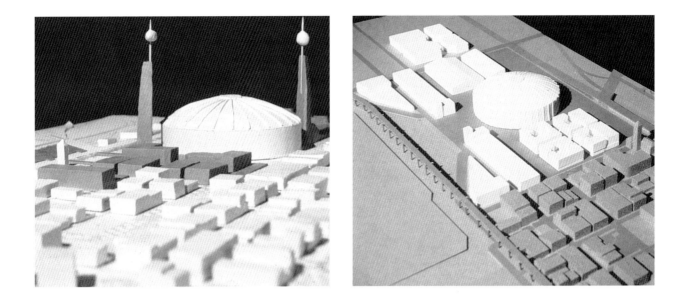

in the south parking lot. Most charrette teams recommended such a parking garage.

There is at least one significant problem associated with constructing four new blocks in the north parking lot. The southern two blocks would encroach on the Kingdome's staging entrance, through which large trucks and rolling bleachers are moved on a regular basis. This could possibly be addressed by raising the pedestrian entrance to the 100-level of the dome, with the truck entrance below. This scenario would require Second Avenue to ramp up a full story before it reached the Kingdome. Several schemes proposed such a level change. Scheme 1 attached a hotel to the drum, the lower level of which could accommodate the staging entrance.

All the teams designed the new blocks to match the existing Pioneer Square blocks in bulk and configuration. They fill up the entire envelope of the blocks with buildings five to seven stories high. They are similar in function, with commerce at the street level, housing and/or offices above, and penthouses on the roof. They are also similar in character, with large shop windows fronting on the sidewalk, masonry construction with punched windows, and penthouses set back from a cornice line that is unusually consistent in height for an American city. Courtyards, lightwells, or parking would penetrate the interiors of the blocks, which would be served by alleys. Sidewalks with street trees and parallel parking would also be the norm. This essentially nineteenth-century urban pattern still proves to be a very workable and very durable model for central cities.

Scheme 2 places the major front on the west side of the building. Here it opens onto a large raised platform, which, in turn, opens onto First Avenue.

The scale of the Kingdome (left), considered by many to overwhelm the district, is reduced by office minarets for the Mariners and Seahawks.

Right: A canal issues into the marina, which faces the front door of the Kingdome. The plaza at the main entrance reinforces the western side as primary, with the Second Avenue axis as a secondary but important entrance.

View from the deck of a boat approaching the Kingdome marina and entry plaza. The plaza is flanked by tower offices for the Mariners and Seahawks and apartment buildings.

A north-facing cross-section cuts through the exhibit hall/basketball arena, apartment houses, Alaskan Way Viaduct, canal, and Port of Seattle container terminal.

This open plaza forms both a front deck for the Kingdome and a reviewing area for parades that march up or down First Avenue. Flanking and helping to define this plaza are two diminutive office towers, one for the Mariners and one for the Seahawks. Across the street is a yacht basin, where pleasure craft and ferries could dock for events. This marina for transient moorage is connected by a canal to Elliott Bay. In this and other schemes, the south parking lot and the open land south of Royal Brougham Street are given over to parking, new exhibit space, and a new basketball arena.

Scheme 4 departed in several ways from the other three. First, it cast a wider net, intervening in a wider area of the city. It took the position that the Pioneer Square Neighborhood should be more continuous with the downtown

to the north, the International District to the east, and the industrial areas to the west, without discrete gateways and edges. It also argued that the Pioneer Square District should be much larger in area and population. Accordingly, it developed new mixed-use blocks to the east and west of the Kingdome. The scheme, however, did not infill the north parking lot with four new blocks—a second major departure from the other schemes. Instead, it proposed a large civic square there, contending that Seattle does not yet possess one (Westlake Square being commercial rather than civic in character). This rectangular plaza would stage public events ranging from flea markets to outdoor operas. Third, this team argued passionately for a rigorous typological approach, stating that a very limited number of building types were appropriate for the area. Specifically, they would allow three types: a perimeter block building of five to seven floors with residential above retail; a perimeter block building of similar height with offices above retail; and a five- to seven-story parking garage above retail. Each type would be crowned by a penthouse on the roof. All other types were thought to dilute and confuse the consistent character of the district. They also took a strong stand on removing parts of the Alaska Way Viaduct, arguing that the rights of drivers to high-speed and convenient vehicular access are secondary to the rights of residents to cohesive neighborhood.

All schemes reinforced linkages to public transit. Direct pedestrian connections to the King Street and Union Station rail and bus stations were proposed. The waterfront trolley was extended closer to the Kingdome. Bus service would be improved. Several schemes proposed new parking garages above the railroad right-of-way to the north, as well as to the south of the Kingdome.

The plaza to the north of the Kingdome would be a civic livingroom for the city, to complement the commercial plaza at Westlake.

This team, led by Stefanos Polyzoides and Galen Minah, emphasized the importance of typology as a link between architecture and urban design. It limited development to three building types, all tripartite. Each had storefronts and lobbies on the ground floor, 4 or 5 stories of parking, offices, or apartments above, and a penthouse or office on the roof. Major horizontal divisions would mark the base, shaft, and top of each building, which would typically occupy a quarter of the block.

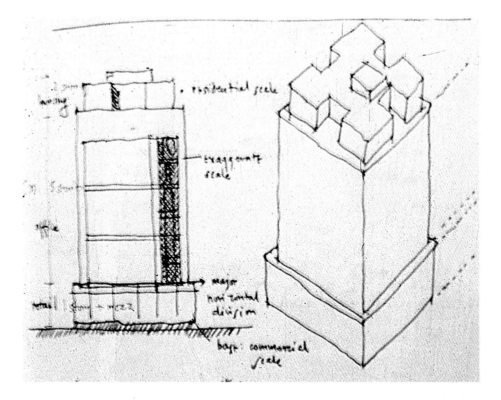

After the charrette, presentations of the results were made to a half-dozen groups and government officials, who were quite receptive. Tom Byers and John Savo, two stalwart advocates of the project, drafted a proposed ordinance for consideration by the city and county, a copy of which follows. As a result of these efforts, City and County Council members convened an historic meeting to hammer out the language for a jointly sponsored study for $100,000. It was followed up by a second study of similar size several years later. A mixed-use agenda was considered in each case and the Pioneer Square District remains hopeful that such a development will come to fruition.

A Joint Resolution of the City and County Councils

Whereas, the Pioneer Square Historic Preservation District was the first historic district to be designated within King County and represents a substantial cultural and historic resource for the region; and,

Whereas, the Pioneer Square Community Council has been organized to represent the diverse interests of the District in formulating plans to strengthen the community; and,

Whereas, the Community Council, through the Pioneer Square Summit process, has identified the need to greatly expand the supply of housing in the district; and,

Whereas, the City and County cooperated in sponsoring a design charrette conducted by the University of Washington in April of 1990, which explored the potential of creating 1000 units of housing and commercial resources on the North Kingdome Parking lot; and,

Whereas the design charrette produced a number of promising ideas for creating housing which appear to be viable; and,

Whereas, it is the policy of King County to focus residential development in urban areas of the County in order to manage growth and prevent sprawl; and,

Whereas, the City of Seattle's Downtown Land Use and Transportation Plan identified the North Kingdome Parking lot as a special target area in which a mix of housing and commercial development would be encouraged by city action; and,

Whereas, the North Kingdome Parking lot is one of the largest publicly owned sites in Seattle on which housing might be developed; and,

Whereas, the site is well-served by public transportation and nearby the region's largest industrial and commercial employment centers;

Therefore, be it resolved, that the City and County Councils finds that it is in the public interest to investigate the feasibility of developing the North Kingdome Parking lot to provide housing for a range of incomes, as well as other commercial, retail and park resources necessary to a healthy urban neighborhood.

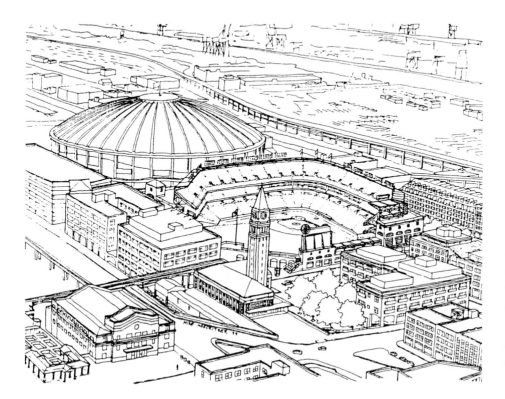

Another use considered for the Kingdome's north parking lot was a downtown baseball stadium. The King Street Grounds, proposed by a group of local design professionals, was a traditional ballpark design that fit snugly into this urban site. It is well served by buses, trains, and ferries and is in close walking distance from downtown offices, apartments, restaurants, bars, and parking spaces. (Drawing by M. Moedritzer)

AFTERTHOUGHTS: THE BASEBALL STADIUM

Since the charrette, a Public Facility District has been formed to site, design, construct, and operate a new major league stadium. Both retractable-roof and open-air facilities were proposed. Some citizens, including the author, argued that the best ballpark site in Seattle, if not the U.S.A., is the north parking lot of the Kingdome. This location allows a sports venue that is within walking distance of downtown offices, restaurants, bars, hotels, apartments, and public transit and is an even higher and better use of the site than housing. A group of volunteer architects and engineers, named the King Street Grounds Crew, developed a design for a traditional open-air ballpark that fit snugly into this large, urban room, with close-up views of the skyline. The ballpark would have been more than a great place to watch baseball. It would have been a great place to celebrate civic solidarity and urban life. Alas, the north lot was turned down in favor of a site immediately south of Royal Brougham Street—a site that will need considerably more urban life and fabric to match the magic of the north lot.

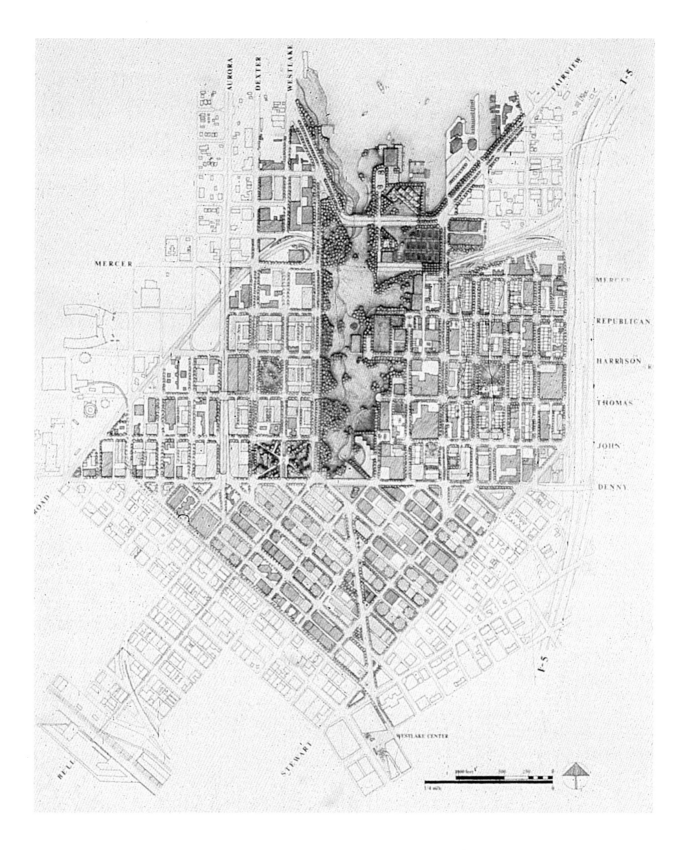

AURORA DEXTER WESTLAKE FAIRVIEW I-5

MERCER

MERCER
REPUBLICAN
HARRISON
THOMAS
JOHN
DENNY

ROAD

I-5

BELL STEWART WESTLAKE CENTER

The Seattle Commons Charrette
Envisioning an Urban Village

*"The measure of any great civilization is its cities
and a measure of a city's greatness is to be found
in the quality of its public spaces, its parks and
squares."*—John Ruskin

The area between Seattle's downtown core and Lake Union has long been
recognized as underutilized. Like the Denny Regrade, it is not blighted or
derelict, but it is underdeveloped for an area so close to downtown. Con-
sisting mostly of low-rise commercial and light industrial uses, the area contains little housing or open green space and vast tracts of parking and
abandoned, unused, or underused buildings. Many of the streets in this part
of town are congested as traffic passes through the area; the most severe congestion is on Mercer Street, a.k.a. the "Mercer Mess." The fact that the area
affords the last chance to create a large downtown park, originally envisioned
by The Olmsted Brothers, is another reason to redevelop the area. Whether
one's interest is in a new downtown park, low-income housing, traffic mitigation, or increased commercial development, there seems to be no way to
pursue those interests in isolation. There is a unique opportunity to develop
simultaneously all of those uses in a sympathetic, symbiotic manner.

The Seattle Commons charrette was undertaken in 1992 in conjunction
with the Committee for the Seattle Commons, and was underwritten in part
by both the City of Seattle and the State of Washington. It was the first large-
scale envisioning process for the area, allowing several glimpses into what
this neighborhood might look like.

THE PROGRAM

That the charrette program was considered to be both reasonable and feasi-

Master plan for the
Olmsted scheme, designed
by team led by Anthony
Walmsley, David Wright,
and the author. With
the addition of small
"parklets" on Westlake
Avenue, the park stretches
from Westlake Center,
in the heart of the down-
town shopping district,
all the way to Lake Union.

ble is an indication of just how underutilized the area is. In addition to redistributing current commercial and residential uses within the 280-acre planning area, teams were asked to include a park of at least 40 acres, upgrade and redesign the area's transportation, including arterial streets (all of which are currently operating at or above designed capacity), increase bicycle and pedestrian accessibility, and consider high-capacity transit, as well as accommodate 15,000 new residents. Additional concerns included creating buffer zones around major businesses in the area (i.e., Washington Natural Gas, the *Seattle Times*); incorporating smaller neighborhood parks; making environmental improvements, such as upgrading water quality and storm drainage; introducing regional amenities; and considering overall economic, social, aesthetic, and functional integration.

Washington's Growth Management Act requires Seattle to absorb a large number of new residents in the coming years. Mayor Rice took the politically courageous stance that Seattle should absorb even more than its share of the region's growth. Because the Seattle Commons would use an existing physical and institutional infrastructure and would be very close to the major employment centers in downtown Seattle, the Commons area was thought

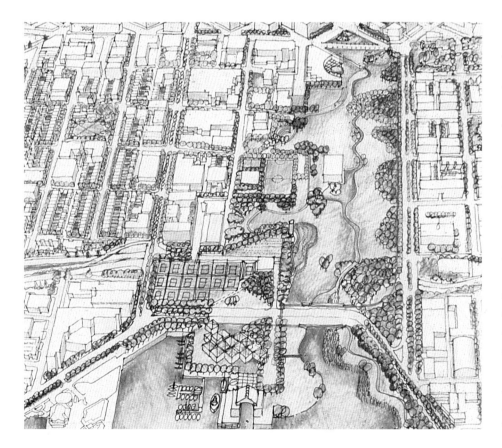

Aerial perspective of the Olmsted scheme. It is a variation of this basic design that the Committee for the Seattle Commons pursued in their efforts to realize a redevelopment scheme. Main features include a large central park, a partially lidded Mercer Avenue, dense new construction along the park's west edge, and infill development in the Cascade neighborhood to the east. The design includes conversion of the Naval Reserve Pavilion at the south end of the lake into a boat-shed for passenger ferries.

The Olmsted scheme proposes three new neighborhoods surrounding the park. The Cascade Neighborhood would be a mix of existing businesses with new low-income subsidized housing. Denny South, with its higher apartment towers, would attract singles and seniors. The West Commons, with ground-related, market-rate housing, would house more families

to be one of the largest and most feasible locations for this new growth to occur. Development of the Seattle Commons was seen to allow the city to absorb new growth without adversely affecting its single-family neighborhoods, while simultaneously adding a park to the heart of the city.

The "Olmsted" Scheme

This scheme organized the area into four distinct zones—the central park, and three neighborhoods of different character surrounding the park on the east, west, and south, linked by treed boulevards. The park is the central organizing element of the scheme, linking Westlake Center with the lake through inviting "parklets" on the triangular half blocks along Westlake Avenue that lead down to the park.

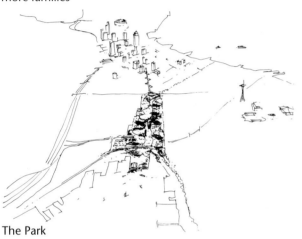

The Park

The Cascade Neighborhood

The Denny South Neighborhood

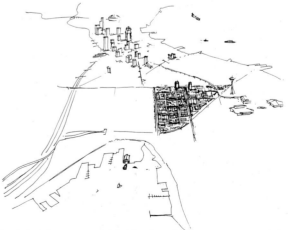

The West Commons Neighborhood

The major theme of the park is established in these parklets, with their repetitive water features, as the park recreates a spring-fed stream that once flowed down the valley between Capitol and Queen Anne hills. Emerging from a 70-foot-high rockworks and fountain at the south end of the park, the recirculating stream meanders north through the park, picking up surface runoff, finally ending in a marsh and ecological water treatment facility that mitigates the effects of storm overflow from downtown streets.

Mercer Street is sunken for four blocks near the north edge of the park, with a planted lid over the western two blocks. Little east-west traffic mitigation is planned in this scheme—the team members believed that congestion on the collector streets that feed Interstate 5 is a result of backups on the freeway itself, backups that can only be reduced by substantial changes in auto use throughout the region. They do hope to see some lessening of area traffic as more downtown employees begin to live in the Commons, although these changes would be slow in coming.

Surrounding the park, the team envisioned three distinct neighborhoods. The large, triangular shaped area south of the park would become the **Denny South** neighborhood. Zoned mostly for mixed-use high rises, it would provide housing for up to 7,500—single persons, couples without children, and elderly who value view, security, and city life—and some expansion of office space from the CBD northwards.

The **West Commons** neighborhood forms a "hard" edge along the west edge of the park. The West Commons is modeled after the upper stretch of Central Park West in New York, with a consistent six-story front along the park, with mid-rise and walk-up market-rate housing for couples with older children who like city living and accept a mix of office and retail uses with residential. Up to 5,000 residents could enjoy proximity to downtown, Westlake Center, the new park, and Lake Union.

Existing

The **Cascade/Eastlake** neighborhood offers the most inexpensive walk-up housing, new row housing and single-room occupancy hotels. It is a good neighborhood for subsidized low-income and live-work housing and could probably carry up to 2,500 residents. It preserves old frame homes and brick apartment houses, along with churches, meeting halls, serviceable businesses, and light industry. Because of the desire to preserve buildings along portions of Terry and Boren avenues, the east edge of the park has a broken, serrated, "soft" edge. The intent is to let selected buildings stand in the park, and have the park spread into and envelop portions of the built fabric.

Olmsted scheme

The park reconnects the city to the lake and unites the three neighborhoods. It reveals the lost watercourse. It achieves a landscape gradation from wetlands to upland forest, representative of the region. It addresses traffic and walkability. It incorporates sound environmental standards, besides displaying natural methods for improving water quality that are cheaper and

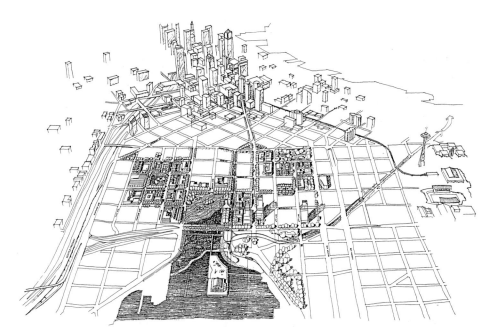

Aerial perspective of the Mercer Marsh scheme by team led by Linda Jewell, Ron Kasprisin, and Anne-Vernez-Moudon. Key features include a 20-acre wetland along the lake, bridged by a viaduct at Mercer Street, a number of smaller neighborhood parks, trolleys to downtown, and gradual growth through a number of different infill housing types.

more effective than engineered solutions. It continues the historic initiatives of the Olmsteds and others of structuring urban development around connected open space. The park is the social center around which the new neighborhoods could grow and flourish, despite their distinct differences in character and socioeconomic mix. It is intended to be a truly public realm, where different social and ethnic subcultures can meet and rub shoulders.

The "Mercer Marsh" Scheme

This team's principal goal was to create the framework for a vibrant place in which to work and live. Unlike the previous team, members of this team were less interested in focusing on the Commons as a major open space with regional significance than in seeding the foundations for a community or a group of neighborhoods in close proximity to the city center. This position stemmed in part from the deep impression that the site itself made on the team—they were convinced that between the steep hills, the Terry Avenue bluff, the towers of downtown, and the lake itself, a "mega open space" would be superfluous. The team interpreted the idea of the Commons broadly: to extend the existing resource of Lake Union and to prolong it with a localized and intimate network of parks and parklike streets for the emerging, dense residential neighborhoods.

The Mercer Marsh team developed a number of design concepts that guided their proposal. First and most importantly, they wanted to unite the idea of the Commons as a major *new* open space with Lake Union as the major *exist-*

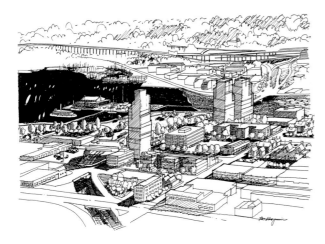

ing open space. Rather than create a competing space that would downgrade the lake's beauty and importance, the team chose to develop an open space that literally grows out of the lake, an extensive twenty-acre wetland and marsh that unifies the land and water, serves as an interpretive and educational device, and contributes to cleaning and filtering runoff. Mercer street is expanded for both pedestrian and bicycle use and to accommodate more traffic, as it becomes the northernmost arterial in the district, crossing the marsh on a viaduct. If people are going to have to sit in traffic, reasoned the team, they might as well have a magnificent view. The lake invades the land, with the marsh extending to the original shoreline near Republican Street. Other traffic modifications include depressing Aurora for three additional blocks north of the existing tunnel to improve links between the area surrounding Seattle Center and the Commons and the transformation of Broad Street into a pedestrian green street uniting Seattle Center and the Aurora neighborhood. Additionally, the team recommended two streetcar systems: one along Terry on the existing railroad right-of-way and another along the proposed Mercer–Seattle Center linear park linking south Lake Union to the Regrade, lower Queen Anne, and Elliott Bay.

The Mercer Marsh team structured the area around four neighborhoods, linked together by a network of open spaces and green streets that flow through and "irrigate" the neighborhoods. The team envisioned districts of distinct character in the **Cascade Area**, along the eastern hill; the **Westlake Valley**, along a north-south axis; the **Aurora Area**, along the western slopes; and **North of Denny Way**, in the area created by the manmade edge of the street grid change. Linkages between the neighborhoods are also encouraged by the strategic location of services and grocery stores.

The team based their concept on phased and incremental development. Street restructuring allows most existing buildings to remain, with new devel-

Left: View of the south end of the district, including the "marsh" and infill housing, including several "landmark" luxury towers whose construction would help subsidize other parts of the development.

View north along Terry Avenue, with light rail and a "wholesale" milieu not unlike the Pike Place Market

Left: View down alley with accessory units over garages

Infill housing (right) would raise the density in the Cascade Neighborhood to around 30 to 40 units per acre.

opment taking the form of infill and eventual replacement of some existing buildings. The team also developed a detailed infill housing strategy that offers six different types of infill housing all based on the same basic lot increment. The team deliberately developed housing types that are both traditional and recognizable: Cottages (one story with habitable attic), Skinny Row Houses and Square Row Houses (two stories with additional attic), Big Houses (walk-up structures with four to eight units), Tall Houses (walk-up or elevator-served, double-loaded buildings up to eight stories), and Very Tall Houses (luxury elevator towers up to fifteen floors). The team rezoned the area to allow these housing types, with placement determined by appropriate street type. Perhaps the most surprising move was to suggest several "landmark" luxury towers along the lake shore, whose high profits could perhaps underwrite less profitable development.

The City Beautiful Scheme

"Ten acres of inner-city land is equivalent to one acre on the water."—F. L. Olmsted

This was perhaps the most radical of the schemes, eschewing the model of Central Park for an eighty-acre greenbelt that curves along the waterfront. Westlake and Broad streets become major tree-lined boulevards, as well as light-rail routes, linking the new neighborhoods with downtown and Elliott Bay. Three east-west streets become minor boulevards: Republican, Thomas, and Denny. Aurora is lidded to north of Mercer, reconnecting the grid of streets; while two new bridges, similar to the Denny Street overpass, span Interstate 5, returning the Cascade district to its pre-freeway neighbor, Capitol Hill. An open arcade supports a public pedestrian esplanade above Mer-

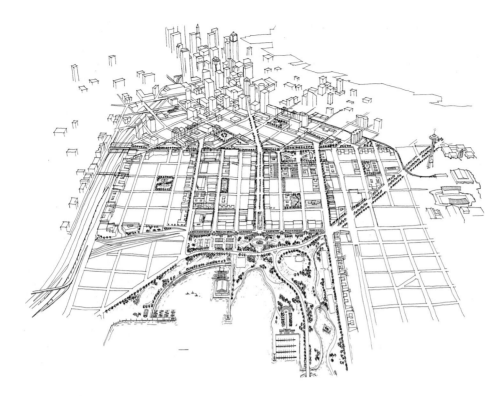

Aerial perspective of the City Beautiful scheme by team led by Elizabeth Moule, Mike Pyatok, and Daniel Glenn. Working from the premise that 10 acres of inner city land is the equivalent of a single acre of waterfront, this team proposed a large, 80-acre park stretching along the lake, while preserving most of the existing building stock in the area.

cer Avenue, while preserving motorists' views. Dramatic stairways flow down into the park itself.

North of the esplanade are recreational areas and ball fields. To the east are the filtering marshes and a small marina; to the west, a curved walk leads along the waterfront to boat tie-ups and a sailing school, enclosing a small bay. In the center is the Maritime Museum in the restored Naval building, along with restaurants, pavilions, and a lighthouse/lookout.

By preserving a larger amount of intact space in the center of the redevelopment area, the City Beautiful team could envision no less than six separate small neighborhoods. All six neighborhoods are served by the retail along Westlake Boulevard. Instead of a park in the center of the site, which would divide this relatively small district in half, a street like Westlake Boulevard could become a Main Street and provide a central location for retail that could be dense enough to act as a magnet for the entire area, while having a large enough market to ensure commercial success. Westlake would be lined on either side with five- and six-story residential apartments over offices and retail on the lower floors.

The **Cascade Neighborhood** is an existing area to the northeast of the site. This area would retain affordability with infill housing, primarily two- and three-story townhouses along the streets and one- and two-story accessory units along the alleys. Density would increase to around 30 units per acre,

The Beaux-Arts scheme distributes open space more evenly throughout the area, with smaller area parks linked by green boulevards. This team proposed modest new construction, along with the addition of alley units to increase density.

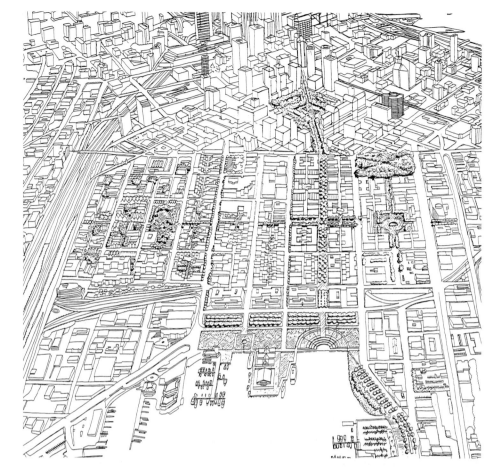

centered around an expansion of the existing Cascade playground. The **Boren Park Neighborhood** would be centered on Terry Avenue, mixing existing industry with live-work housing in converted lofts and new infill. East of Westlake and south of the proposed park would lie the **Dexter Park Neighborhood**, containing a mixture of light industry and commercial with densities of 30 to 40 units per acre. As in the Cascade Neighborhood, these densities would be achieved through infill townhouses and alley accessory units. Along the south edge of the park, densities would increase to 100 units per acre in view apartment buildings lining the Mercer esplanade. The **Denny Park Neighborhood** would infill the blocks surrounding Seattle's first park with family housing at around 40 units per acre, with taller buildings and higher densities along Denny Way. Densest of all would be the two new neighborhoods in the "triangle" north of Denny Way. At a density of 80 to 100 units per acre, these neighborhoods provide for the elderly and single and professionals and are centered around jewel-like open spaces modeled on New York's Gramercy Park.

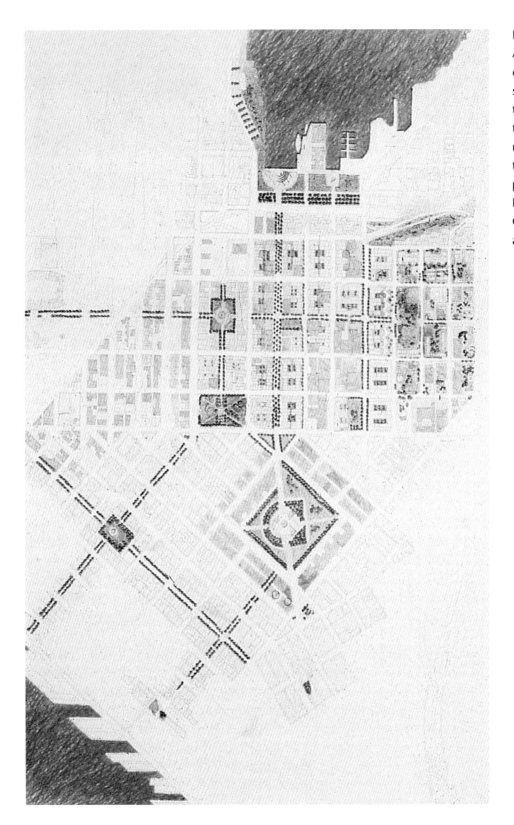

Master plan of the Beaux-Arts scheme shows the distribution of several smaller parks throughout the area. Green Park, the largest, is shown near the bottom of the plan and in the perspective to the right. Design team led by Lee Copeland, Jack Dunn, and Peter Staten.

The "Beaux-Arts" Scheme

Perhaps the most modest of the charrette proposals, the Beaux-Arts scheme was based on three main premises. First, the team concluded that it was preferable to provide several smaller parks throughout the South Lake Union district, rather than a single large park. Smaller parks require less dislocation of sound businesses and serve as nuclei for development in a wider area. Smaller parks also provide more perimeter than larger parks. The second objective is to preserve as much of the existing building stock, businesses, and healthy uses in the community as possible. And third, the team wished to foster improved linkages between the new neighborhoods and their established neighbors.

Pursuing these premises, the team arrived at an organizational framework familiarly called a "dumbbell scheme." Two parks—one at the south end of Lake Union, the other at the intersection of Westlake and Stewart—would be linked by a remodeled Westlake Boulevard. Westlake and Terry are developed as paired streets, each carrying two lanes of auto traffic in each direction, with a center median for landscaping and two lanes for bicycles in each direction. The west side of Westlake and the east side of Terry have parking and loading lanes. Northbound trolleys travel on Terry, while southbound travel on Westlake.

Minor landscaped axes were developed that cross Westlake: one at Harrison Street connecting two local neighborhood parks (Cascade Park and Harrison Square), another connecting the Westlake axis to a new Regrade Park (at Battery and Third Avenue), and a third along Roy Street connecting South Lake Union with Seattle Center. The small parks at the ends of the Harrison Street axis (Cascade and Harrison Square) were deliberately positioned to interrupt the street grid in order to provide a view of green space from the busy arterials, but to discourage through traffic that is unrelated to neighborhood uses.

The development of neighborhoods is to take place almost exclusively through infill, with many small parks throughout the neighborhoods. Commercial development is clustered along Westlake, Denny, and Fairview so that businesses and services will be mutually reinforcing. Neighborhoods include **Cascade** (families, moderate income, medium density), **Boren** (mixed-use, live-work, and light industry), **Westlake-Terry** (ground floor retail with four to five floors of housing above), **Harrison Square** (urbane mix of housing, entertainment, and professional/commercial uses), and **Green Park** (tall buildings—160 feet—serving as a backdrop to the southern end of the "dumbbell"). By addressing traffic and preserving existing business, with smaller-scale interventions, the Beaux-Arts scheme may well be the most economically and politically feasible of the schemes.

AFTERWORD

Following the charrette, there was a well-publicized effort to realize the Seattle Commons, spearheaded by a private, nonprofit organization that assembled land and promoted the project very aggressively. Although the UW charrette did not initiate this effort, it did help clarify and inspire some alternatives. The design adopted by the Committee for the Seattle Commons most resembled the Olmsted Scheme. Their design was developed by a full-time staff, with considerable input from the city and citizen groups. Progress toward implementation of the scheme was a *tour de force* in private initiative for a civic cause—at least until the autumn 1995 and spring 1996 city-wide votes shot down the initiative.

For better or worse, the Seattle Commons represents a unique, remarkable, and even heroic attempt at *private* urban renewal. Rather than the public sector buying, clearing, and banking land for development by the private sector, the roles were reversed: a private group, with the deep pockets of Microsoft cofounder Paul Allen, assembled and held properties for eventual development by the city as a public park. The private group was quick and efficient and involved many groups and talented people in its planning process. The city first watched at arms' length, then nudged and pushed the project in certain directions and downsized it after the first vote. If Jane Jacobs is correct in *Systems of Survival*, the public/private reversal is unnatural and unsustainable. She asserts that the private sector is by nature a conflicted guardian of the public good and generally fails when it tries to assume the mantle of government.

This project received a great deal of attention from both sectors. Indeed, the sheer attention it grabbed may have been its most worrisome aspect. If it takes *that* much energy, media attention, volunteerism, boosterism, hubris, and donation of money and services for *one* civic project of this magnitude, our cities are destined to see as few as one such effort per generation. Although one grand civic initiative per generation is better than none, we must find a less demanding formula for civic projects. Otherwise, good citizens will either shrink from initiating them or, if they do forge ahead, find themselves too busy or fatigued to work on less glamorous, everyday urban problems. If, on top of this Herculean effort, the initiative fails to gather enough public support, as it failed to do in this landmark case, citizens will be even less inclined to volunteer their services and support.

Probably never in Seattle's history has so much citizen effort for a single civic project been in vain. This unfortunate waste of energy and civic goodwill can be mitigated if the city can salvage some of the better ideas from the five years of analysis, design, consensus-building, and investment. The area is sure and soon to be transformed by commercial interests and will need the hand of the public sector if it is to add up to a place greater than the sum of its land uses.

David Brewster wrote a pessimistic post mortem. "The crushing defeat of the Seattle Commons proposal, cruelly abrupt and with no proper funeral, will long reverberate in Seattle politics. . . . Nor will the opponents, in a few years, be able to claim a victory. Very few of the businesses 'saved' from the Commons bulldozers will be around in a few years, since land values and developers will soon buy them out. As for new housing and low-income housing for the area . . . there will be dramatically less. . . . The Commons was an epic and noble effort at a middle course, at reviving the Seattle spirit in our politics. The proponents really did try to involve all sorts of different interests. They opened the Pandora's box of design-by-democracy, progress-by-consensus. . . . The Commons, which could have been the great example of the democratic way to make tough decisions, has instead become Exhibit A in the case for governance by a hidden elite."[4]

CHAPTER 6

Urban Neighborhood
The Forgotten First Ring

Urban neighborhoods have become the orphanage of many American metropolitan areas. Lacking the political and economic clout of either downtown or the suburbs, they have often fallen into a gray zone between the city center and the bedroom suburbs on the periphery. Although the urban model of concentric rings of growth radiating with arterial spokes from a single core no longer prevails in American cities, downtowns are still valued. They are often regarded as the most visible sign of the health of a city and receive a great deal of care and feeding. Suburbs, in the meantime, have been getting the lion's share of new housing, retail, and jobs. It's the urban neighborhoods in America—the inner city and the first-ring suburbs—that have not been getting enough investment, funding, or subsidy. Nor do their depressed tax bases generate as much revenue. As problems mount and tax monies dwindle, the death spiral of neglect has accelerated.

In many cities, urban neighborhoods were once the prosperous neighborhoods of the wealthy, full of big homes and beautiful parks. Many were fashionable streetcar suburbs, others were solid middle class communities of more modest means. Some were working class neighborhoods of bungalows. Now many urban neighborhoods are faded Victorian and Edwardian dowagers at best, blighted ghettos at worst. Whether boarded up, faded, or vibrant, they represent a valuable asset to the emerging American metropolis. They are close-in and well-infrastructured, often with stately trees and buildings, and are finely gridded with narrow streets and alleys for easy mobility of both pedestrians and vehicles. The residential lots are usually narrow and deep, with the short sides of their vertical, two- or three-story detached houses facing the street. Unlike suburbs, where lower and more horizontal houses spread their long dimension along the street, urban neighborhoods can achieve densities of sixteen units per acre, including accessory units. This essentially single-family pattern is dense enough to support bus transit. It's only a matter of time before the inner ring will enjoy a renaissance. Indeed, many urban neighborhoods, such as Beacon Hill in Boston and Georgetown in Washington, D.C., are among the most prestigious in their entire metropolitan areas.

Seattle, fortunately, has been spared decay and destruction in most of its urban neighborhoods. Mount Baker, Madrona, Capitol Hill, Queen Anne, Fremont, Ballard, Wallingford, Leschi, Denny Blaine, Washington Park, and Madison Park are healthy, functional neighborhoods. Some are wealthy, others are well within reach of the middle class. On the other hand, areas such as the Central District, Rainier Valley, and Beacon Hill are suffering from disinvestment, racial segregation, and poverty. In general, though, the upper and middle classes have not fled the first ring, which is one of the city's strongest vital signs.

One of the reasons the center has held in Seattle is the high number of beautiful inner city or urban neighborhoods. Because there are so many, gentrification has been less of a problem than in other American cities, where spot concentrations of reinvestment have displaced fixed- and low-income residents. A rising tide that slowly lifts many neighborhoods has proven more equitable than a torrent of investment that spectacularly gentrifies a few blighted neighborhoods. The views, extraordinary building stock, landscaping, and proximity to downtown have held the value of a critical mass of urban neighborhoods for over a century. Despite large areas of poverty and declining real estate, the average 1995 house price in Seattle was higher than in Bellevue, one of Seattle's most affluent suburbs. Maintaining and enhancing these healthy urban neighborhoods in Seattle and elsewhere will require conscious help and constant attention. (On the other hand, lifting poor neighborhoods out of poverty will take structural changes in our economic system that are beyond the scope of this book.) The City of Seattle's Department of Neighborhoods is a good beginning for the kind of ongoing place management that its many neighborhoods need. With the demise of the neighborhood church and neighborhood school, the provision and coordination of government services are all the more essential.

Many of the design studios at the University of Washington's College of Architecture and Urban Planning regularly focus on these urban neighborhoods, particularly the neighborhood commercial centers with which Seattle is so blessed and for which it is rightfully renowned. However, only one of the dozen UW charrettes to date has focused on the inner ring of the city's residential neighborhoods—perhaps because these areas have been so well attended to in studio projects. Also, because they are mature and complex communities, some of them are more difficult to help with a five-day workshop. Like a climax forest, they are not easily improved. Nonetheless, the 1995 charrette tackled the University District. After ten years of the UW advocating ideas to other neighborhoods, districts, and jurisdictions, it seemed

With the demise of the neighborhood church and neighborhood school, the provision and coordination of government services are all the more essential.

only right to practice in its own backyard what it has preached elsewhere!

Because the University District is necessarily skewed by a very large student population, it is correctly named a "district" (like a theater district or warehouse district) rather than a "neighborhood," which stands for a more balanced mix of uses and population. Once dubbed "Seattle's second downtown," it is densely mixed in use and population. It is demographically and architecturally extraordinary due to the University of Washington's commanding presence. The University's daytime population is 50,000, of which 22,000 live in the District. Every day, it experiences 18,000 transit work trips, the second highest in the region after downtown. Buses that ply the entire region pulse through the District at headways of a couple of minutes. Many of the riders are the students who have so shaped the area into a unique place.

How did this charrette and its follow-up studio stack up against the theory from Part I?

COSTS OF SPRAWL

No area of the city would profit more from increased density than the University District. Students are captive and willing candidates for commuting by foot. The more of them that live within walking distance of campus, the fewer the vehicle miles traveled. This logic also applies to faculty, few of whom in recent years have been attracted to live within the University District. There is no faculty/staff housing provided or sponsored by the University for active or retired employees. Fewer faculty and staff shop in the District than a generation ago, and this, coupled with the great number of parking lots and vast amounts of vacant or underutilized land, make the District ripe for more housing of all types. Another factor in favor of greater density is the excellent bus service available. The District has always figured prominently in rail transit plans for the region. There are 2,200 housing units officially proposed for this area, which the City's Comprehensive Plan officially designates an Urban Center. If built, these units would prevent more than a square mile of sprawl.

CRITICAL REGIONALISM

The University District, which dates back to the first decade of the century, has some of the state's most distinguished architecture. The campus is full of outstanding buildings, well designed and built of substantial materials. Ironically, the architecture of the many Neogothic, or Collegiate Gothic, buildings has nothing to do with regional history, building practices, or culture. It is a direct import from East Coast universities, which, in turn, transplanted it whole cloth across an ocean and several centuries. In both cases, the architecture was imported to lend an instant legitimacy and to improve the universities' reputations as much as the beauty of their campuses. The University of Washington campus is stunningly handsome and coherent—as are the District's brick apartment houses with Neogothic, glazed terra cotta trim similar to that which graces many of the campus buildings.

Recent buildings added to the campus have skillfully reinterpreted the Collegiate Gothic architecture, which has been around long enough now to constitute a local tradition, even though its roots are transplanted. Indeed, the organic and irregular spatial conceptions and motifs of Gothic architecture are in direct contradiction to the axial formality, symmetry, and clarity of the Beaux-Arts campus plan. (So much for authenticity and integrity.) Some of the most authentically regionalist buildings in the University District are not university or even institutional buildings. They are maritime buildings along the waterfront of Portage Bay on the south edge of the District. Also, some of the Arts and Crafts houses in Ravenna at the north end of the District are good examples of regional bungalows and cottages. Lastly, the two elementary school buildings—University Heights and Latona—are examples of the architectural excellence that Seattle public schools have represented over the years. Most of the charrette schemes picked up on and maintained the bulk, character, and scale of these buildings.

TYPOLOGY

The District is well represented typologically. There is the normal urban array of architectural types, plus the campus typology of library, auditorium, classroom, laboratory, studio, and administrative buildings. A campus, by intent, is usually more architecturally consistent than ordinary urban fabric. There is the opportunity for overall clarity, in this case achieved with strong axes and well-defined quadrangles. Like the military base at Sand Point in chapter 7 or any institutional campus, there is the potential for more unity in terms of both architectural type and style. Single ownership and operation, as well as common aspirations and goals, make it easier. Even when the architectural styles change over time, the clarity of types holds a campus together. (This local unity is bought at the expense of unity with the greater community, but in the case of institutions that benefit from some degree of separation from daily life, it seems justified.)

In a looser way, typology also holds the rest of the District together. There is a relatively consistent quality to the street wall along University Way, with a common typology of retail establishments on the ground floor, hard against the sidewalk, and offices or apartments above. The commercial buildings along Roosevelt Avenue are a melange of standard, one-story pancakes, except for some new multistory, brick medical buildings. The residential typology is also unconvincing, with a myriad of house and apartment types lined up on any given block. A critical mass of low- and mid-rise brick apartment houses is almost achieved, but it falls several buildings short. The residential streets north of 47th Street have greater consistency in both architectural and typological terms. Some are in fact *tours de force* in Seattle bungalow and bungaloid architecture.

The charrette teams found that for the most part they did not need to invent new architectural types. Although jumbled and deteriorating, a sufficiently broad palette exists, especially for residential functions. (After thousands of years of building dwellings for an almost infinite number of situations, there is very little new under the sun in housing.) It was more a question of knitting dwellings into the existing context in sensitive and sensible ways. Nonetheless, there were several new types that this charrette, like every charrette to date, invented. Mike Pyatok's team proposed magnet parking garages—essentially multistory parking structures with small student-dwelling units attached like barnacles to the sides and top. Michael Shaw and his University of Liverpool students added some new apartment house models and accessory unit models to the American typology. Jill Stoner's "contrada" reinterpreted a traditional Italian neighborhood type for America. The follow-up studio developed several new types: a scattered site, a shipping-container youth center, and a parking garage that over time can reconfigure itself into apartment housing.

NEW URBANISM

Urban neighborhoods are the most challenging area in the cross-section of the American metropolis. They do not lend themselves to sweeping master plans, grand visions, or wholly new templates.

Urban neighborhoods are the most challenging area in the cross-section of the American metropolis. They do not lend themselves to sweeping master plans, grand visions, or wholly new templates. They require microsurgery, while the suburbs need organ transplants and pulmonary bypasses for their weak, and in some cases, nonexistent hearts. They present the untidy, messy problem of a more mature community. They have in many cases been the dumping ground for society's "Lulus" (locally unacceptable landuses) and the breeding ground of disadvantage and pathology. Although many of Seattle's urban neighborhoods are humane, integrated, stable, affordable, and livable, some are in need of restoration and investment. Others are not assuming their fair share of society's burdens. (My north Capitol Hill neighborhood, for instance, fought the conversion of a large house into a halfway house for homeless women and the use of a church parking lot for commuter van pool parking during the week. Some residents have asked for a quarter-billion-dollar lidding of nearby Interstate 5. This kind of NIMBYism and sense of entitlement from people who are otherwise solid citizens illustrates how myopic our vision and selfish our civic ethos can be.)

New Urbanists have been slower to embrace these inner city challenges, where small-scale infill is needed more than Welcome Wagons and toxic clean-up is needed more than high school car washes. The old chesterfield urban neighborhoods of grand homes and green trees are too comfortable and stuffy to be worried, and the ghettos are too down-and-out to turn themselves around without massive funding. Although the periphery is where the endless imprint of suburban development is now being laid down as fast as we once laid railroad track and highways across the continent, the urban neighborhood is where future battles must be fought and won if our society is to survive intact.

The University District charrette tried to build more common place for town and gown, which are often at odds with each other. It generated visions, but they were more modest than ones to come out of the Seattle Commons, the New Communities, and the Interbay charrettes. If the New Urbanism is to rise to its full potential, it will need to take on more than suburban greenfield sites and urban brownfield sites. It will have to help struggling urban neighborhoods that sit quietly between the high-pitch, high-profile center cities and droning, low-profile suburbs.

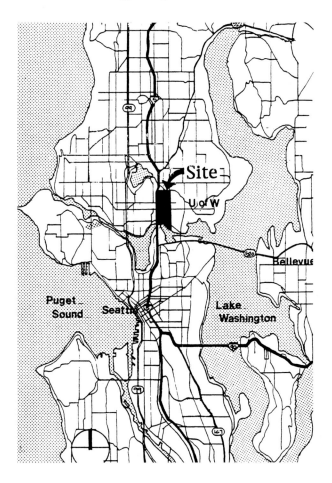

Site of the University
District Charrette

The University District Charrette and Studio

"The avant-garde rejects all forms of convergence. It is based on the romantic idea that creativity can only prosper outside the constraints of what is shared. It claims autonomy for the sake of art, but confuses the autonomy of the form, which is real, with the autonomy of the author, which is a fiction. It does not see that invention and originality need to grow from a common field."—N. John Habraken[1]

HISTORICAL OVERVIEW

The University District emerged from a community called Brooklyn.[2] The early development of Brooklyn was single-family residences with a community-oriented business and service core, in keeping with the original idea of patterning Seattle after New York City. The Brooklyn development was annexed by the City of Seattle in 1891. The University of Washington moved to its present location in 1895. At that time the main business street was Brooklyn Avenue rather than University Way. Brooklyn Avenue was intended to be the main street of a business core second only to downtown Seattle. But due to several factors, including the laying of trolley lines, the commercial focus was shifted to 14th Street, later renamed University Way and commonly referred to as "The Ave." The addition of the University to the community caused a gradual shift from a community-based business sector to one that provided institutional business and services needs, as well as specialized housing and retailing.

From the 1930s until the late 1940s the District experienced a downturn, a depression, and then World War II. The University District followed this economic boom-and-bust cycle with the rest of the region and country, as

Team 3's Plan

Market rate housing above University Heights Community Ctr.

Park, playground and farmers market

Safeway, grocery store, and garage with housing above

50 senior housing units over church parking lots

West University Heights: 200 family units

Neighborhood park

"Magnet" garage for 800 cars; 45 live/work alley units; 95 rooftop penthouses

Office building with affordable alley housing

Market-rate housing (streetside) and affordable studios (alleyside)

Affordable single-room occupancy studios, with social services

"Magnet" garage for 500 cars; 30 live/work alley units; 50 rooftop penthouses

New commercial/University building on Campus Parkway

Married student and faculty housing

Neighborhood playground

University's south rail station

University's southwest parking garage

Southwest Research Campus

Southwest Campus marketplace, restaurants, and plaza

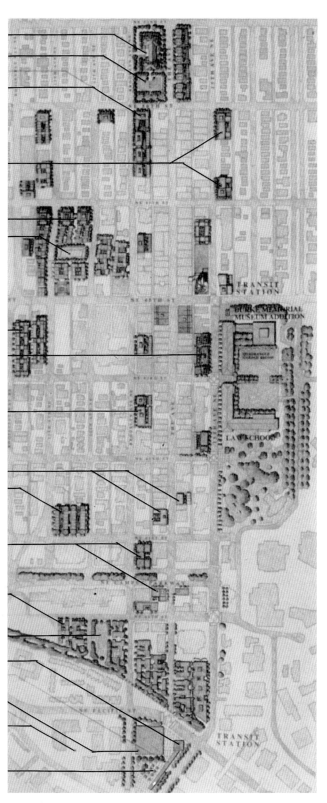

The Ave was Seattle's bustling "second downtown" from about 1910 to 1950, after which it has experienced a slow decline.

it typically has over its 130-year history. During this time several bridges were built or reconstructed that later proved vital to automobile movement to and through the District. This improvement in vehicular access brought more customers into the District to shop.

With the economic prosperity of the 1950s and 1960s, as well as a greater demand for higher education and the G.I. bill, University of Washington enrollment skyrocketed. There were approximately 7,000 students in 1945; by 1960 there were more than 18,000. During these two decades there was a substantial shift in the demographics and lifestyle of Americans. There was a general out-migration of family households from the older urban neighborhoods like the District to new suburban communities. The housing stock of the UW area was thirty to fifty years old and required more and more maintenance. To many district families, a new house in the suburbs with modern conveniences was an attractive alternative. American shopping habits and car usage were also changing. Americans were inventing the age of the automobile, and suburbanization was in full swing. Northgate shopping center opened in 1950 with approximately 500,000 square feet of covered shopping and free parking, both of which doubled in area in 1965. University Village, east of the UW, opened in 1956, also with easy access and free parking.

The 1960s saw the University continue to expand its land holdings, especially in the southwest quadrant of the District. Much of the West Campus expansion was aided by the federal Urban Renewal Program. This move to condemn and tear down houses and other buildings was met with community resistance and litigation. By 1971, after eleven years of court delays, the University of Washington had added a total of sixty acres in its westward expansion. In response to this development pressure, several local organizations were formed to protect community interests.

THE SITUATION TODAY

In recent years the Ave's commercial, physical, and social environments have deteriorated. This is evidenced by a growing number of vacant shops, poor maintenance of building facades, graffiti, litter, and increased crime. An increasingly narrow retail mix and the growing number of street youth and panhandlers have discouraged some people from frequenting the Ave, which has also been negatively affected by the closure of University Heights School. The housing stock and mix have become less amenable to families with children.

The Ave is still dominated by the overwhelming presence of the University of Washington. This huge and growing institution sits one block away and transforms what would be a "neighborhood" into a "district." The UW also has its own needs and aspirations and, like most urban universities, is facing community resistance to expansion. How and where it will grow is a challenging question that requires a closer look at the nature of the American campus in general and the UW in particular.

THE CAMPUS

There are several physical models for universities.[3] There is the Anglo-American tradition, which started with Oxford and Cambridge in the early thirteenth century. This model had its origins in the medieval monastery. It

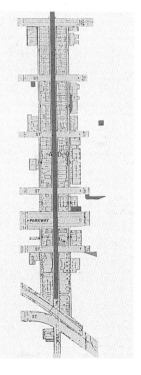

The Ave is a taut thread with frayed edges.

View over the ship canal to downtown Seattle from the University District. The District is designated an Urban Center Village in Seattle's new Comprehensive Plan.

was a sanctuary set aside from the life of the city, with courtyards, cloisters, lawns, and, later, playing fields. The English universities erected exemplary buildings of Gothic, Renaissance, Neoclassical, and Modern architecture, using the finest architects of their day. When this model came to North America, it became less urban, with expansive lawns and buildings that were free-standing. Closed courtyards in separate colleges gave way to larger, more open quadrangles in a single enclosure, first called a "yard" at Harvard University and later a "campus" at Princeton University (after the Latin word for field). Numerous colleges and universities located themselves in small towns, where their leafy campuses dominated the townscape. In the late nineteenth and early twentieth centuries, many campuses became more geometrically formal, with symmetry, axes, and vistas set within Beaux-Arts plans. Many also became more architecturally consistent, even thematic. They adopted Victorian, Richardsonian, Neogothic, Neoclassical, or Neocolonial styles in an attempt to unify and legitimate themselves as universities, as much as to unify disparate building types.

The University of Washington campus was laid out at the turn of the century by The Olmsted Brothers, the nation's premiere landscape architecture firm at the time. Its core is an excellent example of American Beaux-Arts campus planning, with some of the grandest axes and most dramatic vistas in the country. Somewhat contradictory was its adoption of the Collegiate Gothic style, which is based on an architecture and urbanism that is much more organic and less grand than the axial and symmetrical planning. Nonethe-

The University of Washington central campus is one of the most beautiful in the world and its axes and quadrangles are among the most memorable designed spaces in the region. The Anglo-American campus model may need to give way to a more continental European model for the West Campus, where town and gown could mix functions in an urban fabric that integrates academic, research, residential, retail offices, and other institutions.

less, the campus is home to some of the finest examples of Neogothic architecture on the West Coast, especially the many works of Bebb and Gould. The University has generally taken its architectural and planning responsibilities seriously, setting up one of the nation's first architectural commissions in the 1960s to select architects and review their work.

On closer inspection, there are arguably five UW campuses: the Anglo-American, Beaux-Arts central campus, the Health Sciences megastructure, the athletic complex, the newly emerging Southwest Campus, and the West Campus. There is always the question of whether to try to unite a large campus into a single whole or to divide it into separate precincts. Should the university, for instance, try to extend the formal principles of the central campus into the West Campus, or should it adopt a completely different model—that of the original continental European university? This model, which originated in Paris and Bologna a century before Oxford and Cambridge, is fully integrated into the city. Academic, administrative, and research buildings are mixed into the urban fabric and are sometimes indistinguishable. Students live in apartments rather than in college dormitories and eat in cafes rather

The University of Washington campus enjoys a sixty-mile view of Mt. Rainier, surely one of the longest and most spectacular axes anywhere. *The Fountain and Mountain*, by Norman Johnston of the College of Architecture and Urban Planning, describes and illustrates the campus and its history.

than college dining halls. Does this model make sense for the West Campus and the lower Ave? Does it represent a symbiotic way for both the University and the community to grow? What are the formal implications when an essentially nonresidential educational institution wants to become more integrated into the community and sympathetic to the daily lives of its neighbors? These are some of the questions that precipitated the design charrette.

THE DESIGN CHARRETTE

Team 3's Statement

Our approach to this urban design challenge envisioned a revitalized University District through a series of incremental steps. In contrast with the grand and all-controlling gestures of "Master Planning," we believe that the District can be strengthened within its current patterns and without imposing a singular, exclusive vision. We sensed a strong community interest in diversity and in maintaining and strengthening the unique qualities of the area and the Ave. Through a series of interrelated strategies, our approach builds on and celebrates many of the positive qualities that can be found in this distinctive part of Seattle. This project includes five key sets of overlapping issues:

View of proposals for the alleys, including the development of pedestrian amenities, housing, and commercial spaces. Team 3 was led by Gordon Walker, Cynthia Richardson, and Peter Hasselman, who did this and the next two drawings.

1. **Transit strategies.** These are critically important to the local setting of the District and the regional matrix of transportation. This proposal involves an underground light rail traveling below 15th Avenue, with stations at the northwest and southwest edges of the University campus. Several other linked ideas involving other forms of transport (cars, bicycles, buses, pedestrians) support this initial assumption.

2. **Integration of the University and community.** There is a rich symbiotic relationship between "town and gown" which has not been fully realized. The University can take an approach which engages the community rather than turning its back; both will benefit from a reinforced sense of mutual dependence and involvement.

3. **Exploration of housing strategies.** A wide range of housing options are developed to accommodate diverse groups within the community. Residential construction sites are identified in existing "open" areas of parking or low scale and underutilized sites. This strategy encourages growth of over 2000 units of housing within the district, thus building a more stable socioeconomic foundation for the area. The increase in density and a reinforcement of residential character are essential to the District's long term viability.

4. **Jobs.** Through sensible growth, employment opportunities can be projected within the twenty-five-year period of this proposal. A strengthened Ave would produce an increase in employment, as would the development of several key areas of research and support functions for the University in the Southwest Campus, the West Campus, and the 15th Avenue corridor.

5. **The Ave.** This project celebrates the positive and distinctive attributes

View of proposed low-rise multifamily units in the residential neighborhoods north of 45th and west of the Ave

View of proposed Campus Parkway open space, which has been enlarged by eliminating the east-west rights-of-way. Only the Ave and Brooklyn Avenue pass through the green space.

that can be found on the Ave and its alleys. Our development strategies and incentives along the Ave imagine a slow transition over time. The qualities of the Ave and the adjoining alleys are seen as different conditions. The development of these distinct qualities would support a rich diversity of retail and residential use for a range of income and age groups within the University District.

Housing Strategies

The University District's future retail and employment opportunities depend on an increase in residents with discretionary income. These new households should be in close proximity to the Ave and its transit links. Therefore, this approach did not consider any new higher-density housing developments north of 50th Street (other than the former University Heights school). Approximately 2,250 units of housing are proposed south of 50th with the following unit count:

Affordable: 29% of total

- 250 (11%) live-work studios along alleys in the Magnet Garages (500 sf)
- 150 (7%) moderate income family units (900 sf) in new family-oriented districts
- 100 (4%) mini-studios (250 sf) for special needs populations on the Ave with services
- 150 (7%) low income seniors (550 sf)

Market Rate: 71% of total

- 1100 (49%) family units (900-1,400 sf) in new family-oriented districts
- 350 (15%) singles, couples (600-1,000 sf) near the campus on 15th and for married students and young faculty near the southwest campus along the Burke Gilman Trail
- 150 (7%) market rate seniors (550-700 sf)

"Still Life with Cigarettes" —Private balcony over-looks the east alley, which could become as busy as the Ave.

Magnet garages are big enough to collect a large quantity of cars in strategic locations and are sited for convenient pedestrian access to the Ave. Their sides and top would be devoted to a layer of student apartments.

Mixed-income housing with units along the alleys and below-grade parking

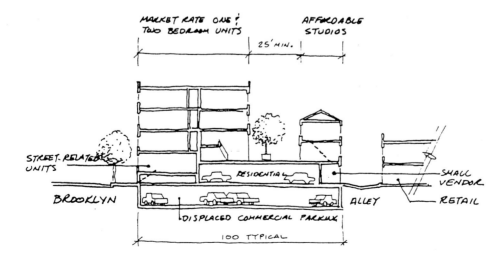

The Ave

The Ave suffers from a lack of a shared vision and cooperation among the property and store owners. The mix of street level misses the full range of potential for users of the Ave. The alleys could absorb uses that cater to the youth and student population; catering to these uses on these public rights of way could free up the Ave for more upscale shops and restaurants, without displacing the lower-end market. Decentralizing the markets could also help alleviate the density on the Ave. Many of these smaller businesses need only 10-20 feet of depth to operate. Cheaper studio apartments can be built above these small shops, entered from the alleys. More upscale housing can be built facing the broader streets. Several incentives in the zoning code could improve the pedestrian life of both the Ave and its neighboring alleys. A development may take advantage of incentives to achieve a full height of 75 feet.

Team 4's Statement

The design challenge, in this relatively dense, socially and culturally complex district, elevated the importance of searching for potential within existing physical conditions, and the searching for identity within existing demographics. This approach eschews the idea of the "Master Plan," with its implication of large areas of removal and radical alteration. We rather took the metaphor of microsurgery, an approach that would leave few scars on this already rich terrain, while repairing the fabric with small rather than large interventions.

Our analysis resulted in a series of diagrams around issues such as the perceived problem of the separation of "town and gown," the potential for smaller neighborhood groups within the district, the difference between a "district" south of 47th Street and a "neighborhood" north of 47th Street, the implications of regional transit for the community, and the relationship of the Ave to its context.

It seemed to us, as architects, that the building itself represents the best surgical approach within an urban fabric tending to greater density. One building on an empty lot not only provides new programs, but helps to reinvigorate the buildings on either side, and in turn might inspire another building farther down the block. The siting and programming of these new buildings were determined by searching for micro-districts, each of which might become the client for an architectural act. These small districts we called "contrada."

West Campus

Latent in the west campus is a different model of development for the University and its campus. Rather than the Beaux-Arts model of the central campus, with its axes, quadrangles and buildings in the green, the west campus

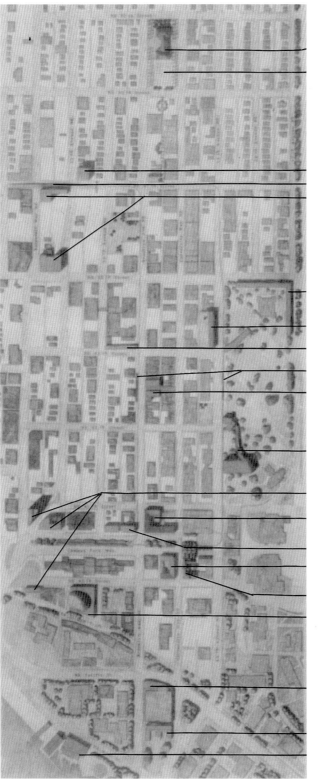

Team 3's Plan

Elementary school

Public market

Elderly housing

Transit stop

Research facilities

Addition to Burke Museum

Parking garage

Infill housing

Transit stop

Mid-block pedestrian mall

Law School

Research/office buildings

Retired faculty and staff housing

Apartment building

UW Information/Employment Center

Expanded College Inn

Velodrome

Retail addition to parking garage

Day care center

Renovated police station

Aerial view showing the relationship of the University of Washington, the University District, I-5, and the ship canal. New residential development is proposed along Campus Parkway and research facilities along Roosevelt Avenue with a major employment node north of 45th Street around the proposed rail stop. A student quarter is defined by Campus Parkway, Roosevelt, the Ave, 47th Street, and 15th Avenue.

could develop with urban buildings with courtyards. This figure-ground reversal puts the green within the building rather than the building within the green. These courtyard buildings could combine retail offices, classrooms, recreation facilities, parking and residences. Typically they would fill their lots, front directly onto streets and be three to five stories in height. Because the University's athletic and recreational facilities are concentrated on the East Campus, we also propose siting a sports facility on the West Campus. Specifically, a velodrome and swimming pool could be built.

Campus Parkway

At present, Campus Parkway seems spatially unresolved, with many missing teeth and unclear function. We propose filling in these gaps with market-rate housing, including at least one retired faculty and staff apartment house. A mixed use building, incorporating the UW ticket office, information center and employment office should be built on the corner of Campus Parkway and the Ave.

Research Corridor

Land surrounding a research university is more appropriately devoted to university-related activities than an ordinary mix of commercial, institutional and residential land uses. The Roosevelt Avenue corridor, with excellent access to I-5 and the proposed RTA, as well as the University, seems the ideal place within the District for research enterprises. We propose transforming the auto-oriented commercial area, which consists primarily of auto dealerships, into a research area. Car dealerships are unrelated either to the Ave or the University and big box retail proposed for the area actually threatens the retail life of the Ave. This linear research zone could widen at its northern end, around

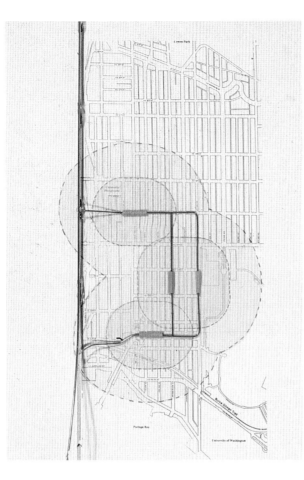

This RTA scheme proposes a light-rail trunk line that runs parallel with I-5, with a slower moving surface line through the District. Every other train could peel off the main line, thereby eliminating the need for transfers. Transit stops are shown as gray rectangles.

our proposed RTA stop at 47th Street. A major employment center with mid-rise, even high-rise office and elderly housing towers should cluster around this transit stop, which is located in an area that is presently underdeveloped and peppered with many parking lots. The bulk of new development along this corridor and around the transit stop should be research companies and institutes befitting the proximity to a major research university. A research office tower at the south end of the corridor marks the entrance into the University District.

The Parking Garages

One garage at the foot of the Ave is already under construction. We propose wrapping it with a thin layer of retail shops, to bring more commercial activity to the Southwest Campus. We also suggest a park or plaza, and day care center south of the garage to better terminate the Ave. A new garage is proposed for the empty lot behind the University Bookstore. It is roofed with a lawn of sod, sloping gently to the south.

Collage showing proposed vertical signage along the Ave

Retail that is distinctive to the Ave, such as used-book stores and student-oriented restaurants, should be encouraged as part of a culture that is more local and authentic than that of the University Village Shopping Center.

University Heights

Ideally, the structure would be returned to its original use as a school. In the meantime, we propose to remove the chainlink fence around the old playground and install a pergola or shed around its perimeter to provide cover for markets, fairs, etc.

Student Housing

An SRO (single room occupancy) apartment building integrates small room student housing at the exterior with larger student/family housing facing an interior courtyard. By beginning to make carefully designed housing for students in the District south of 47th Street, the larger houses north of 47th, now broken up into rental units or boarding houses, can be returned to single-family residences.

Cottages

On a block-by-block basis, the "contrada" north of 47th can begin to frame their own zoning concepts, including backlot and garage accessory units that can bring the student community into the neighborhood on a more controlled basis. They also provide income for owners, thus making this housing stock more affordable for middle-income families, including University faculty and staff.

The Ave

Reinvigorated businesses now selling such items as flowers, food, clothes, chairs, books, and shoes begin to lend their own design elements to the public realm. We turned the store signage perpendicular to their building faces. Also we recommended widening the sidewalks from 9 feet to 11 or 12 feet by narrowing the cartway from 13 to 11 feet and the parking strip from 8 to 7 feet. This would have the desired effect of slowing vehicular traffic while easing pedestrian congestion. Moving parking meter stanchions, signs, and other pieces of urban furniture closer to the curb and/or removing them would also help sidewalk circulation. Metered parking could be replaced by free parking with posted time limits and enforced by parking police, thereby increasing sidewalk space and competing with the free parking at University Village.

Research Area and Family Housing

Parking Garage with Housing

Market Rate Housing

Burke Museum Addition

Market Rate Housing

UW Information and Extension Center

Married Student Housing/ Recreation Center

Mixed-Age Housing

Community Oriented Housing

Nondenominational Chapel

The design studio generated building designs for twelve different sites in the District. Like most of the charrette teams, it relied on strategic interventions in the form of single buildings rather than on a grandiose, master plan. In general, there was an attempt to increase and diversify the District's population and to nurture interaction through cross-programming academic, research, commercial, and residential uses in various combinations within single buildings. The projects tended to be modest buildings that attempted to reinforce the relatively fine-grained, low-rise, high-density fabric of this urban center without demolishing buildings or altering the existing street grid. A generation earlier, a similar academic studio might have wiped much of the slate clean and started over with large-scale buildings, more futuristic and more highly zoned planning and design.

THE DESIGN STUDIO

A design studio of thirteen undergraduate and graduate architecture students continued the work of the charrette. Because the visions generated in a charrette are always hastily and imaginatively conceived, they need to be tested, edited, consolidated, and elaborated. The first task of the studio was to adopt a master plan quickly by picking and amalgamating what it considered the best ideas from the charrette.

The range of possible building types was broad, both in size and function. The buildings designed were academic, commercial, institutional, residential, or a mixture of these uses. Some were foreground buildings, others were background or hybrid buildings. Students used existing programs or developed new ones, including cross-programming new combinations of functions that reflect new and emerging realities and imperatives for the District and contemporary times.

Youth Center with Satellite Shelters

This project takes advantage of "left over" space to provide shelters for homeless youth. It consists of a center base camp with several satellite shelters. The base camp is located in the lot adjacent to the UW School of Social Work. This facility would maintain a 24-hour drop-in center, located in the building along the street, and a communal cafeteria and bath house, both retrofitted into the existing concrete block structures located on the alley. The outdoor court adjoining these structures is intended to remain open and flexible. It may, for instance, serve as a bicycle repair shop and training center during the day and double as a gathering place in the evenings.

Shipping containers are retrofitted as housing on rooftops and over alleys for homeless teenagers. (Prentis Hale)

Existing concrete block buildings are retrofitted with a bike workshop and a common bath for homeless and jobless teenagers.

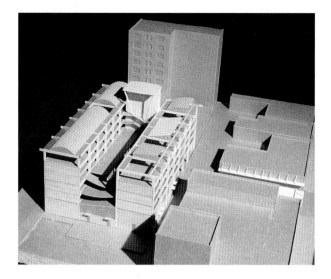

Left: Organized in three bays, the garage allows for incremental dismemberment of the middle bay to accommodate the retrofitting of housing as the demand for parking decreases. (Kenneth Last)

Section of the garage cut at the midblock pedestrian passage, which includes stalls for vendors

The satellite shelters are meant for those youth who have demonstrated responsibility and earned a more private dwelling. The lack of bathing facilities in the satellite shelters is intended to link them to the base camp by drawing the youth to the common bath on a frequent basis. There are two satellite dwellings explored in this study. The first takes advantage of the unused space under the parking lots where the level change requires a retaining wall along an alley. These cavelike dwellings receive natural light through skylights that sit in the parking lot above. The second type of dwelling sits on top of buildings. These units are built from shipping containers which are structurally independent and can span their own length, with bearing points at either end. They might sit directly on a building roof or span the alley.

Parking Garage Cum Housing

This design proposes a parking facility and a food market located in the surface parking lot on Brooklyn Avenue. The idea behind the garage center is its ability to be retrofitted with housing as parking demands diminish over the long-term future of the District. The facility is a simple rigid-frame structure organized in a grid of three bays by seven bays. The less permanent design of the middle bay allows for its incremental disassembly, floor by floor, to provide a lightwell for the housing units as they come on line. The design also reinforces an east-west, mid-block pedestrian passage by allowing people to traverse a path from Brooklyn Avenue to University Way, passing through the garage structure on the ground level and through the open-air food market.

CHAPTER 7

Suburb
In Search of Place

"Suburbs, composed of endless variations on the ranch-style house, epitomize the complete separation of work and home, paradoxically inverting the original relationship of ranch house to land. The suburban development, more centrifugal than centripetal, disintegrates into a dispersal of dwellings across underdeveloped terrain, disrupting plant and animal habitats and commodifying land in ever-dwindling parcels. This scattered, decentralized, and noncommunal pattern of settlement results in environmental degradation and the careless, wasteful use of land and other human and natural resources."
—Barbara L. Allen

At the dawn of what has been called in America the suburban century, it is fair to declare that the suburbs are winning the war against the city. They are now home to the majority of Americans. Many urban and rural communities are scrambling to adopt suburban norms. The worst-case inner cities have given up the hope of recovery. It is a sad commentary on shifting political power and priorities in America—sad because it is likely to bankrupt the nation ecologically and economically.

The two projects that follow deal with very different areas within the suburbs and with very different challenges. The Sand Point charrette focuses on a second-ring suburb, albeit a military community. The site is beyond the first ring of streetcar suburbs (e.g., Madison Park, Wallingford, Queen Anne). Most of the houses were built in the 1950s and 1960s, although some predate World War II. The site itself, the Sand Point Naval Air Station, dates back to the 1920s. It reached peak activity as a military base during World War II,

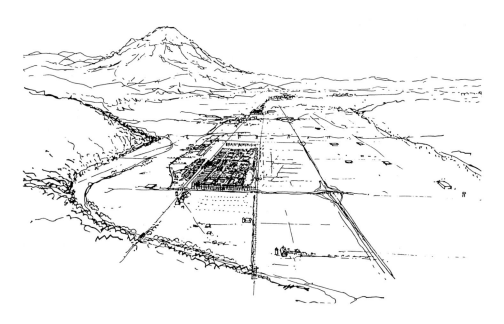

The 1988 Pedestrian Pocket charrette looked at suburban infill for a site south of Seattle in Auburn. It is not included in this book because it has been fully documented in *The Pedestrian Pocket Book,* a national bestseller in its field, published in 1989 (Princeton Archectural Press).

ceasing operation as an airbase in 1970. The charrette addresses the question of what to do with the 150 acres and 50 buildings that were not turned over to the city when the airfield was decommissioned and Magnuson Park built. It is not a situation in which most residential communities find themselves, nor is it altogether unusual, as the U.S. armed forces convert hundreds of military facilities to civilian use around the country.

The second project, a design studio, deals with a third-ring suburb (although these concentric rings of growth are not as clear or circular as the annular rings in the trees they cut down). Lacey, Washington, could be many places in America. Built out after Interstate 5 was constructed in the mid 1960s, it has boomed in recent decades. Lacey is primarily a bedroom community, although it is home to a large mall, a small college, and a new campus for state office buildings. It lacks a clear center, primarily because it has experienced most of its growth after the automobile was the dominant form of transportation. Lacey's planning staff had asked for help in bringing identity and form to what they too perceived was an anonymous physical place. Half the design studio looked at how to retrofit a downtown core, through selective replatting of streets and infilling of buildings. The other half of the studio looked at an arterial commercial strip, ubiquitous throughout the U.S.A. It asked what can be done to improve the mall itself and what can be done with the vacant land that lies between the mall and the cul-de-sac subdivision behind it. This vacant strip is a classic American phenomenon—fallow land that is a sort of DMZ separating a purely commercial function from a purely residential one. How to knit together these two zones, or at least put to use the empty land, was the studio problem.

COSTS OF SPRAWL

The capital costs of implementing these projects are not excessive relative to the benefits. In the case of Sand Point, the buildings and land are essentially free. They have already been paid for once by the taxpayers through their federal tax dollars. Some of the buildings, especially the brick officers' and enlisted men's housing and the former aircraft hangars, represent an extensive and well-constructed physical inventory. Not to recycle them would represent a major economic loss to the neighborhood and region. As for Lacey, it fits tightly the description of sprawl given in chapter 1. It demonstrates and suffers the many problems of sprawl as much as any community in the region. This landscape of consumption and cars may offer moderate-cost housing to individual residents, but its patterns of land use and transportation are expensive for society.

CRITICAL REGIONALISM

There is nothing particularly regionalist about Sand Point, because of its federal pedigree. It exudes the faded glory and character of an old military base. There are some honorific buildings and parade grounds, although most of the buildings are standard government issue. When the first 150 acres of runways were donated to Seattle in the 1970s, the park that was soon developed by the city was an attempt to restart regional landscapes and vegetation. Some of the public art, for which the park is justifiably famous, picked up on regional themes and qualities.

As a gated, planned community, the military base doesn't suffer the same low level of definition as most second-ring suburbs. (To be more historically precise, it was built during the era of streetcar or first-ring suburbs, but later found itself situated within a second-ring community.) There is a definite sense of limits and of bounded community, with a single entry gate. A long shoreline, a hill to the south and west, and a major boulevard form emphatic and natural edges. As a consequence, it lacks physical connections to the abutting neighborhoods.

As elaborated in chapter 4, gated or bounded communities are not wrong if they contain a full spectrum of people and functions. If inclusive, they can be a healthy and sustainable community. That's what a medieval walled town was—a gated but inclusive community, with almost all the members of its feudal society welcome inside the gate. It's when the gates and fences keep out people from the same society and enclose an exclusive, private realm that they become socially shortsighted and dangerous. With the addition of a broad range and sufficient number of residents and businesses, Sand Point could grow into a successful community. But it needs a sufficient and bal-

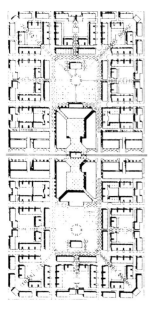

The Pedestrian Pocket, shown here as an idealized diagram that has not been inflected to a particular site, is bounded but not walled or gated. Unlike gated subdivisions, there is a broad cross-section of income and age groups, as well as diverse land uses and building types.

anced population to endure. Concentrating many homeless people there, without a large influx of other household types, would be just as unbalanced and ultimately as unsustainable as a socially elite enclave.

Lacey, on the other hand, lacks regional identity and architecture, primarily because it is a young town. It will be challenging to make a there there—to develop a critical sense of place, of nature, of history, of craft, and of limits. It will take great political will, a richer architectural typology, and good design.

TYPOLOGY

There is a well-developed architectural typology at Sand Point, primarily the result of its being planned and operated by a single owner, a hierarchical one at that. The U.S. Navy has imprinted its own order and brought its own architectural types. In many ways, a military base is the quintessence of typology, with its clear chain of command and status and its emphasis on teamwork embodied in architecture as much as protocol. Highly specific architectural types are reserved for highly specific functions. There is an architecture of common vocabulary and materials—other hallmarks of typology.

Like many post–World War II suburban towns, Lacey lacks a clear or legible hierarchy of architectural types. If footprint is the measure, the Fred Meyer store would be the most important building in town. The impoverishment of architecture, the reduction in the number of building types, and the loss of legibility and meaning in the built environment are fully evident in Lacey. The primary type is the one-story commercial building. The proposed designs, for both downtown and the arterial strip, are meant to bring more typological variety and rigor to this low-definition townscape.

NEW URBANISM

Sand Point is a coherent example of an older suburban society, in this case a military one. Ironically, it demonstrates many of the principles of the New Urbanism. With more inhabitants, more mixed-use, and more integration with the surrounding neighborhoods and city, it could quickly shed its military stigma. It also needs to repair some of the physical fabric. If it implements these changes, it could become a model of New Urbanism, as well as a model of military base conversions. Lacey, unfortunately, has a much looser and less defined structure with which to work. It will need to make major physical changes to realize the basic principles of New Urbanism. The studio proposals illustrate the magnitude of change needed on both sites. Developed over a ten-week period, the studio suggests how to phase this transformation, something most design charrettes don't have enough time to delineate in detail.

The Sand Point Charrette and Studio

Reinvesting the Peace Dividend

WITH DANIEL GLENN

(Drawing by M. Twohy, © 1993 The New Yorker Magazine, Inc.)

"This one is for converting a military base into a crafts center."

The 1993 charrette tackled one of the most important and one of the largest single design projects facing the City of Seattle: the reuse of 150 acres of land and 1.5 million square feet of building on Sand Point's Naval Air Station and its integration with the adjacent 150-acre Magnuson Park. This large parcel of land and buildings is located in a low-density section of Seattle on a point in Lake Washington. The base was intended to become available for public use by 1995 as a result of the 1990 Congressional Defense Base Closure and Realignment Act. The base closure presents a historic opportunity for Seattle to convert a former military use to civilian needs on a large scale. With affordable housing a critical need in the city and the federal McKinney Act requir-

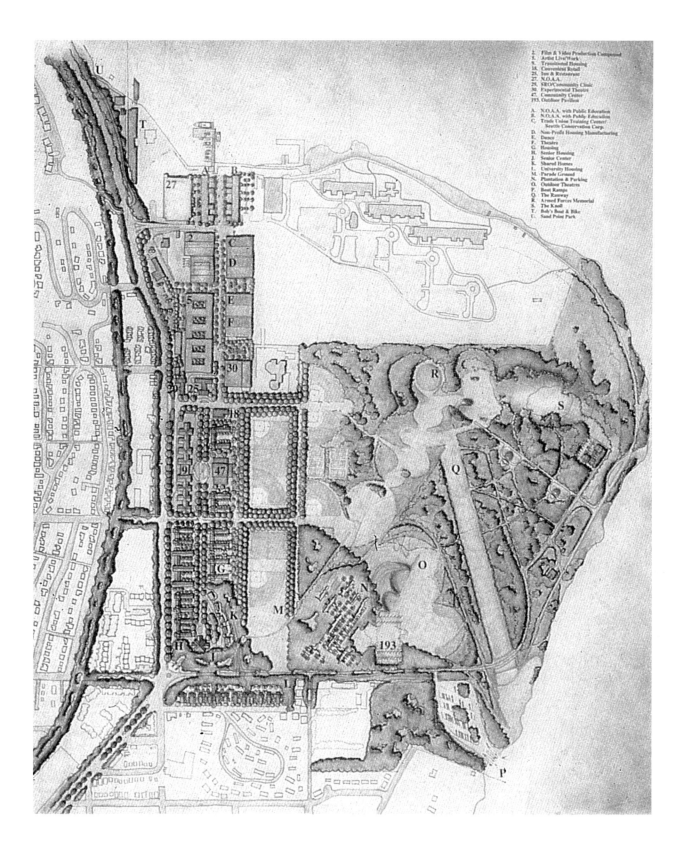

ing that housing for the homeless be given first priority on federally surplused property, housing on the site was a major priority for the charrette. Design teams had the task of incorporating that housing into a larger whole that includes the development and expansion of Magnuson Park and a mix of recreational, cultural, educational, commercial, and other residential uses.

The Naval Air Station opened in 1925, serving primarily as a reserve facility for Navy and Marine training. During the thirties, the site was leveled, and Pontiac Bay and Mud Lake were filled to construct a large runway. The base reached the height of its activity during World War II, providing repair and logistical services to the Pacific Theater. After the war, most flight operations were transferred to other bases and, in 1970, all flight operations at Sand Point were suspended, making way for the donation of 150 acres to the City of Seattle as Magnuson Park in 1973. During the seventy years of military occupation, a vast stock of buildings was erected (including several large hangars that are some of the largest clear-span buildings in the Seattle area), housing for several hundred personnel, and administrative, recreation, and storage facilities.

Many local groups expressed interest in using the facilities at Sand Point. Rather than turning all these groups loose for a congressional land grab, the city attempted to incorporate all groups into a single vision. Among the interested groups were the Sand Point Neighborhood Liaison Committee (a well-established community group that represents the adjoining neighborhood), the Seattle–King County Coalition for the Homeless (an advocacy group), the Sand Point Arts Coalition (a group of artists seeking to convert some of the buildings to live-work studios), the Washington State Motion Picture Council (seeking to use several hangars as movie sound stages), the City of Seattle Sailing and Tennis Advisory Councils (seeking more outdoor and indoor facilities, respectively), the Seattle Parks and Recreation Department (seeking to implement public recreation facilities), and the University of Washington (seeking to expand its married-student housing).

All these significant and seemingly reasonable proposals had been considered in light of the city's Sand Point Community Plan. This vision for the property states the following goals: (1) preserving and enhancing recreational opportunities and facilities; (2) creating a multiuse community which will add to the area's aesthetics and opportunities; (3) developing and maintaining this community with the least burden on taxpayers; (4) ensuring meaningful and logical connection between the future uses of the base; (5) exercising sensitivity to ecological and environmental concerns; and 6) creating uses compatible with the character of the surrounding neighborhood.

In this charrette, there were more parties that had a legitimate claim on the future of the site than in any other charrette. This competition is a natural outcome of the federal surplus process. In addition to listening to these

The "Magnuson Park and Village" scheme introduced a modest amount of new infill housing along Sand Point Way, expanded the park, and suggested turning the north end of the site into a "street of arts and industry."

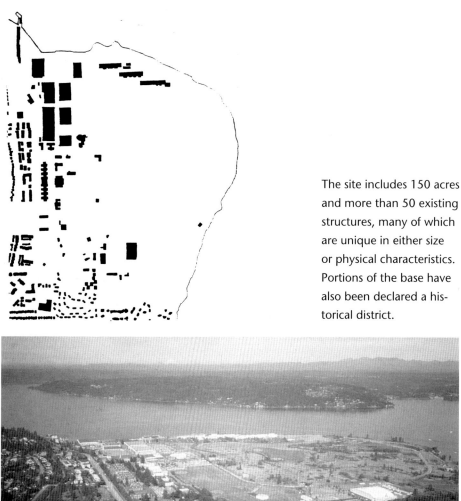

The site includes 150 acres and more than 50 existing structures, many of which are unique in either size or physical characteristics. Portions of the base have also been declared a historical district.

often contradictory voices and goals, the charrette teams were charged with looking closely at the site itself and discovering what *it* wants to be.

This charrette marked the first time the City of Seattle Planning Department officially incorporated a UW charrette directly into the city's formal planning process. The design teams used the city's Sand Point Community Plan goals and plan as the program for their designs. The charrette intentionally did not result in a "solution" for Sand Point; however, a number of interesting ideas and valuable proposals resulted from the process.

GENERAL CONCLUSIONS

- The site, with its vast amounts of built and open space, lends itself very well to both the creation of a new community and the enlargement of Magnuson Park. The park is a regional resource, not just a neighborhood or city amenity. The conversion of the naval base offers an excellent opportunity for improvements in the design of the park. Indeed, as the largest public, open parcel of real estate in the city, the site cannot be treated as an isolated planning problem, but must be part of a larger vision of Seattle and the region.

- Though there appears at first to be an insurmountable number of competing interests in the property, the site and its extraordinary building stock are large enough to handle most, if not all, of those needs. In fact, several team members commented on the problem of finding too little programmed space to fill the built square footage. It also became apparent that competing interests can in fact create a complementary, as well as lively, mixture of uses on the site.

- Housing was recognized by all the teams as a vital and feasible element of the site. The number of units remains a social, political, and economic question. The team solutions varied from a few hundred units to over two thousand. Some retail, commercial, and industrial activity on the site is also vital to the economic future of the project, as well as to its viability as a part of a larger vision of Seattle and the region.

- Transportation to, from, and within the site is an important determinant of the design and the use of the site, given the fact that the neighborhood is relatively disconnected from downtown Seattle and the greater region and that patterns of automobile usage in the surrounding neighborhood are more typically suburban than urban.

THE DESIGN CHARRETTE

Of the vast number of ideas to spring from the charrette, one of the most universally acclaimed was the "Plowshare Commons" scheme to redevelop the main entrance to the park with a grand diagonal that would extend the angle of Sand Point Way into an entry boulevard. All schemes proposed expansion of the existing park, most to a final size of 200 to 250 acres, making it the largest park in the city. As such, there is recognition that the current "side-street" entrance to the park is inadequate. Most schemes also recognized that current parking and boat-launching facilities in the park are heavily overloaded. On sunny weekends, lines of boats waiting to be launched often extend as far as Sand Point Way. All four schemes also proposed an extension of the heavily used Burke Gilman bike trail (which skirts the west edge

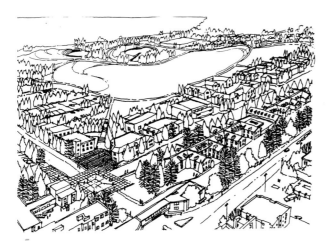

The "Plowshare Commons" scheme emphasized expanded access to the park, with many new links through the built area and a grand new diagonal entrance to the park. Infill housing and a new commercial node line the edge of the enlarged Magnuson Park.

of the site) into and through the site, providing bicycle access to all the recreational facilities of the park.

Another well-received idea was the revival of the now-filled-in Mud Lake, once a popular fishing destination. Several schemes proposed bringing back the lake, either as a separate entity, or as a shallow lagoon that connects to Lake Washington. Other recreational additions included stripping the siding from the old base exchange building and turning it into an open sports pavilion, and constructing an open air theater on the shores of Mud Lake. One team embraced the proposal of the federal Fish and Wildlife Department (their Seattle facility borders the site) to build handicapped-accessible fishing ponds, expanding the proposal by designing a small riparian zone and wetland interpretive trail from the ponds to their outlet into Lake Washington.

Several teams proposed some variation of a major municipal small boat center on Pontiac Bay at the north end of the site where a small marina already exists. All of the city's boating facilities are operating at full capacity, and there is much support for a new facility modeled on Vancouver's highly suc-

The "Planes, Trains and No Automobiles" scheme, while dealing seriously with issues of housing and access, also followed the credo: Living in cities should be fun. The scheme attempted to create an environment where the arts were integrated with the daily life of the community in an entertaining and whimsical manner.

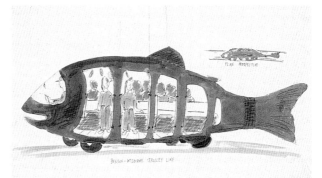

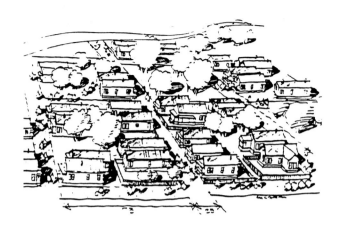

Incubator or starter housing can grow (or shrink) with household size and income.

cessful Jericho Bay Center. Several teams proposed new landscaping for the body of the park that recalled the naval air station runways; however, this was an idea that apparently held more appeal for designers than for area residents. The concept was roundly criticized because the runway orientations were open to the prevailing wind gusts that sweep across the lake. Other citizens felt that the sooner the era of naval aviation was forgotten, the better.

Many schemes proposed additional vehicular and pedestrian entrances to the site along Sand Point Way to integrate better the new community with the existing one, as well as to provide more views to the lake and beyond. Additional streets would also break up the existing enclave of military buildings into more easily developed and accessible city blocks. Access to the park was dealt with in many ways. A modest proposal was to open the NOAA parking lots on the north end of the site to weekend park use and the extension

One team, led by Rich Haag, Ron Kasprisin, and Cheryl Cronander, proposed using the site for a future world Olympiad, which would leave behind a legacy of housing and sports venues.

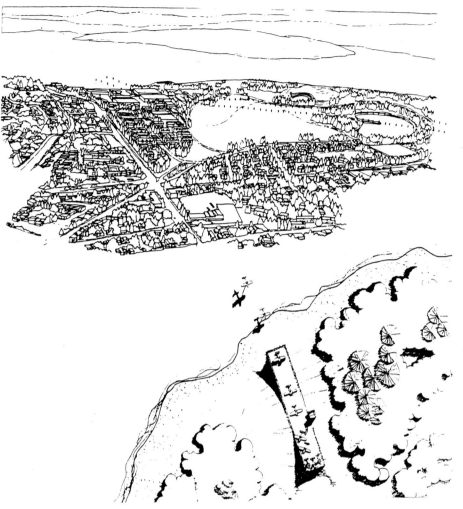

One of the most popular ideas to emerge from the charrette was to create a grand entrance to the regional Magnuson Park, along with a view corridor and transit links.

Several schemes suggested recalling the aviation history of the site in public art or landscaping.

of a loop road surrounding new ball fields on the western perimeter of the park. A more radical idea was a colorful "fish trolley" to connect the park with the University District and downtown. Several schemes also stressed the importance of opening up pedestrian access through the built-up portion of the site down into the park. There was also considerable balancing of jobs and housing, as well as several suggestions for the new community becoming more of a transit node, with either trolley or increased Metro service. Two schemes also proposed Sand Point as an appropriate stop for commuter ferry service on Lake Washington from the Eastside to downtown Seattle at Westlake.

The teams also reached a consensus on the most appropriate locations for many potential user groups. The civic and commercial center of any new development would be best at the existing administrative core of the base,

Despite the claims of some community groups opposed to new development at Sand Point, new housing of up to four stories could be built without infringing on the views of the hillside neighborhood.

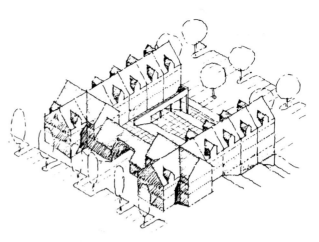

Typical housing proposed to infill along Sand Point Way, while high density, is of relatively low impact. During the quarter following the charrette, a design studio at the UW further explored infill housing at Sand Point.

where 70th Avenue enters the property. Building 2, an expansive double hangar was judged to be best suited for the movie soundstage, with its attendant needs for a securable location and easy access for large support vehicles. The vast Building 5, with its 300,000 square feet of built space, could provide more than adequate space for all the public access TV, drama, music, and art groups, including facilities for Pottery Northwest and a metal foundry. There was considerable support for a vibrant "Street of Arts and Industry" in the northern portion of the site, where many different creative enterprises would intermingle on the broad pavement of what used to be a taxiway between the two rows of hangars. Three groups also suggested converting the brig into some sort of museum. The large, brick Building 9, already serving as short-term housing for base residents, was considered the easiest and most cost-effective way to fulfill the requirements for transitional housing for the homeless. However, it was the strong belief of most charrette participants that housing for the homeless on the site should be part of a larger community that includes low-income, moderate-income, and market-rate housing and community retail and services. To achieve these ends even the more conservative schemes proposed more housing than the minimum numbers set out in the Sand Point Community Plan.

All schemes recommended both the reuse of existing building stock and infill of new housing. Virtually all teams emphasized that housing should be mixed-income, incorporating the Coalition for the Homeless's proposals for long-term transitional housing, married-student housing, senior housing, live-work housing, and mixed-income family housing. One team even proposed building housing above the large parking lots that lie on the south portion of the NOAA site. All groups proposed this new housing at densities above the norm for the surrounding neighborhood.

Housing and density became the largest points of contention in community response to the charrette. The Sand Point Neighborhood Liaison Committee, representing an influential and affluent neighborhood, strenuously objected to the large amount of housing, especially in the density and price ranges proposed. Regardless of this resistance, the teams seemed to come independently to the conclusion that a critical mass of housing is required to create and sustain a vibrant community. The potential for such a community, with a large arts center and diverse housing, was seen as an opportunity, not a problem. Additional housing, especially in the higher income ranges, was also seen as necessary to keep housing for the homeless from becoming isolated from the rest of the community.

Along with increased housing, all teams included in their charrette solutions greatly increased retail and commercial facilities. Currently, the only retail outlets within walking distance of both the Sand Point site and the surrounding View Ridge community consist of a dry cleaner and a single convenience store. The schemes proposed a variety of village centers and shopping streets centered around the intersection at 70th Avenue, where the base's main street jogs between the northern and southern half of the base.

THE DESIGN STUDIO

After the completion of the charrette, a dozen architecture students engaged in a follow-up design studio led by Michael Pyatok and Daniel Glenn. No single charrette scheme was followed exclusively. Nor was a new site plan developed. Rather, students explored specific designs for infill housing on the site. Students were encouraged to incorporate specific ideas from the charrette, particularly the diagonal entry of the Plowshare Commons proposal.

Schemes varied from twenty to sixty units per acre in density, and automobile allowances varied from 0.5 to 2 cars per unit. This exploration confirmed the extent to which parking tends to drive contemporary design, and how the current zoning requirements for two cars per unit virtually eliminates lower income/higher density housing. Schemes also varied in intended resident income levels, from low income and assisted living to high-end market rate.

One housing design for the portion of the site south of Building 9 along Sand Point was christened the "stealth unit." It was an innovative proposal to defuse neighborhood resistance to high-density housing by designing four- to six-unit "big houses," deeper than they are wide, that appear from the street to be large single-family houses. Distributing quarter- to full-block

Student designs for housing of high and moderate density on the Sand Point site. Many designs emphasized human and neighborhood scale elements to defuse community resistance to large, bland apartment buildings and condominiums. (Forrest Murphy; Jennifer Mundee; Glen Phatok)

parcels between different developers would assure architectural diversity among these apartment houses posing as mansions. This scheme and some of the other housing designs pulled their parking into mid-block parking courts, blocking the view of parked cars from the street.

Few, if any, of these student solutions are likely to be implemented. What they do show, however, is a large number of ways to incorporate increased density housing at a variety of income levels while minimizing the impact on the character of the existing neighborhoods.

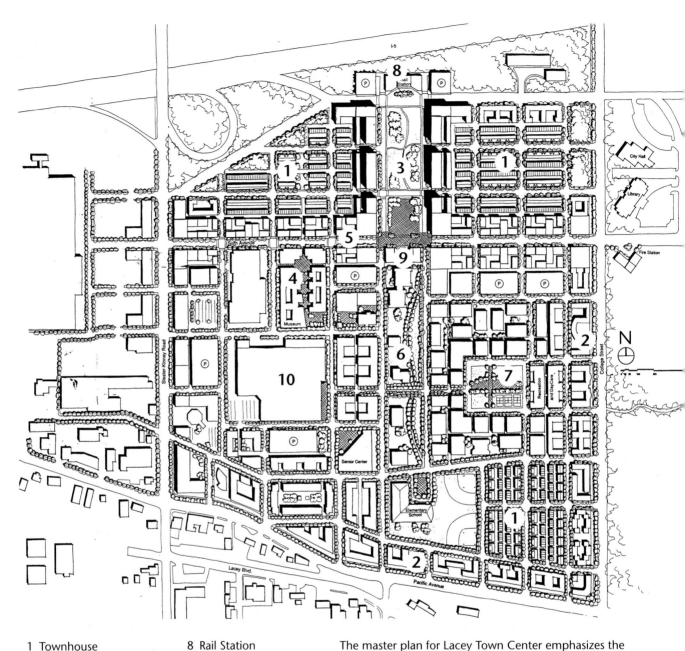

1 Townhouse
  Neighborhoods

2 Multi-Family
  Perimeter Blocks

3 Town Square

4 The Paseo

5 Main Street

6 The Promenade

7 "Office Park"

8 Rail Station

9 Bus Station

10 Public Market

The master plan for Lacey Town Center emphasizes the reintroduction of the grid to the suburban core, with jogs in the grid to preserve as many existing buildings as possible. A train station for the proposed high-speed line from Portland to Vancouver is located along Interstate 5. It is paralleled by a new "Main Street" four blocks south, which has civic buildings in the green campus surrounding St. Martin's College at one end and a regional shopping mall at the other end.

The Lacey Studio
Centermaking in Suburbia

WITH RICHARD MOHLER

"These new settlements, plowing haphazardly through rural and suburban communities, cannot accurately be called cities or suburbs. They have no core. They lack linkages among their fragments. They do not have a continuous fabric or coherent structure of buildings and landscapes."—Robert Geddes[1]

At most architecture, landscape architecture, and design schools, the primary mode of education is the design studio. Typically, one professor works on a tutorial basis with a group of 10 to 15 students on a design problem, such as a building, landscape, or area of a community. Some explore more theoretical and speculative issues, some simulate or deal directly with a real program and/or site. The four studios in this book—Sand Point, University District, Lacey, and Interbay— are of the latter type.

This subchapter[2] is devoted to a quarter-long architectural design studio which examined how to integrate both the retail highway strip and a typical suburban town center with higher density housing and how to relate these uses to adjacent single-family residences. In particular, the studio examined the transitional zone between the commercial strip and the detached single-family residence. For the purposes of this study, the suburban town center is defined as that portion of a suburban community that can be loosely described as its "downtown." Largely built after World War II, this type of community lacks a traditional "main street" and is often located at or near a freeway interchange. The suburban core generally contains civic institutions such as the town hall, library, and fire station, as well as office and retail facilities such as shopping malls and strip development. Some evidence of a street grid or other municipal development pattern may exist, but the area consists primarily of large zones of single use development. Due to segregated patterns of zoning, housing is limited or absent from these areas. The proximity to the freeway makes the suburban core a candidate for a regional transit stop and for greater reliance on public transit in the future.

ISSUES OF SUBURBAN INFILL

In addressing the urban design problems of suburban infill, the design studio uncovered a number of issues to be considered in attempting to integrate and order a suburban center.

Parking

Parking may seem like an odd place to begin, but it drives much of suburban design. Parking regulations are so overpowering (code mandated parking often takes up more of a given site than the building footprint) that architects often look at them first.

With public transit and increased pedestrian connections between residential, commercial, and retail uses, overall parking requirements for commercial and residential uses can be reduced. It is important when mixing retail, office, and residential uses along the same street that the parking for those uses be clearly coordinated, as they have very different requirements. Retail and commercial parking must remain independent of residential parking during working hours in any mixed-use neighborhood, and their entries must be obvious from a high-volume thoroughfare. Residential parking must also remain separate from any retail or commercial uses and have its own private, secured entries, preferably from quiet, less traveled streets. While retail lots must be large and connected to permit continuous searching for spaces by shoppers, residential lots should be small and compartmentalized to create a greater sense of connection among neighbors who share the lot. Parking lots, after all, are often the place where neighbors interact—a type of public or semi-public space that we need to design better.

Typical solutions to parking and parking access in suburbia should be reconsidered. The typical configuration for parking in suburban retail strips and town centers is in front of the building, i.e., between the building and the street. While this provides a clear and convenient access for the automobile, it severs the important relationship—found in more traditional "main streets"—between the sidewalk and the storefront. Frequent curb cuts are hazardous and discourage pedestrian activity. On-street parking is one traditional strategy that should be reconsidered for suburban centers, especially along retail streets. This strategy at once provides visible and easily accessible parking for short-trip automobile shoppers, as well as a physical barrier between automobile traffic and the pedestrian.

Another effective strategy is to park near the center of the block rather than at its perimeter. Residential parking may be located beneath the dwelling units in garages behind storefront uses. Retail parking may be gathered into larger lots behind shops to serve the larger shopping district. This provides a more pedestrian-friendly environment and recognizes the value of street frontage, especially along retail streets. In this case, pedestrian access to retail should not be at the rear of each store but in mid-block pedestrian passages which periodically connect the parking area to the street frontage. This configuration encourages shoppers to stroll past more shop fronts and enlivens the district as a whole. Parking behind buildings in the center of the block also hides the parked cars from view and better defines the sidewalk and street space. Coupled with short-term, on-street parking, it is urbanistically preferable to parking lots between the building fronts and the sidewalk.

A traditional component that affords parking within the block is the alley. By allowing vehicular access to the center of the block at limited locations, the alley enhances the street front for the pedestrian. As discussed below and elsewhere, the alley also provides opportunities to mediate between different scales of building and to increase residential densities unobtrusively and affordably.

Circulation

In order to provide a more pleasant environment for the pedestrian and automobile alike, the two must be more closely integrated within the suburban downtown. The typical condition of the "superblock," currently found in Lacey and Bellevue and throughout suburbia, thwarts efforts to provide a workable pedestrian realm. The development of smaller blocks and narrower streets is critical to the creation of a viable pedestrian environment in the suburban town center.

In addition, it has been demonstrated that the post–World War II legacy of cul-de-sacs, collector roads, and arterials not only hampers the pedestrian but also creates more, not less traffic congestion. It also forces unnecessarily long vehicular routes. Smaller, more numerous blocks and narrower streets

The traditional street grid, provides greater lane capacity than the post--WWII hierarchy of cul-de-sac, collector street, and arterial road. In many cases, the grid provides shorter travel times and in all cases provides shorter apparent travel times. These advantages are primarily the result of having more intersections at which to turn left. The traffic lights in suburbia not only seem longer, they *are* longer because left-turn lanes and signals are standard. Suburban grid-lock is to a large extent caused by a treelike rather than a latticelike network of roads. This heirarchy forces vehicles through fewer and fewer branches as they near the trunk arterials and allows no access between one cul-de-sac system and the next.

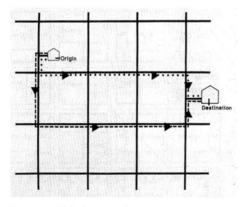

Dense gridded network

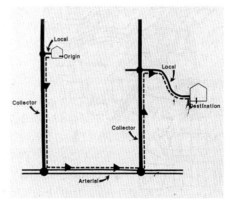

Conventional suburban heirarchy

provide an environment more scaled to the pedestrian. They shorten the actual and perceived travel times for most automobile trips. The shortened travel times are a result of more intersections. The interruptions of left turns are spread out over a large grid rather than concentrated in a few intersections that usually require left-turn signals. The reason for traffic congestion in many suburban communities is as simple as it is maddening: there aren't enough places to turn left. In addition, the grid provides more street frontage for dense, smaller-scaled incremental development.

The addition of streets and alleys in the existing suburban downtown or behind strip commercial developments is an important area of investigation. Whether achieved by easements through new and existing development or by new public rights-of-way through privately held land, establishing a sense of connection and permeability is essential to the development of lively, mixed-use pedestrian environments in suburban downtowns and along arterial strips.

The reason for traffic congestion in many suburban communities is as simple as it is maddening: there aren't enough places to turn left.

Public Open Space

One of the most noticeable elements lacking in many of today's suburban centers and commercial strips is clearly defined open space. Parking lots, with all their agoraphobic breadth, are usually the largest, if unintended, public open spaces and act as a sort of surrogate public realm. Open space is a critical element in establishing a sense of community and quality of life for residents; it becomes even more critical as levels of density increase.

The main commercial/retail streets require special attention to create a pedestrian-friendly environment. When they are considered as boulevards rather than traffic arterials, they can become amenities rather than liabilities to the community. Widened sidewalks, street trees, furniture, projecting canopies and signage, and generous shop windows are important elements that encourage strolling. Issues related to alternative parking strategies have been discussed above. Buildings with ground-floor retail spaces should be pulled forward to the sidewalk. Generous floor-to-floor heights for retail spaces should be encouraged. Entries to residential uses above the retail should be clearly legible, perhaps by being recessed deeper within the street wall than store entrances or treated with canopies of a very different scale and character than those designating the retail spaces.

Public parks and town squares are important elements of community life in the traditional town and help to encourage pedestrian activity, community awareness, and civic pride. They provide a venue for public activities such as fairs, markets, concerts, exhibits, etc. A clearly defined open space at the center of the suburban downtown can also lend a strong and identifiable center to the town as a whole. Residential and/or commercial uses should

Live-work units, with apartment above a work-space/garage/studio, make for an excellent buffer between commercial and residential areas. If situated on an alley, the work can spill into the public realm. (Steve Matthias)

surround the parks or square so that there is surveillance of the open space, as well as a sense of ownership of the space among the local community.

The scale of the open space must be consistent with the building fabric that surrounds it, as well as its intended use. For example, smaller scale pocket parks or tot lots should be located in residential neighborhoods, while a larger scale, more formal village green might be surrounded by multifamily development, transit stops, or civic buildings. Playgrounds and athletic fields associated with public schools provide an excellent opportunity to establish dual purpose open space within the suburban downtown.

CASE STUDY 1: THE SUBURBAN COMMERCIAL STRIP

The Site

Roughly three miles east of the town "center" along I-5, the site is a gently rolling 47-acre parcel bordered by the interstate highway to the north, by a strip shopping-development fronting Marvin Road to the east, by Martin Way to the south, and by an existing single-family residential development to the west. The residential development to the west is typical in that it consists of detached dwellings set on lots of 6,000 square feet. The street pattern is that of a discontinuous grid without alleys. Because of the discontinuities, one must drive a considerable distance west in order to gain access to Martin Way and the shopping mall, which is, as the crow flies, less than a quarter mile to the east.

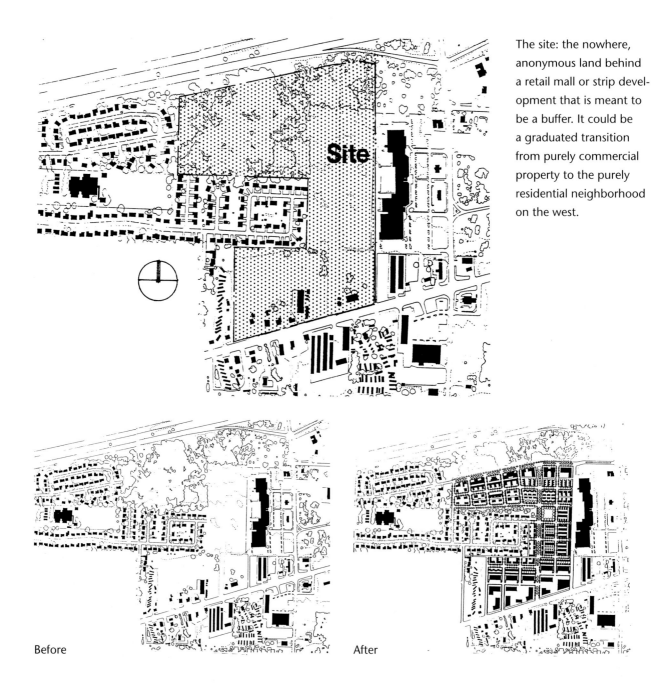

The site: the nowhere, anonymous land behind a retail mall or strip development that is meant to be a buffer. It could be a graduated transition from purely commercial property to the purely residential neighborhood on the west.

Before

After

The southern edge of the site fronts on Martin Way (Route 99). Uses along this stretch of the strip development include retail, service (mini storage), light industrial, and some trailer park residential. The blank wall of the shopping strip forms the eastern boundary of the site. The building is roughly 20 feet tall and nearly 1,000 feet in length. It is an internally focused mall with parking lots on the east side facing Marvin Road. The rear of the building is used for access to loading docks and dumpsters and for employee parking.

The northern boundary of the site is defined by Interstate 5. A mature forested area forms a significant visual buffer between I-5 and the open portions of the site. The topography, sloping upward to the north end of the site, also helps to visually block the freeway.

"Converting underutilized commercial sites in residential neighborhoods is going to be a major opportunity in the future."[3] This strip mall near single-family houses is a good example. Such a site offers the opportunity to develop a more continuous suburban fabric extending from the currently severed edge of the residential zone to the blank rear wall of the shopping mall. Residential units could be introduced into an otherwise exclusively retail zone. In addition, alternative strategies for development of retail and light industrial uses are suggested along the south edge of the site at Martin Way. In so doing,

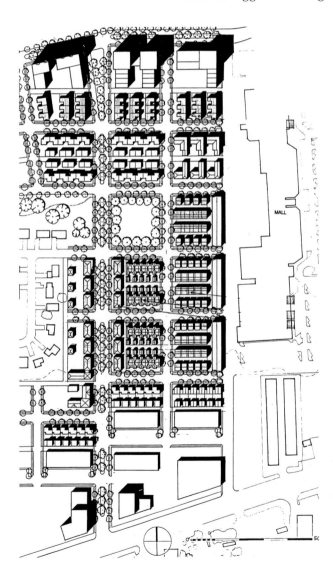

Platting streets, alleys, and lots shapes the character, scale, and ownership of a neighborhood.

a number of land use goals may be achieved. A transition in scale from the monolithic mall building to the smaller scale of the single-family residential use is also important along with a greater intensity and mix of uses to encourage interaction between the two existing uses. Finally, a stronger link between the uses is established for pedestrians and vehicles alike.

Goals and Objectives

The studio sought to establish a basic conceptual framework for the master plan. The following goals and objectives were emphasized:

- To establish a comfortable interface and transition in scale between the monolithic nature of the strip shopping mall and the existing detached single-family dwellings.
- To incorporate a comfortable transition in intensity and character of use between the purely commercial and the purely residential areas.
- To develop a comfortable transition from the commercial strip uses along Martin Way to the forested buffer at Interstate 5.
- To increase connections for vehicles and pedestrians between the site and surrounding parcels and adjacent neighborhoods.
- To establish a greater sense of the pedestrian/public realm.
- To take advantage of the topography and views from the northern portion of the site.

Design Proposal

The master plan provides a regularized street grid. The grid is intended as a means by which the site can accommodate a series of transitions in intensity and character of use across the site. The grid adapts itself simply and directly to changes in topography and provides ample opportunity to connect to the pattern of streets in the existing single-family neighborhoods to the west. All land parcels in the proposal are accessible from both street and alley.

A divided, tree-lined boulevard moves through the center of the site in the north-south direction. Rather than establishing a major east-west axis through the site, connecting to the existing shopping mall, a consistent pattern of secondary streets traverses the major boulevard. The space between the mall and the proposed development is conceived as a wide, light-industrial work street. Moving west from here, the use changes from commercial/light industrial space to work-live units to live-work units to duplex units and finally to the existing single-family houses. Moving north through the site, the uses change from commercial uses along Martin Way to live-work

Duplexes along the boulevard give the sense of large, grand homes along a traditional residential boulevard. (Susan Busch)

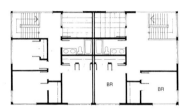

UPPER FLOOR PLAN

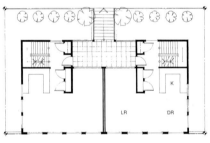

MAIN FLOOR PLAN

LOWER FLOOR PLAN

units to primarily single-family and duplex units along the boulevard. The northernmost portion of the site, where potential views are found, is occupied by attached terrace housing and mid-rise apartment buildings.

Central Boulevard
The boulevard is the primary north-south circulation route through the site. It connects Martin Way with the community park at the center of the site and terminates in the forested area at the northern boundary of the site, which is designated a public greenbelt. The boulevard is fronted by a variety of building types, ranging from commercial buildings along Martin Way to duplex units at the center of the site to attached single and multifamily housing at the northern end of the site.

Duplex Units
These units are designed to appear as large single-family houses fronting on the boulevard. Raised on a parking plinth and with very simple massing, these buildings are intended to present a scale appropriate to a boulevard.

Live-Work Units
Located behind the duplex units to the east, these simple three- to four-bedroom designs provide a flexible space on the ground floor that is easily adaptable for use as a home office, small day care facility, or rental unit.

Work-Live Units
Further east of the live-work units, the work-live units provide a transitional use between the light-industrial uses adjacent to the shopping mall and

Boulevard Duplexes

residential uses to the interior of the site. These units are comprised of a smaller residential unit pulled forward to the street with a larger two story accessory structure at the rear of the lot accessible from the alley. This accessory structure is a large, two-car garage on the ground floor which is easily converted to home office or workshop. Above the garage/workshop is a generous studio apartment.

Terraced Housing

At the northern edge of the project, terraced housing units are sited and oriented to take maximum advantage of southern exposure and views. These attached three-bedroom units are entered from private garden walks that extend from the street to the alley. The rooms are organized around a paved southeast-facing courtyard, which, in turn, opens onto a private rear garden. The design explores the possibilities of orienting housing units to take maximum advantage of sun and view within the generic street pattern of the grid.

Live-work units have a small workspace that shares the ground floor with living spaces. In work-live units the entire ground floor is devoted to a home office or shop. (Susan Busch)

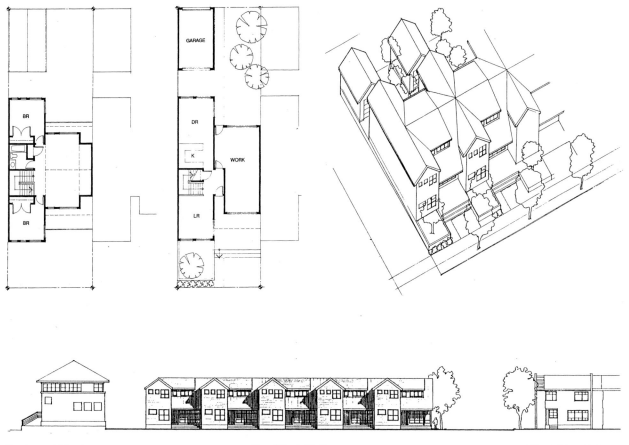

Boulevard Duplexes   Live-Work Units   Work-Live Units

CASE STUDY 2: THE SUBURBAN TOWN CENTER
The Site

The Lacey town center is defined as the 170 acres bordered by College Street to the east, Slater-Kinney Road to the west, Interstate 5 to the north, and Pacific Avenue SE to the south. The area was originally platted in 1897 as a grid of blocks roughly 200 feet square. However, few of the platted street rights-of-way were established to the east of the site across Martin Way. In this area, St. Martin's College exists as a wooded campus. In the mid-1960s, I-5 was constructed, with interchanges at Martin Way and at Slater-Kinney, which make the site very accessible. Shortly after the construction of I-5 came the construction of the South Sound Shopping Mall in 1966. The mall, located just off the interchange at Slater-Kinney, was the first regional shopping mall between Portland and Tacoma.

In the 1970s, the city hall was constructed across College Street from the site at the terminus of Sixth Avenue, nearly on the college campus. More recently, the Lacey public library was constructed adjacent to the city hall to form a small group of civic buildings in a wooded setting. Recent development on the site includes the encroachment of mall-type retail construction across Slater-Kinney from the shopping mall and the development of suburban office buildings flanking the two sides of Sixth Avenue.

Current zoning for the area suggests that the town center is envisioned as a short term destination for employment or conference purposes. The area is zoned to allow buildings up to 250 feet high. This zoning allows for primarily office buildings and hotels of roughly twenty-five stories. Presumably, a core of taller buildings, set back slightly from the street, is intended to be a landmark from the freeway to mark both employment and conference facilities. Sixth Avenue would remain as the primary vehicular arterial through the site. While there is some allowance for residential uses in the town center, it is clearly incidental to office and retail uses.

The site shows great potential to become a strong and identifiable town center for Lacey for a number of reasons. The site's proximity to I-5 offers the opportunity to establish a regional transit link within the town center. The overall site, as determined by the boundaries listed above, is slightly less than one half mile on a side. This provides for a clearly bounded precinct within which pedestrian access from the center to the perimeter is highly feasible. The quarter mile walking radius is entirely consistent with standards established for new Pedestrian Pockets, TODs, and TNDs.

St. Martin's College and its extensive wooded areas across Martin Way from the site offer recreational opportunities which would augment parks and recreation within the town center. Currently, a strong east-west axis is formed by Sixth Avenue, which is terminated at its east end by the city's major public institutions, the town hall and library, and at its west end by the South Sound shopping mall.

Goals and Objectives

The following goals and objectives were emphasized as a conceptual framework for the master plan:

- To take advantage of existing axes and connections within the site and between the site and the surrounding area, as much as possible.
- To subdivide the existing superblock configuration of the site while maintaining existing buildings to the greatest extent possible.
- To reestablish the original platted grid wherever possible.
- To establish a clear hierarchy of streets and open spaces within the town center.
- To reverse the current figure/ground relationship between buildings and open spaces so that buildings define public space as opposed to being free-standing objects.
- To provide a rich mix of uses throughout the town center while at the same time imbuing smaller neighborhoods with their own character and identity.
- To establish a clear hierarchy of building and architectural types within the town center so that public buildings, such as the transit station, become foreground buildings.

Design Proposal
(master plan on p. 214)

The first step in the development of the master plan was to recognize and reinforce Sixth Avenue as the major east-west vehicular path or "main street" in the downtown plan. A major north-south axis was then established. The north-south axis is distinct from the east-west axis in that it is primarily pedestrian and consists of a series of linked open spaces. The north end of this axis is terminated by the new light-rail transit stop while the south end is terminated by a new elementary school building.

Superimposed on this framework is a gridded network of streets established to retain as many of the existing buildings on the site as possible. These streets follow the original platting of the area where possible and jog to avoid existing structures. Within this new grid of streets and avenues, six overlapping neighborhoods were established. While each neighborhood is mixed use in nature, the intent was the development of a dominant use and character for each that would be derived from existing uses on the site. Two neighbor-

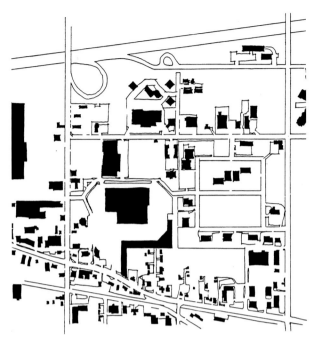

Before: With no edges, vacant lots, missing "teeth," large parking lots, there is not a legible town center.

After: Platted streets break up the existing superblocks. Apartment houses form a legible edge around the perimeter. Parking structures replace surface lots. The figure-ground relationship of buildings and open space is reversed.

hoods are north of Sixth Avenue and are primarily residential in nature. Two are immediately south of Sixth and are primarily commercial. The two most southerly neighborhoods are, again, primarily residential.

A pattern of open spaces was then established and overlaid on the major and secondary street pattern. These open spaces provide for recreation and begin to engender a sense of hierarchy within the town center. Major exterior spaces are scaled to the town center as a whole, while smaller parks are scaled to provide uses and an identity appropriate to the neighborhoods they serve. In addition, the parks provide for uninterrupted pedestrian circulation, linking the various neighborhoods within the town center.

Finally, the resulting block forms were platted to establish a pattern of lot sizes consistent with the uses intended for each block. Incremental development, the measure and rhythm of which would be determined by the platting dimensions, was presupposed by this strategy. Platting dimensions would be tested during subsequent phases. Avoiding a uniform, cookie-cutter or even an architecturally coordinated set of buildings in favor of incremental urbanism was considered essential to avoid the uniformity and boredom of a master-planned suburban community.

Main Street

As stated above, Main Street is to be established using the existing alignment of Sixth Avenue. The street is conceived as not only the primary east-west vehicular route through the town center but as the primary retail and service street as well. The current curb-to-curb width is retained and on-street parallel parking is provided. The overall street right-of-way, however, is to be increased to allow for wider sidewalks than currently exist.

To achieve the feel of a traditional Main Street, incremental development (and ownership) is necessary. Accordingly, a consistent platting width of 60 feet was established for 100-foot-deep lots. This dimension was deemed appropriate as it would provide the minimum adequate dimension for a double-loaded parking garage within each building and accommodate adequate flexibility for retail and residential uses. This same lot size is found in many mixed-use urban neighborhoods such as the Denny Regrade in Seattle.

The prototypical building for Main Street has a 14 -to-16-foot-high base story containing store-

Phasing: The grid is incrementally infilled, leaving selected existing buildings but also trying to establish an overall order and better access by foot and vehicle.

The large footprint of the existing Fred Meyer discount store has been subdivided into a public market of smaller vendors. Across the street is new housing above shops and offices.

front retail with enclosed parking behind, accessible by alley. Above are two stories of residential/office use. This prototype reverses the relationship between street, building, and parking currently found on Lacey's commercial streets where the storefront is severed from the sidewalk by the parking lot.

Town Square

The town square is the northernmost of a connected series of open spaces that form the major north-south axis through the town center. At the head of the town square is the transit station on I-5. The square is conceived as a large outdoor room which is defined along its eastern and western edges by the tallest buildings proposed in the town center. It is essentially three blocks, one of which is paved and two of which are landscaped. It is seen as the entry into Lacey from the transit station and is scaled to the town as a whole. The south end of the town square, at its intersection with Main Street, is the functional and symbolic heart—the 100 percent corners—of Lacey. Here is sited the bus station, which would connect the Lacey town center with the surrounding communities.

The buildings defining the square's east and west edges consist of a 14- to 16-foot-tall retail base with an optional mezzanine space topped by about twelve stories of residential apartments. With its convenient access to Main Street shops and the transit station, these buildings are assumed to house primarily, but not exclusively, elderly residents.

The Promenade

The promenade is a less formal, linear open space that extends to the south and connects the town center elementary school with the town square. It is seen as the major pedestrian link between the northern and southern halves of the proposal. The promenade includes meandering bike and walking paths that pass between existing freestanding office buildings on the site. These buildings are some of the few freestanding buildings in the precinct and are architectural remnants of the previous suburban spatial order.

The Paseo

Extending to the south behind the retail street wall of main street is the paseo. Inspired by the pedestrian retail street of the same name in Santa Barbara, California, the paseo is intended as a "discovered" mixed-use enclave that suddenly opens after a narrow pedestrian passage at the heart of the commercial portion of the scheme. Ground-floor retail with garage parking behind is beneath three stories of offices and housing. The paseo is the most internally focused block in the town center. Housed within it are sidewalk cafes, fountains, and a small children's museum.

Office Park

To the east, across the promenade from the paseo, is the office park. The park forms the heart of this precinct, which consists primarily of office and related uses. It provides recreational opportunities for office employees, including tennis and basketball, as well as a pleasant venue for lunch breaks. The park is connected to other open spaces in the scheme by a series of pedestrian ways.

Townhouse Neighborhoods

To the east and west of the town square and, to a lesser extent, to the west of the elementary school are the single-use residential portions of the scheme. Buffered from the arterial streets by commercial and multifamily uses, these blocks contain attached single-family and duplex units. The lots are in widths of 25 feet and 30 feet and are 100 feet in depth. All units are served by alleys and contain detached garages with accessory units or home offices above.

A block devoted to multifamily housing. It is dense enough for a town center but perhaps too uniform architecturally. (Tom Jordan)

Multifamily Perimeter Blocks

The bulk of the multifamily housing is located at the perimeter of the scheme along College Street and Pacific Avenue. The buildings are meant to define the edge of the town center by being higher than adjacent housing. These three-to-four-story buildings consist of walk-up units above a courtyard terrace on a single-story parking plinth set partially below grade. By partially submerging the parking, the courtyard level of the building is elevated and protected from the street, allowing transitions from street to court to unit. The buildings are set on half-block lots and some are served by alleys.

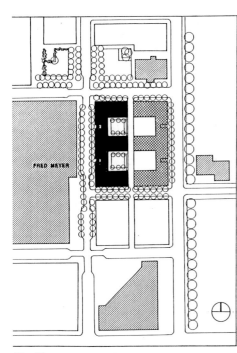

Site Plan

Housing over shops and offices. Open stairs rise from the sidewalk to two raised, landscaped courtyards above a parking garage, which occupies the center of the block and is accessed from the alley. (Cynthia Esselman)

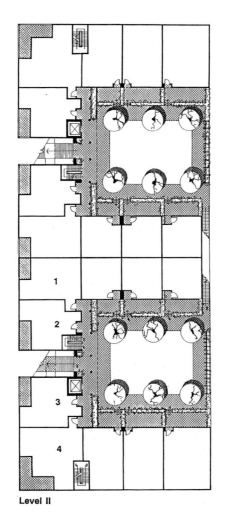

Level II

Units 1&2

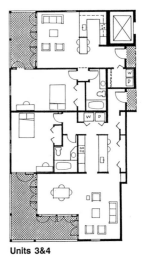

Units 3&4

CHAPTER 8

Small Town
Maintaining Rural Identity

There are many small towns that were once rural but now find themselves within the gravitational field of a metropolis. Unlike bedroom suburbs, these rural towns may not have sought or welcomed this fate. Some of them resent being swamped by the tsunami of metropolitan growth. The Seattle Region is replete with examples of once rural towns that are now hardly recognizable as distinct settlements. Renton, Kent, Issaquah, Woodinville, Redmond, and Fife come quickly to mind. Others have remained relatively intact, usually because they are farther out or enjoy some degree of separation by virtue of topography or water. For example, Steilacoom, Monroe, and Snohomish are far enough out; Black Diamond and Bothell are separated to some extent by topography, Duvall by a floodplain, and Winslow by Puget Sound. Even these towns suffer from too much nibbling at the edge. In the best of all worlds, they would maintain their identity by dedicating agricultural land, greenbelts, floodplains, and recreational open space as circumferential buffers around their outskirts and accommodating growth within. Unfortunately, they often spread shapelessly into their hinterland with low-density development and an increasingly fuzzy edge. Main Street is threatened and often killed by larger stores that accumulate on the highway bypass—supermarket, cineplex, shopping strip or center, big box discount stores, gas station/convenience stores. This pattern of destruction is by now so well known that some rural communities in Vermont are refusing to permit Wal-Marts at the edge of town.

Winslow, on Bainbridge Island, was the subject of a charrette in late 1993. The charrette looked at ways to maintain a small town atmosphere while doubling the town's population. As a rural town of about 3,500 population in the clutch of Seattle, Winslow enjoys several advantages and suffers from a common malady. Its separation from Seattle by Puget Sound has kept it insulated from suburban creep, but frequent ferry service has kept it well connected to downtown Seattle. In some ways, it offers the best of both worlds—rural character and urban proximity—what suburbs have always aspired to but rarely achieve these days. As a consequence, there are many commuters to downtown Seattle. The jobs there raise per capita income higher than in a typical rural town, where the economy might be based on lower paying agricultural or industrial employment. The commonplace malady Winslow must deal with is the shopping center. Despite having a pleasant and workable main street, a shopping area has sprung up a mile north. It is smaller than many of its counterparts elsewhere, but it sucks economic life out of the traditional center. It is single-use and auto-dependent, with an expansive asphalt parking lot and cheaply built, Postmodern architecture. While it serves an island-wide automobile clientele, it serves few households by foot. It needs multi-family and zero-lot-line housing with accessory units within walking distance.

Here's how this small town project makes manifest the theory of Part I.

COSTS OF SPRAWL

It is very much in the region's interest and Bainbridge Island's interest to absorb half of the island's growth in downtown Winslow and to preserve the bucolic environment of the rest of the island. For all the economic, environmental, social, and architectural reasons reiterated frequently throughout the book, concentrating growth in compact, twenty-four-hour, walkable centers is essential to long-term community health. The center of Winslow is already a model of this kind of mixed development. It simply must be intensified to accommodate more housing and jobs—both downtown and uptown. The design paradigm is in place. It is now a question of political will and civic discipline more than technical expertise or clever design.

CRITICAL REGIONALISM

The town of Winslow is a fine example of regionalism. With its working harbor and docks full of ferries and boats, its natural surroundings and views, and its small-scale building stock, it is a picture postcard of a small maritime and rural community in the Pacific Northwest. Winslow Way, Ericksen Avenue, and Madison Avenue are full of well-crafted and well-maintained buildings. Although it lacks an honorific Town Hall and the main street is too wide, the townscape is generally legible and understandable. There is a sense of place, of history, and of craft. The downtown ravine and the waterfront park provide a sense of nature at the center. It is the sense of limits that is wanting. The center of gravity of downtown is beginning to shift to the new uptown shopping center. Another challenge is how to maintain the historical, small-town character of Winslow without crossing the thin line that separates Neotraditional design from kitsch and Disneyland. This is more an issue of architecture than town planning. Because this charrette, which was 2 1/2 rather than 5 days long, did not have time to illustrate its urban design concepts with building designs, the issue remains open. There is also the important challenge of establishing new building types and places with as much lasting power and integrity as some of the old ones along the waterfront, the main street, and the older residential avenues.

TYPOLOGY

Like many traditional towns, Winslow is typologically coherent. From waterfront sheds to trailer park to the relatively consistent storefronts to the larger houses, there is an overall coherence and order. There is a balance between a sufficient but finite number of architectural types and a rich array of variations on those types. Despite this working balance, the proposals introduce several types new to Winslow: the townhouse, the apartment over shop, the accessory unit over garage, the parking lot infill building, the mixed-use ferry terminal, and the above- and below-grade parking garage.

NEW URBANISM

Most of the charrette teams naturally and unselfconsciously employed the principles and patterns of New Urbanism. Small towns are, after all, one of the New Urbanist archetypes. The application of these principles resulted in many common proposals. The ferry system and bus system were illustrated as fully integrated with each other and with new development around the ferry terminal at the east end of Winslow Way. Proposed development was always low rise and mixed use, always in compact configurations. Existing neighborhoods in and around the center of Winslow were scrupulously preserved. Walkable distances from activity nodes were maintained. Several superblocks were broken up with proposed new streets and alleys. The shopping center north of downtown was transformed into a more walkable, integrated, and residential upper town center. The natural ravine that cuts through the main street was enhanced. Runoff from paved surfaces was minimized. Air pollution was decreased by more pedestrian-friendly and transit-oriented development. And, in the process, it was shown that, indeed, half of the proposed population growth for all of Bainbridge Island could be accommodated within Winslow proper.

Rendering of the common elements on which most of the charrette teams agreed—from a local newspaper supplement, a good way to publicize charrette results. (Andy Rovelstad)

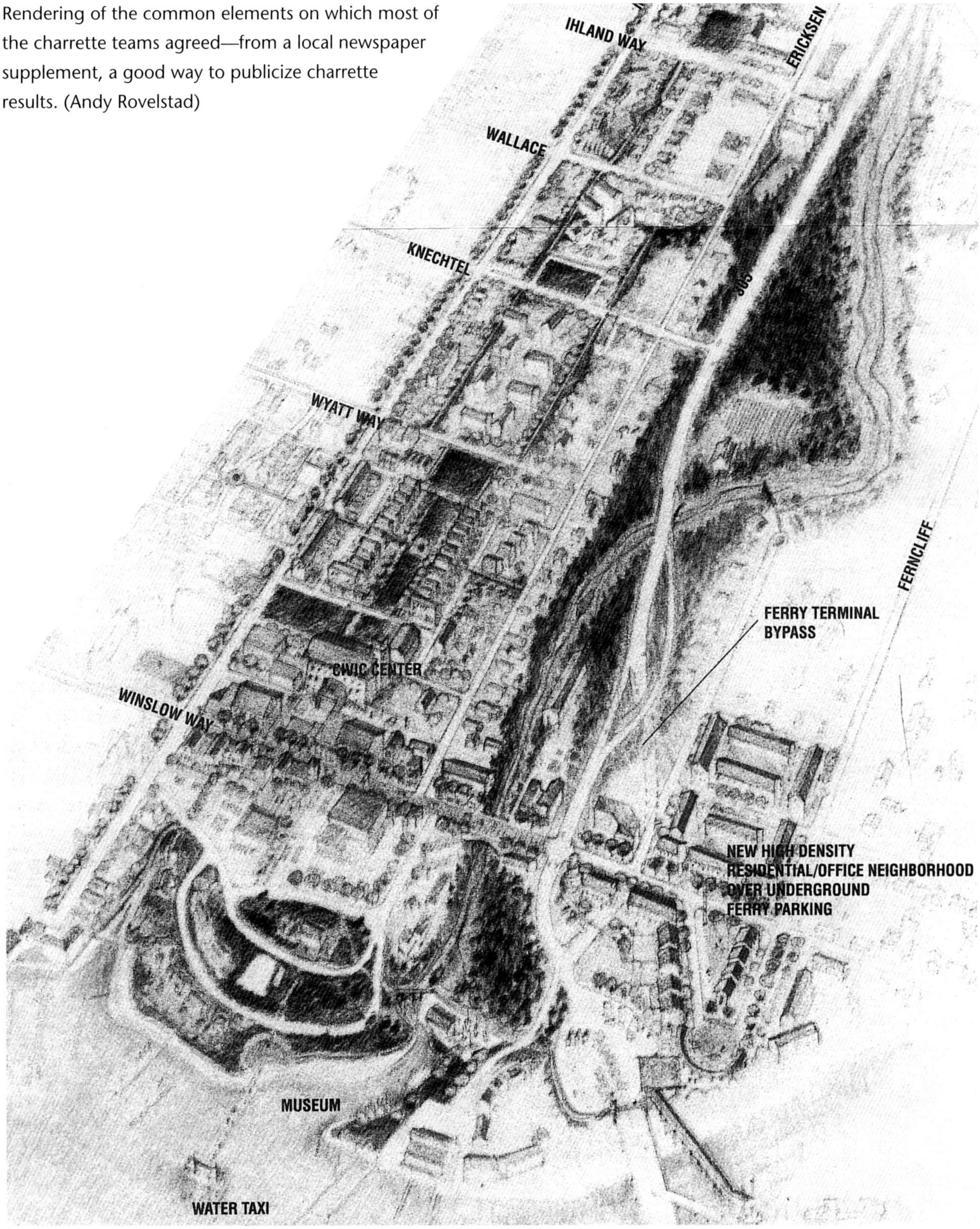

IHLAND WAY

ERICKSEN

WALLACE

KNECHTEL

WYATT WAY

FERRY TERMINAL BYPASS

FERNCLIFF

CIVIC CENTER

WINSLOW WAY

NEW HIGH DENSITY RESIDENTIAL/OFFICE NEIGHBORHOOD OVER UNDERGROUND FERRY PARKING

MUSEUM

WATER TAXI

The Winslow Charrette
Planning for Growth in a Small Town

Winslow is a town in an unusual situation. Located on Bainbridge Island in Puget Sound, it is surrounded by farms and undeveloped open land like most rural towns. However, it is also a mere twenty-five-minute ferry ride from downtown Seattle's ferry terminal, which is at the foot of the city's densest concentration of high-rise office towers. A considerable number of Island residents commute into the city every day, and Winslow is subject to intermittent rush hour traffic that can rival a city of much greater size. The state's Growth Management Act required that Bainbridge Island develop a Comprehensive Plan that accommodates at least 6,000 new residents over the next twenty years. Winslow is expected to absorb roughly half of the expected growth.

The charrette was convened with two primary goals: planned development to preserve and improve Winslow's small-town character in the face of rapid growth, and mitigation of the effects of ferry commuter traffic, which will grow heavier as the Island's and Kitsap County's population increases. More than fifty Island design professionals and citizens participated in the weekend charrette, augmented by a number of University of Washington student volunteers. In addition to developing plans and drawings to illustrate the Draft Comprehensive Plan already developed by a volunteer citizen advisory committee, the charrette teams were also asked to contribute new ideas and improvements to the plan.

Winslow's core is made up of three distinct areas: Winslow Way, High School Way, and the area along and between Madison Avenue and Highway 305. The charrette teams envisioned enhancing and connecting these areas to create a more unified town. Adding residents to the town's core would enhance its vitality, making it a more inviting place for both residents and visitors. Importantly, it would also preserve and, by contrast, make more vivid the rural character of the island. Winslow also contains a number of residential neighborhoods outside of the core area which contribute to its small town

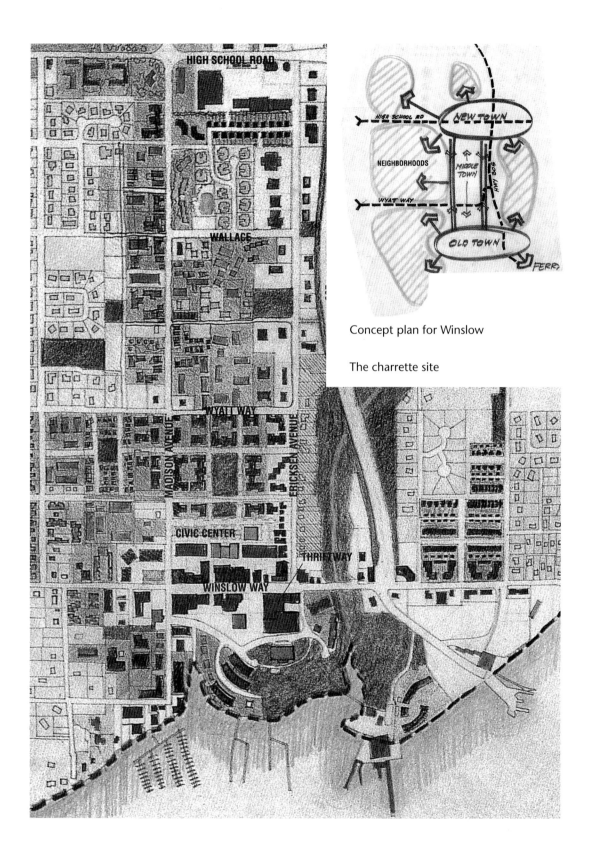

Concept plan for Winslow

The charrette site

character. The Draft Plan envisioned retaining the existing character of these neighborhoods while connecting them to the core area. Also of critical concern was some kind of modification to the ferry terminal area.

There were seven questions asked of the four design teams:

1. What is Winslow's urban boundary?
2. What is the urban design structure of Winslow?
3. How can Winslow best accommodate 3,000 diverse new residents while retaining its small-town character?
4. How should people transport themselves through and within Winslow?
5. What is the open-space plan?
6. What are the public service needs and solutions?
7. How can residential, commercial, and employment opportunities be encouraged within Winslow?

COMMON IDEAS

There was a remarkable amount of overlap among the teams, especially in terms of general design principles. The short time period of the charrette and the strength of its originating document narrowed the scope of the teams' efforts. For the most part, teams differed from each other only in the areas in which they offered specific designs. A summary of commonalities among the four schemes would include:

- Encouraging the development of a high-density residential core that contains a system of open space and connects the Winslow Way and High School Road retail areas.
- Creating smaller, more pedestrian-oriented blocks out of the superblocks that currently exist between Winslow Way and High School Way and between Ericksen and Madison Avenues.
- Developing a new network of streets with design standards that are pedestrian friendly and help create better vehicular access as well as additional places to park.
- Developing extensive pedestrian walkways and an open-space system.
- Developing a new civic center with City Hall adjacent to the Bainbridge Performing Arts Cultural Center.
- Preserving of the Lower Ericksen Historic District.
- Locating of new housing along the edge of Waterfront Park and along lower Madison Avenue.
- Limiting ferry parking, including underground parking.
- Creating a ferry terminal neighborhood with high-density residential/office space and underground ferry parking.

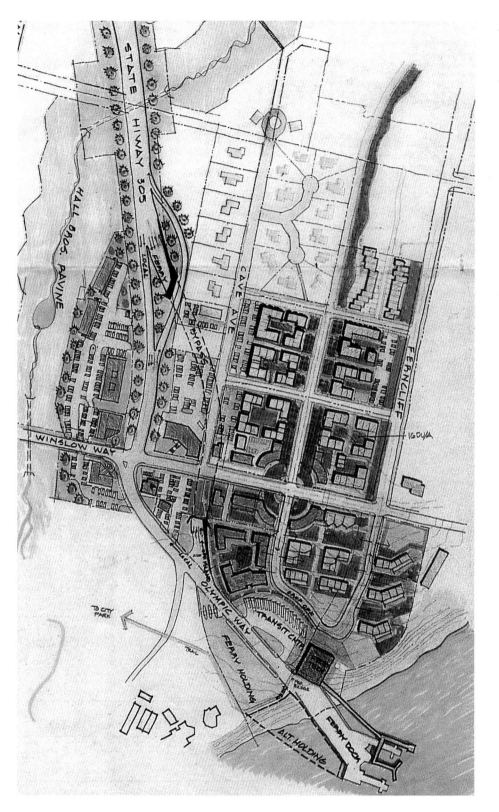

A ferry district proposal, including a vehicular underpass for northbound traffic coming off the ferry

Suggestions for calming traffic and making pedestrians more comfortable on High School Road

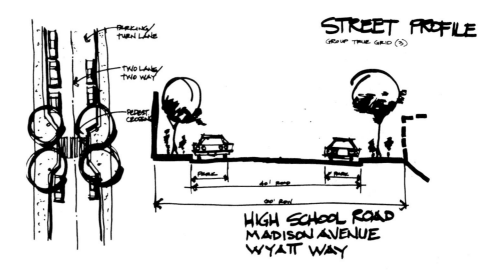

STREET PROFILE
GROUP TRUE GRID (3)

PARKING/TURN LANE
TWO LANE/TWO WAY
PEDEST. CROSSING

HIGH SCHOOL ROAD
MADISON AVENUE
WYATT WAY

- Creating a better pedestrian and visual connection between the ferry terminal and the Winslow Way retail center.
- Separating ferry and local traffic.
- Connecting Ericksen Avenue to High School Road.
- Providing a new connection along Wyatt-Ericksen-Knechtel to Highway 305.
- Encouraging on- and off-island public transportation systems and the creation of other regional ferry hubs.

SOME SPECIFICS

Downtown Winslow

Teams agreed that Winslow Way would ideally retain a strong mixed-use and retail flavor, while additional parking could be developed off Winslow Way. By developing the parking lots of the Thriftway supermarket into a pedestrian plaza, pedestrian access to the waterfront could be improved. North of Winslow Way, a civic center could be developed by joining a new City Hall to the existing Bainbridge Performing Arts Center. The area north of the civic center should be developed as a high-density (17 – 28 units/acre) residential area, with new streets and parks on a smaller grid within walking distance of the town center.

Accommodating New Residents

New housing developments could be located throughout the area between Madison Avenue and Highway 305 and between Winslow Way and High School Road. There could be a new residential development of considerable size and density north of the ferry terminal and one on the edge of Waterfront Park. In addition to new development in the core area, infill and accessory dwelling units would accommodate growth in the adjacent neighborhoods. Garage apartments would be an appropriate, low-impact way to absorb growth, as outlined in chapter 4.

To make Winslow more pedestrian friendly and a more pleasant place to live, work, and shop, new streets were proposed that would result in slower traffic, less congestion, and better landscaped vehicular corridors. This new system of streets would act as part of the pedestrian network of paths and trails connecting housing to transit stops, shopping, the ferry, and a system of urban open spaces.

Ferry District

The area to the east of the ferry dock is currently separated from the rest of Winslow by the flow of high-speed commuter vehicles rushing from the ferry onto the highway. Several teams recommended ways to unify this area with downtown Winslow and proposed residential areas west and north of the

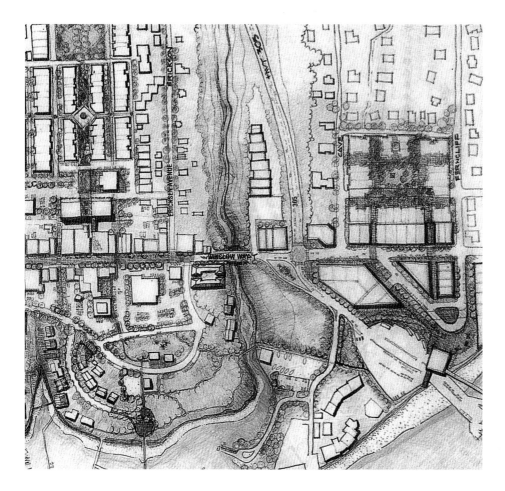

Winslow proper,
the old town

ferry terminal. Suggestions included limiting commuter parking and locating some parking beneath a new residential/office development at the ferry terminal. Also suggested were increasing transit opportunities both on and off the island, as well as developing off-island park-and-ride lots.

PRIORITIES

Because the town is unable to proceed with all these changes at once, three strategies should be given the most immediate priority:

1. Draft and adopt design guidelines that deal with High School Road development before the area is totally suburbanized. Guidelines should encourage:

- Mixed use, including residential
- Smaller footprint buildings and smaller lot sizes
- Parking in rear of commercial buildings, in lots broken down in scale by landscaping
- Better defined street "walls"
- Parking and planting strips along roads and streets
- Greater floor/area ratio (FAR), including multistory buildings
- Better bus service, especially a loop or shuttle bus to downtown Winslow

2. Plat and develop the eastern end of Winslow Way, north of the ferry parking lot. Build the maximum number of dwelling units, with office and limited commercial space at ground level. Terrace the ferry parking structure into the hillside. Create a pedestrian spine that connects the ferry to the town, lined with commercial and institutional uses (including perhaps an honorific part of City Hall). Reinforce the terminal building as a public anchor, perhaps even as a meeting hall. Ask the state to build a vehicular bypass/underpass for ferry traffic headed north to off-island destinations, people who literally use Bainbridge Island as a bridge to the rest of Kitsap County.

3. Develop an alley or intimate street with parking behind the commercial buildings on the north side of Winslow Way, with small dwelling units above or in the rear of buildings. Possibly locate City Hall and a public marketplace in the vicinity of the Bainbridge Performing Arts Center. Landscape Winslow Way in a manner that will make its width less apparent.

After the charrette, Mike Burroughs, an architectural illustrator who is a local resident, volunteered to do the aerial perspective (see page 244). It illustrates many aspects of Winslow's Comprehensive Plan, which was adopted after the charrette and includes many of its ideas.

Rural towns, which are being suburbanized by the automobile and shopping center at an alarming pace, need growth boundaries and infill development to reverse their dissolution into nebulous scatterings. As main street falls prey to the commercial strip on the highway bypass, stronger planning controls and political backbones will be required if small towns are to retain their rural character.

CHAPTER 9

New Town
Beyond the Fringe and At the Center

There is a long and venerable tradition of New Towns in America, stretching back to the early colonists and pioneers. These towns were usually founded by religious groups that were dedicated to a spiritual or communal ideal. In New Haven, Connecticut, on the East Coast or in New Harmony, Indiana, in the Midwest or in the scores of Mormon towns out West, these new towns were located and laid out self-consciously and deliberately. They were not spontaneous settlements that sprang up where they were economically necessary and possible—whether for an agricultural market, overland or maritime trade, or extractive or manufacturing industry. They were not like the religious centers of Medieval Europe that were pilgrimage destinations at the site of important shrines. Nor were they like their European Renaissance and Baroque predecessors, which were more geometrically elaborate and absolute. Like other frontier towns, New Towns were typically gridded, rather than radial or circular, befitting the American ideal of egalitarian economic opportunity and political equality.

The Garden City Movement, started by Ebenezer Howard in England at the end of the nineteenth century, was essentially a New Town movement. It influenced early American suburbs, especially around New York and Chicago. Earlier this century, company towns were modeled on New Town practices, but for the economic production and security of a single employer. In the United Kingdom, Scandinavia, and France, satellite new towns were the centerpiece of national planning during the 1960s and 1970s. Reston, Virginia, and Columbia, Maryland, were the two major American efforts during the same period. Recently, the New Urbanism movement has revived the notion of New Town, although often on a smaller scale and within a suburban context rather than as a stand-alone community in the countryside.

Unlike the last four chapters, all of which dealt with infill development, this chapter deals with stand-alone development. New Towns are bigger than

Pedestrian Pockets, Transit-Oriented Development, and Traditional Neighborhood Development. They are also more autonomous, in that their population and size is large enough to support and accommodate their own schools, recreational and religious institutions, a supermarket, and industry. They are big enough to be twenty-four-hour-a-day communities and to be self-governing. Rather than the 1,500 to 3,000 residents in a Pedestrian Pocket, these New Towns house 10,000 to 20,000 residents or more. (The last New Town in England, Milton Keynes, has grown to a population of almost 150,000 people.)

New Towns are typically conceived of as satellite communities beyond the urban growth boundary or greenbelt that surrounds the metropolis. Sometimes they are proposed right in the heart of the metropolis, a New-Town-in-town. These downtown versions are often complete communities but usually not as freestanding. Battery Park City in lower Manhattan is a well-known recent example. They are often built on or over underutilized or abandoned industrial land and railyards or on landfill. The Interbay charrette is just such a project, proposed for the underutilized maritime landfill and rail corridor between two established residential areas. At the other extreme, the New Communities charrette looks at a New Town for 10,000 to 15,000 residents on a green plateau beyond the urbanized area of Seattle and beyond the region's urban growth boundary.

COSTS OF SPRAWL

New Towns are considerably bigger investments and more ambitious propositions than the suburban infill strategies such as Pedestrian Pockets. The satellite versions require completely new infrastructure. They require the aggregation of more land and, importantly, the aggregation and coordination of economic demand—something that the American market and weak public sector have been less successful at than the stronger governments in Europe and Asia. Indeed, lack of public sector cooperation and/or clout has hamstrung most modern American efforts to realize New Towns. Either a strong public/private partnership or a powerful public development corporation or authority seems to be essential. Whereas TODs and TNDs are smaller and can be realized by a private developer with a sympathetic local government, New Towns need more help from local and state government. Despite this Achilles heel, they can play an important role in the American metropolitan project. If properly conceived and organized, they are both feasible and cost-effective—as the economic and fiscal studies of Interbay show in some detail. They are effective both in the center and beyond the urban fringe, because they are compact uses of land and resources and are large enough to eliminate commuting trips through a jobs/housing balance.

CRITICAL REGIONALISM

New Towns are free to be regionalist if they want to be. Because they start from scratch on rural greenfield sites or urban brownfield sites, they offer the opportunity to celebrate local differences and regional characteristics. Because greenfield sites have more natural than human history, they need to listen carefully to the *genius loci* of their site. Because they are planned anew, their sense of place and history must be teased out of natural determinants. A sense of architectural craft is especially important to develop, because there is little if any well-crafted building stock from earlier periods to set a standard or lend human scale and character. A sense of limits and scale is especially critical to a satellite town that is both physically freestanding and functionally stand-alone. Natural or imposed boundaries need to mark a walkable, compact territory. In a new-town-in-town, the built context offers more architectural and urban cues from which a critically regionalist design can develop. In a historic in-town setting, like Pioneer Square, the temptation might be the reverse of a greenfield site—to be too literally historicist and risk crossing the line into kitsch and nostalgia.

TYPOLOGY

Because New Towns are usually built on open sites, typology is essential. It becomes a primary ordering device and a way to bring a common language and understandability to a brand new community. The following two charrettes are fairly ruthless about architectural type, block type, and street type. Indeed the laying out of streets, the shaping and sizing of blocks, and the platting of building lots are the major focus. These two projects attempt a consistent and complete taxonomy of block, street, and building for their sites.

The architectural types on the Sammamish Plateau project are lower rise and lower density than at Interbay. The rural site is designed with two- and three-story fabric. Housing is background and public buildings, such as city hall, churches, and schools, are foreground. Townhouses, apartment blocks, shops with apartments and offices above are the norm for residential development, as are alleys with accessory units. In one case, they are deployed within a Cartesian tartan grid; in another case, along curving streets that wrap around and hillclimbs that run from the valley to the plateau.

At Interbay, the block types and architectural types at its center are dense, with five- to seven-story perimeter block buildings containing retail, office, and residential uses. Two highrise buildings mark this center, which is an intermodal transportation node as well as a public place. As the density declines toward the edges, the architectural types get lower and are much like the Sammamish Plateau project. Alleys with garage apartments are a low-income housing type in both projects. There is a formal hierarchy of street types, with varying sidewalk widths, street widths, landscaping, and building setbacks. Without a deliberate and rich typology, these two projects would be a denser but amorphous version of suburban sprawl.

NEW URBANISM

Both these projects are exemplary New Urbanism. They embody principles and practices already enumerated many times, although the mid-rise perimeter block housing at Interbay pushes the American housing market beyond TOD and TND densities. What sets new towns apart from city and suburban infill projects is their size and their autonomy. As communities get larger the necessity and desirability of comprehensive planning increase to meet the expanding complexities. On the other hand, because build-out takes longer, phasing and regulations must be more flexible. Governance and planning are more complicated. (This book has not dealt with the question of governance, leaving this important issue to political scientists.) These new towns are large enough to require a municipal government with fire, public safety, public work, finance, and social service departments. These issues beg questions about public policy, to which the book will turn in chapter 10.

The New Communities Charrette

A New Town Out of Town

" . . . slowly nature will recede, to be replaced by growing islands of development. These will coalesce into a mass of low-grade urban tissue, having eliminated all natural beauty."—Ian McHarg[1]

In attempting to manage both its existing and anticipated growth, the State of Washington has adopted a dual strategy. First, urban growth boundaries limit the sprawl of existing cities. Second, development outside the growth boundaries is limited to new communities that are compact, bounded, and fully contained. This charrette focused on the latter. Sponsored in part by the Washington State Department of Natural Resources (DNR), it attempted to illustrate what form and character these new communities might take.

SITE AND PROGRAM

The site is a square mile of completely undeveloped DNR land on the Sammamish plateau, a rural area about twenty-five miles east of Seattle that is quickly being absorbed by the encroaching suburbs. The surrounding eight square miles is of very low density, including hobby farms, forests, and five-acre residential lots. The developable portion of the site represents 450 acres, and excludes steeper slopes on the east side and several small wetland areas. The site is covered by low-value second-growth timber and is not a strong candidate for a park or wilderness preserve.

The program for the charrette is very similar to that of the Pedestrian Pocket charrette, but considerably larger. It includes requirements for a bus station, back office and service office space, neighborhood retail facilities and convenience center, commercial parking (at half the standard requirement to encourage transit and carpools), day-care, school facilities, and civic facili-

ties. A minimum of four thousand dwelling units were to house at least 10,000 residents in a mix of apartments, townhouses, carriage homes, single-family detached houses, and congregate living facilities for the elderly. The program also required 50 acres of parks and recreational facilities, as well as 200 acres of open space (including the steep slopes and wetland areas excluded from the developable area of the site).

AN EXTRUDED PEDESTRIAN POCKET

Kelbaugh/Polyzoides Statement

The New Town for 10,000 residents on the Sammamish Plateau is developed as a community that is both freestanding and stand-alone. Unlike a Pedestrian Pocket, which is also freestanding but not stand-alone, it is large enough to support its own high school, supermarket, municipal government, etc. Surrounded by open space, it is a figure in the abstract landscape originally laid out in the Jefferson continental pattern of one-square-mile sections. This Cartesian pattern, which is slowly being eaten up by the wormy pattern of cul-de-sacs, is reinstated at the smaller scale of street and avenue.

Towns have developed spontaneously where people paused to rest, to trade, or to wait for a crossing. Some towns were linear—the country road town. Others were radial—the intersection town. Still others were binuclear—the town on either side of a bridge. On the other hand, planted towns or planned communities have had their beginnings as conscious acts of establishing roots. They were founded for a purpose, from defense and colonization to the pursuit of social and physical order as an ideal in itself.

The New Town type clearly belongs to the planted town tradition. Nineteenth- and twentieth-century New Towns in Europe and America have been designed and constructed as an attempt to mitigate the results of the uncontrolled growth of cities. Specifically, they have been conceived as a means of responding to social dislocation, environmental pollution, and degradation and as a mechanism encouraging new modes of production and distribution of goods and services.

Successful design strategy in the twenty-first century relies on the primacy of neighborhood and of region. Satellite new towns are a response to the ecological and social problems generated by a car-centered society. The programmatic basis for such towns lies in the possibility of designing a community that lives in closer balance with nature and that produces and consumes without the waste of time, energy, and material so characteristic of sprawl—a community that is equally focused on individual pride, responsibility, and civic duty.

The greenbelt satellite town gains its initial validity by concentrating density in one place and conserving the natural landscape of an area up to ten times its size. The particular form of the town that we designed is based on three personal reflections:

1. Since Radburn, most New Towns have been centroidal in form, expressing the simple diagram of equal access from their periphery to their center. The Pedestrian Pocket is an interpretation of this diagram with its development precinct circumscribed within a quarter-mile radius of the town center, which is punctuated by a public transit node. We have maintained a quarter-mile walking distance, but have extruded it into linear bands on either side

of a main street. We are interested in the possibility of linear new towns, because they also allow for walkable communities that can exceed in size the 2,000 units that can be accommodated within a full-sized Pedestrian Pocket. They also easily allow for growth.

2. We wished to investigate the idea of the grid as a figure. There is a noble American urbanist tradition that considers the grid not only as a neutral field for expansion and change but also as a pattern of particular formal qualities. We investigated various formal characteristics of the grid in our project, including its pattern of streets, its block sizes and geometries, its edge qualities, its land parcel divisions, and its typology of streets and buildings.

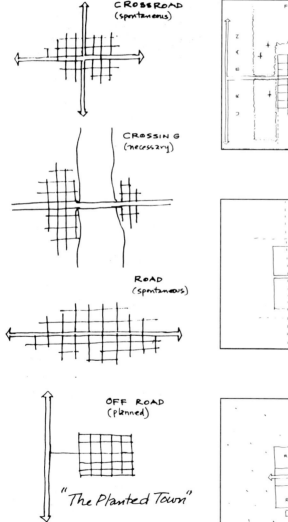

A casual typology of town origins

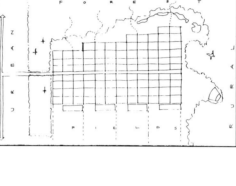

The grid softens into meandering lanes that access cabins in the woods on the north. On the south side, the grid fades out into agricultural fields, orchards, and greenhouses.

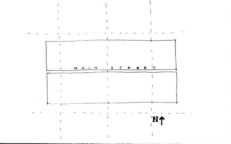

Main Street bisects and is the spine of town, like an elongated Pedestrian Pocket.

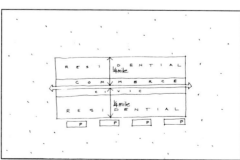

Commercial and civic uses hug Main Street with low-rise, high-density housing within 1/4 mile. Remote parking with shuttle vans is provided for employees working along Main Street.

The New Town falls off with the terrain on its eastern end, as the curving boulevard dives down the hillside with a pedestrian link to an amphitheater nestled in the cleavage of the hill.

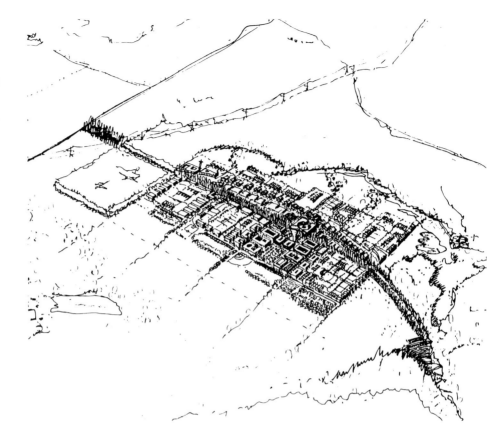

3. The overall form of our design makes reference to the two grand forces that act upon it. On the west it connects to the regularity and predictability of the continental grid. On the east, a long, sensuous, curved road intersects the grid and visually connects it to the open landscape that lies beyond. The town sits on the edge of the metropolis expressing in its form the wish to balance the geometric abstract order of the city with the curvilinear and figural order of nature.

The most important elements of the plan are open spaces. What characterizes large-scale, urban thinking is reference to voids, not buildings. For a building to be relevant to the making of the city, it should share with other buildings the magical power to generate physical presences larger than itself. Thus, small houses can define great streets, modest attached mixed-use buildings can form great squares, and simple civic buildings properly located can become engaging monuments.

Urbanism is at the heart of landscape architecture as well. The making of place by bounding open space, capturing the elements, engaging the earth, the horizon, and the sky is landscape architecture. This project is designed around a number of such gestures that give it its essential social meaning and formal character.

1. The town is conceived as a clearing. The edge of the forest will be a constant reminder of the pioneering act of carving urban life out of the wilderness.

2. At the western entrance into the town, on either side of the county road, we located two large greens. They are meant as places of civic gatherings, celebrations, flea markets, festivals, and games.

3. On the east end of town, a large sloping meadow opens up in the direction of the countryside. An open-air theater is located here. This is a place for quiet reflection by individuals and for performances by groups.

4. On the north edge of town, a series of small ponds and streams gather and channel the urban run-off and return it to the earth.

5. On the south boundary of the town a series of sewage recycling greenhouses define a crystalline frame, an edge between the town and the orchards and community gardens that the gray water, which is cleansed by the greenhouses, irrigates.

6. The design of squares, boulevards, streets, alleys, quadrangles, and courtyards is operative at the scale of the whole town. The heart of the town is organized around two squares. The eastern square gathers both the civic and commercial cores. The western square is a simpler neighborhood anchor. The plan is made up of a series of clearly defined street types. Each possesses a specific section and native planting profile and attempts to define a particular place. Each favors pedestrian experience over vehicular speed.

Urbanism is different from architecture. Architecture is the making of particular, sometimes idiosyncratic objects in response to specific and unique requirements. In the experience of the twentieth century, there have been some first-rate individual buildings to rank with the best of any epoch, but there have been very few first-rate streets, and even fewer if any neighborhoods of note.

Urbanism is about approximating architecture. It concerns itself with the essential ingredients of each building in plan/organization, in section/space, and in elevation/character. Individual buildings constitute the city only if their ingredients are shared or combined to generate a physical entity larger than the sum of the parts. The set of essential formal ingredients for any building determines its genetic imprint, its type. The city is a typological framework, a field of potential buildings. The city, therefore, constantly unfolds as a physical place and is never fixed.

Housing is the common fabric of the town we designed. Its typological structure is as complex as the social structure of late twentieth-century America. It is one of the most astounding aspects of our culture that, in spite of unprecedented social and cultural cross-fertilization, housing types today are in essence limited to the single house on the ground and various manifestations of the apartment on a double-loaded corridor.

The grid, particularly rigorous in this scheme, is a tartan pattern rather than a simple gridiron. The curving boulevard provides relief, as do several parks and squares.

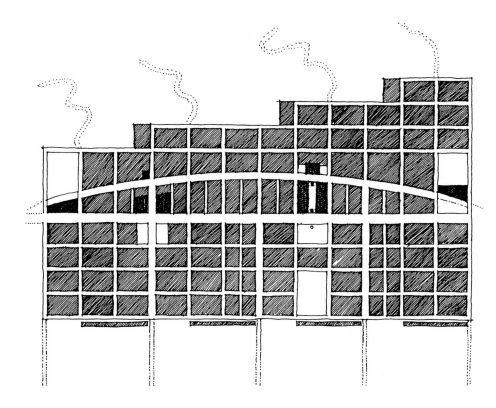

We speculated about the desirability of both old and new types. In constructing this typology, we attempted both to remember and to project:

Urban Cabins: small starter houses that have escaped from the grid and wandered off along meandering roads in the north edge of the town. These houses are partially located in the forest to remind us of their primitive beginnings in the process of urbanizing the West.

Single-family houses with garage apartments: houses that respect the conventions of the most typical American house form, they allow for higher densities by locating apartments above alley garages. They are limited in their location to specific areas in the northern parts of the plan.

Fourplexes: four units assembled into a single front-oriented house form. This housing type follows the compositional rules of the single-family house.

Sideyard and Courtyard Housing: Five to ten units organized around a courtyard. Both these types and the one above combine the advantages of identifiable, separate dwellings with the privileges and economies of living in very close proximity to other families. These relatively denser types are located in the southern portions of the plan. They are generated from a land parcel plan that allows for larger footprints and are arranged so that they define consistent street walls and street spaces.

Live-Work: this type is located in the central linear core of the town. Its central characteristic is its subdivision into three parts: house, garden, and workshop. As houses are arranged to define streets, workshops are arranged to generate yards for both production and selling.

Apartment Flats: traditional housing type utilized in its conventional sense in order to allow people to live in the center of town within easy access to commercial and civic activities. They are often designed into mixed-use buildings with commercial space on the street.

Three civic and commercial architectural types are part of this satellite town. They are treated as unique objects. There is no geometric center in this project. The composition of blocks and districts is serial or linear. Off to the eastern side of the central thoroughfare is the civic center. It is organized around a square and it gathers buildings of various uses and meanings: a water tower (an ecological icon), a library, a police/fire building, an assembly and community building, and a city hall. Two schools occupy the sites at the entrance to town on the east and west, with abutting open space for playgrounds.

An office campus is located near the civic center. An office park is conceived as a work-dominated district where the buildings involved are as penetrable as campus buildings. It was our intention to introduce housing into this district, but we did not determine the best way of doing so. Finally, the main retail activity in this town is located on the east-west Main Street—a kind of link between the two halves of the town. Most large stores are concentrated on the eastern square behind an arcade, although the western square also accommodates neighborhood shops.

Living on the edge of the metropolis should be an opportunity for those who wish to engage in planting roots and in experimenting with the order of things to come. New satellite towns should not be conventional suburban communities or conventional small towns. Nor should they be caricatures of futures whose time has passed. The future might well be less obsessed with progress and more modest in its life possibilities.

SEQUALLIMINE NEW TOWN
Pyatok/Sellers Statement

Much of the thinking for today's new communities (while laudable in its demand for compactness and the resuscitation of traditional smaller-scaled street grids) suffers from a case of excessive tidiness and "designer" cuteness. Part of this is due to the middle- and upper-middle-class origins of planners and architects who are proposing the planning and architectural ideas. They tend to ignore the working classes and their blue-collar jobs, with their messy buildings and the not-so-well-kept streets that industry requires. As a consequence, the new communities, while seemingly more intimate and humanly scaled, overtly express upper-class biases toward a picturesque, recreational

The central meadow crowns the hill, to which the community clings like an Italian hilltown, as designed by David Sellers and Mike Pyatok, the two most inveterate charrette team leaders.

KEY
1 STORM RETENTION
2 SENIORS CLUSTER
3 CIVIC PLAZA
4 REMOTE PARKING
5 MAIN RETAIL STREET
6 MIXED-USE STREET
7 MIXED-USE LOFTS
8 SCHOOL, THEATRE
9 CENTRAL MEADOW
10 SOLAR, WASTE TREATMENT
11 EVAPORATION PONDS

character, almost resortlike in imagery. This attitude removes from the town-scape the rough and not-so-pretty side of a working community of diverse housing.

The organizational elements of this proposal for a New Town are designed to create an active, vital community which grows, changes and reconfigures itself over time, and always accommodates the wide range of work opportunities required by a full range of socioeconomic classes. This can happen within a clear and strong framework of roads, paths, and open spaces along with critical, permanent, institutional structures. A variety of street types, as well as a

Above: Curving streets
that follow the contours
provide a sense of visual
and spatial closure. This
one is Main Street.

wide range of housing types and prices, ensures the presence of a wide socioeconomic mix of residents.

This solution fronted the new village on an enormous meadow. The line of
separation is north-south. The meadow is like an ocean with a western sunset. Its edge is the harbor, where the cultural and commercial action of the
village is located. In this case, the action takes place in the park, as well as
along the street that fronts the park. Enough energy there will justify cafes,
commercial shops, and upper-level apartments overlooking and participating
in the show. This north-south street—Main Street—is double-loaded with open-
ings and invitations, paths and gardens, which bring in light from the great
meadow and which encourage participation. The street is designed for traffic,
buses, bicycles, and inner-village cars (electric, pedal), but largely for pedestrians.

At the north end of Main Street is the civic plaza, where the town tower,
bus stop, and all the civic functions are located. Like a totem, the tower rises
above the old-growth forest top of 150 to 250 feet. The bottom (ground) level
of the tower holds the post office, message center, and bus station. Directly
above are three stories of village offices, town clerk's office, mayor's office, and
community meeting rooms. Above these are ten floors of seniors' housing,
ten units each with porches overlooking the village and the big meadow. Above
these is a 10-million-gallon water storage tank, enough for the entire village
for four days, pumped from an array of wells on the property. There is a pedestrian ramp running down the outside of the tank for five or six stories, which
serves as a public viewing path. Above the tank are a restaurant and public

A singular "town tower"
accommodates a remark-
ably broad range of com-
mercial, civic, and
residential spaces and acts
as a civic symbol at the
end of Main Street.

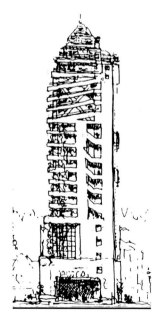

Work Street

A residential street

meeting rooms, and on the very top, an exterior viewing deck. The tower is owned by the town.

At the south end of Main Street are the school and the arts center (theater, galleries, classrooms, studios). To the south of the school is the biological waste treatment plant, where all the town sewage is recycled in greenhouses. The waste feeds the plants and is in turn purified and returned to the water table. This facility is a part of the educational function of the school. Public gardens and a farmer's market are also located immediately south of the school.

Work Street on the eastern edge of the village is designed as a collage of offices, shops, studios, and business and light manufacturing centers. This street is tailored to serve businesses that hire workers of both white and blue collars, and that employ people who may not live in town. Parking lots to the rear of the buildings that line this street accommodate cars of the commuter workers by day and the second cars of residents. The enterprises on Work Street are housed in concrete loft structures of double-height ceilings and generally square plans, which allow great flexibility in uses over time. They are adaptable for live-work studios, light manufacturing, and back offices.

The village itself is a series of grids arranged along 8 percent slopes, descending toward the east. The grids are interrupted with strings of natural water courses, gardens, and pathways connecting the meadow on the west and a natural area to the east, with the intervening human-made living environment of the town. Radial east-west streets cut through the grid and connect Main Street with Work Street. These are lined with local shops, small businesses, and studios, with housing above. As residents descend the slope from Main Street to Work Street and leave the great meadow to the west behind, they can see the distant mountains above the forest to the east. These radial streets serve as linear separators as well as links between the three main neighborhoods.

The north-south streets parallel to the contours serve low-rise, high-density housing, never exceeding three or four floors in height; while back alleys hold garages for each house, with second units positioned above the garages. Running east-west and perpendicular to the contours and the residential streets are narrow, auto-free pedestrian paths. These provide a more intimate walk than the radial streets up and down the slopes between Work Street and Main Street.

The overall scale is pedestrian, bicycle, and intimate, with easy access to open space, back alleys, pathways, and larger recreational and agrarian uses on the adjacent land. A majority of the open forest land will be reforested in the native species, Douglas fir, and managed by the community.

Public costs are substantially reduced by the compact nature of the design. Additional savings are in the water and sewage systems, where the biopurification will make a profit from plant sales. The most significant savings is in terms of the reduced transportation costs to the residents. If one third of the residents, say 2,000 households, reduce their car requirements to one car, the annual savings as a group could be as much as $12,000,000. Intangible savings are in reduced air and water pollution, better community health from increased excercise, and increased awareness of the natural environment on a day-to-day basis.

Finally, the physical integration of different socioeconomic classes in the same community, both in work opportunities and residential options, has the potential to increase the flow of information to those who must toil manually for a living. It can also increase the appreciation of those who process information as a living for those who have the skill to make things with their hands. The cultural consequences of such coexistence of white and blue collar workers, and of management and labor, are admittedly unquantifiable and unpredictable. But we do know that the segregation of classes is taking a measurable toll on continued community, especially its economically underprivileged.

CYRANO DE ISSAQUAH

Fraker/Solomon Statement

We believe that the purpose of a university charrette should not be to practice practice, but to criticize practice. Our design for a new community, Cyrano de Issaquah, is a critical scheme. We chose to abandon the site assigned to us and pick a new one because we believe that building a new settlement out in the woods, five miles from any roads or infrastructure is a bad precedent for American development in the 1990s. It might be a dream architectural commission or an excellent real estate opportunity, but it is not a good idea for five reasons:

1. A long extension of infrastructure—roads, sewers, utilities—to create a small settlement is neither sensible nor plausible. It is a wasteful purpose, difficult to phase and difficult to finance.

2. The ecology of a forest greenbelt around a metropolitan region should not be altered unless there is a more compelling reason than land speculation, regardless of whether the speculator is a private entrepreneur or a public agency.

3. Continued development of an ever more outlying periphery of the metropolitan region leaves the existing periphery in a limbo of semi-development and semi-abandonment that is neither urban nor rural. These places do not foster community or investment and are impoverished environments socially and aesthetically.

4. A distant settlement built all new with no direct connection to anything existing is likely to seem artificial and rootless.

5. The original site assigned to us is not a candidate for transit and would add considerable traffic to an already congested road. It would be a long commute.

For these reasons, we concluded that even the most intelligently designed new community on the site assigned to us would perpetuate many of the bad features of conventional sprawl. We choose to do something different.

The New Site Chosen

Having abandoned the DNR site, the question became how to find a place to locate the program that would address all the criticism implied by rejecting the original site. We sat down with aerial maps and the knowledge our students had of the area and searched for a location out of which we could cre-

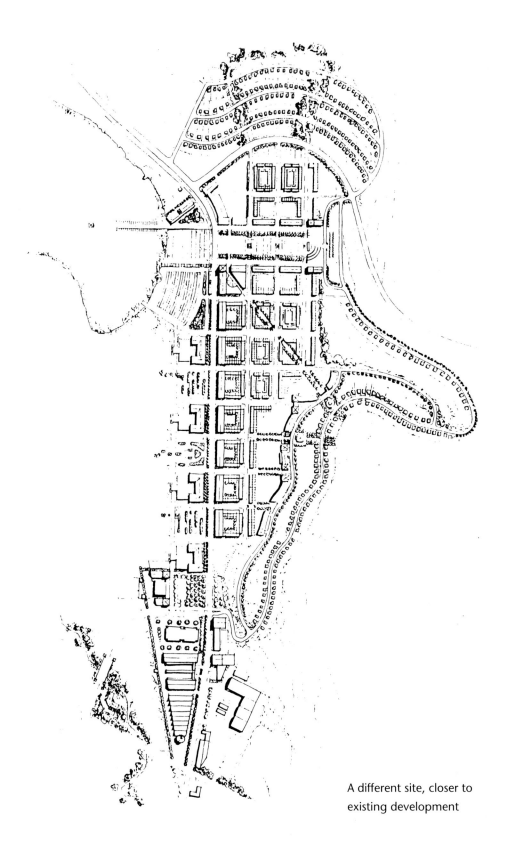

A different site, closer to
existing development

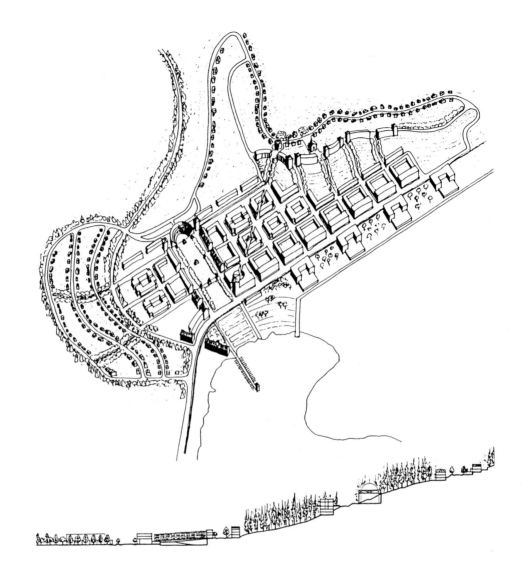

Steep hillside development leads down to Lake Sammamish

ate a unique sense of place. We very quickly focused on approximately 350 acres at the southeast end of Lake Sammamish, just north of the town of Issaquah and north of Interstate 90 (about twenty miles from Seattle). The location is blessed with both natural and manmade features which we thought would enhance our program and create a unique opportunity.

The Plan

The plan of Cyrano de Issaquah looks like a face with a big nose and glasses. The plan is not a contextless abstract universal formula; it is not an ideal. Its form is particular, like a face, because it is part of a particular real place with hills, existing roads, buildings, parkland, and a lake. The plan is based on the premise that place making involves the embrace of the particular and that

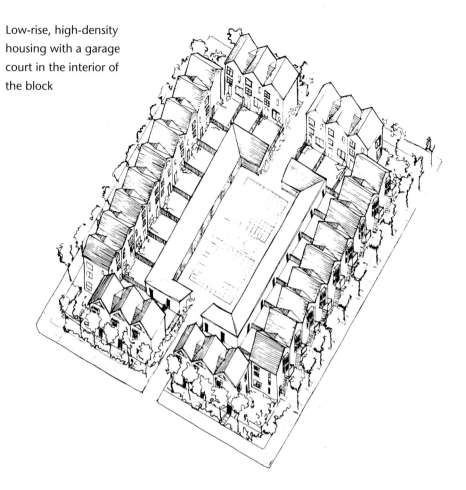

Low-rise, high-density housing with a garage court in the interior of the block

abstract systems like grids have vitality and the quality of place only when they are animated and modified by the qualities of a particular landscape.

Work

Our plan accepts one fundamental assumption about the future of suburbia: for most people, the suburban work place will continue to be the large, low-rise office building. This is driven by the effect of information technology on work, the efficiency of small work groups, and the demands of an ever more affluent and educated work force. This conventional assumption is debatable, but we accepted it nonetheless. Our plan integrated today's large campus-type suburban office building into a compact community in which it is possible to walk to lunch and to accomplish daily errands on foot, as well as walk to work from home or from a transit stop. Our plan takes advantage of a large regional park bordering the town's main street to make an in-town office campus. Main Street has continuous frontage on the east side with a variety of uses arrayed as market conditions dictate. The west side of Main Street consists of large office buildings at regular intervals interspersed with the park edge.

Housing

Plans such as this can only be realized over a period of years. For a plan to endure until it is implemented it must be flexible and not presume exactly what kind of development the economy will sustain some time in the future. But to be a plan at all, certain things must be fixed. The traditional gridiron of the American Town accomplishes this double role. It establishes the public space of a town but allows a great range of density, building type, and unit size. As in Seattle, it is the interaction of gridiron planning and hilly topography that will give Cyrano de Issaquah its character. There are compelling reasons for this approach. First, gridiron planning tends to connect the parts of a neighborhood and encourages street life and walking, in contrast to cul-de-sac planning which tends to isolate and privatize. Gridiron planning provides long vistas and a sense of the surrounding landscape; curvilinear streets close vistas and deny the sense of where one is. Grids are efficient with respect to density. Gridiron planning, when it interacts with hilly terrain, is not monotonous because the grid itself is frequently interrupted and discontinuous. There are many special incidents—stairs, retaining walls, overlooks, deformations of the grid itself—that give the opportunities to create memorable places.

In its central area, the plan establishes only the grid and some rudimentary principals of urbanism. As long as parking garages do not dominate the streetscape, buildings are parallel to streets, there are no large gaps between buildings, and there are frequent entrances along streets, all other aspects of the housing can remain flexible to respond to market conditions over time. The illustrative blocks in the site plan show various combinations of townhouses, apartments, houses with accessory units, and single-family houses. Densities range from seven units per acre up to thirty or more units per acre. There are two places in the plan designated for larger buildings of higher density. On the hill above the gridiron neighborhood, on a curvilinear road, is a series of mid-rise apartment buildings—the Cornice—with commanding views of the town and the lake. The Cornice is broken by public stairs extending from the grid below and passing through the hillside parkland. Each public stair terminates on the hillside at a site for a small church or other community building. The other high density housing site is adjacent to the central square.

The plan of Cyrano de Issaquah is not based on European models. It returns to the tradition of American town planning that existed before World War II. It has been inspired by the qualities of small-town America like those of Galena, Illinois, and Guttenberg, Iowa. It takes all the pieces of suburbia and puts them back together so that they add up to an intelligible and meaningful whole for a single person on foot.

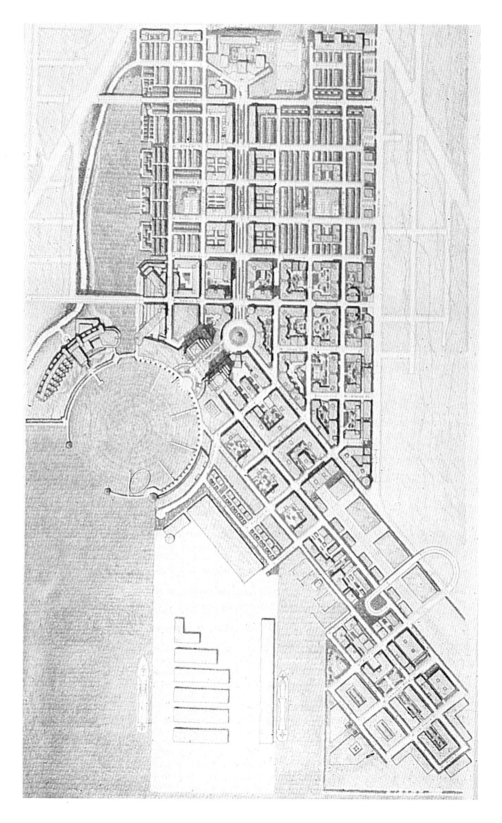

Master Plan for Scheme 5

The Interbay Charrette and Studio
A New Town in Town

The Interbay 2020 study represents the largest University of Washington design charrette. Of the dozen charrettes since 1985, this one tackled the largest area and had the largest number of participants and the largest budget. It also benefited from the longest pre-charrette and post-charrette study, including a follow-up studio and, for the first time, economic and fiscal analysis of the design proposals. The fifth scheme, which builds on the four designs produced in the charrette, was more fully and carefully developed in a ten-week architecture design studio.

Terminal 91 and the Interbay neighborhood represent one of the great development opportunities available to the Port and City of Seattle. The "brownfield" site is arguably Seattle's most underutilized parcel of land, with vast areas given over to car parking and the dumping of fill. As the accompanying map illustrates, the land is largely owned by three parties (the Port, the City, and Burlington Northern). It is extremely well served by rail, including the possibility of trolleys, commuter trains, and intercity trains. It has a deep harbor with two piers that are 2,000 feet long and cover 35 acres. It is close to downtown but also near two of the city's most beautiful and mature neighborhoods, Queen Anne and Magnolia. The southern end of the site enjoys spectacular views of downtown, Mount Rainier, Elliott Bay, and the Olympic Mountains, without blocking views from the two adjacent neighborhoods, which sit much higher above Puget Sound. Lastly, the site is large—over 500 acres that extend north/south the equivalent distance from Gas Works Park to Westlake Plaza or from the Capitol to the Lincoln Memorial in Washington, D.C. Rarely do such advantages come in such complete packages.

There are also problems. The site is not particularly well served by streets and highways, and vehicular access to Terminal 91 is constrained to a few points. Interbay's only north-south arterial, 15th Avenue West, is approach-

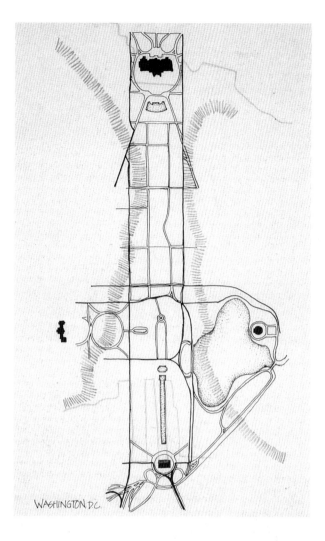

The shaded lines represent the edge of Magnolia to the west and Queen Anne to the east. Maps of the Washington, D.C., Mall (left) and downtown Seattle/Lake Washington (right) are overlaid to illustrate how big the Interbay site is.

WASHINGTON, D.C.

ing capacity already with congestion at peak hours. The Garfield Street viaduct is questionable seismically and in poor physical condition. East-west links are generally poor. The site is noisy with railroad activities, including the building of trains in Balmer Yards. The area is primarily landfill with potentially severe liquefaction during earthquakes. Portions of the site are contaminated with toxic chemicals. It has edges with environmentally sensitive steep slopes and tidelands. There is a poor jobs/housing balance, with little land given over to residential use. Some of the industrial uses on the site are incompatible with on-site residential development. Some of the noisier uses are incompatible with the Queen Anne and Magnolia neighborhoods, which are primarily residential. There are also nonphysical obstacles and costs to development, such as the Port's long-term leases with Datsun and other tenants, as well as the "shortfill agreement" with the community, which limits growth.

Aerial view of the
Interbay site

Although the constraints are formidable, they seem overshadowed by the opportunities the site presents. In any case, a long-term plan or vision for the area is needed, especially as sizeable pieces of Port land are sold or leased to companies such as Immunex and as the City implements its Comprehensive Plan and the Interbay golf course. Accordingly, the Port of Seattle, later joined by the City of Seattle, contracted with the University of Washington for this study. Phase I, carried out by the UW's Institute for Public Policy and Man-

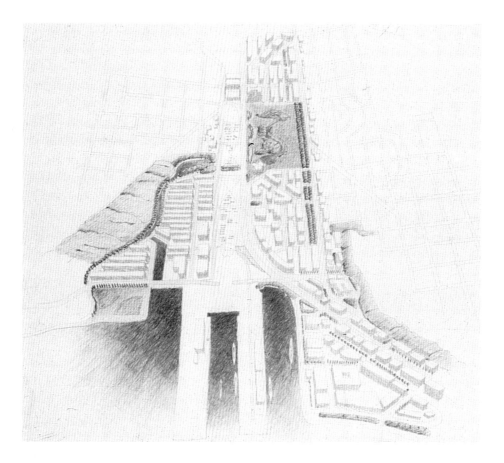

agement, was an inventory and assessment of the existing physical conditions in the area and of the political climate.

Scheme 1

This team divided the 500-acre study area into two neighborhoods and three districts. The first neighborhood is centered at Dravus Street, a major cross-street that would be lined with retail and that would have a commuter rail stop at its west end and a trolley stop at its east end (15th Avenue West). The second neighborhood is along 15th Avenue West, where the National Guard and Goodwill Industries are presently located.

The first district is a platted commercial area for medical facilities occupying the proposed Immunex site and is served by three streets ramped over the railroad tracks. The second district is devoted to heavy industry on Terminal 91 and Port land to the north. It is served by a new and simple bridge without ramps, which continues on to Magnolia. The third district is a platted light-industrial area to the west of T91 across a canal. This final phase would be built after Datsun either leaves the site or parks their cars on a proposed lid over the BN rail tracks. 15th Avenue West is also shifted atop these tracks to allow its present right-of-way to be transformed into a tree-lined boulevard. A small "ecological" golf course is proposed over the former golf course, now covered by a landfill in the center of the project area. At the northern end of the light industrial zone a new salmon stream ends in a spawning pond, to which fresh water is piped from Salmon Bay. Soccer fields are moved from Dravus Street to the former Navy ball fields next to Smith Cove.

The vacant land in both neighborhoods and the Medical Park are platted in 70-foot-wide lots to accommodate double head-in parking and four different building types: courtyard apartments, single-story light industrial, shops with offices with apartments above, and townhouses.

Scheme 2

Team 2 emphasized the strengthening of the city's industrial base, especially maritime industry. Accordingly, it enlarged the industrial zone north of Terminal 91 and carved a large flat rectangle suitable for large and heavy industrial tenants. T90 and 91 are consolidated into one large pier, which would provide sufficient surface area for a new container port that could accommodate up to four ships at a time. An intermodal rail yard would be located north of the Magnolia bridge, which has been shortened so as not to disrupt the Magnolia greenbelt. Just as improvements are assumed in the off-loading and storage of cars, container port technology is assumed to become quieter within the next twenty years. It is proposed because of its efficiency, its visual interest, and the proximity of freight rail, commuter rail, and highways. Containers bound for rail rather than truck transport would obviously be preferred.

A dense, compact residential village is proposed for Dravus Street. It contains approximately 750 new apartments, townhouses, and live-work units, which are laid out on newly platted blocks with alleys and accessory units. An open-air market bridges over the rail yards at Dravus Street.

The Pacific Rim Research Village is proposed at T88. Although not a conventional research or corporate campus, it could accommodate Immunex within its dense, gridded, mixed-use urban fabric. Its Elliott Bay promenade is lined with shops, cafes at street level, and apartments above. The promenades culminate in an amphitheater, to which a diagonal pedestrian spine also leads from new mid-rise housing across Elliott Avenue. When paired with Duwamish Head to the south, this promontory marks the mouth of Elliott Bay. From these two spots, lasers are shot into the night sky on important occasions to form a gateway to the harbor.

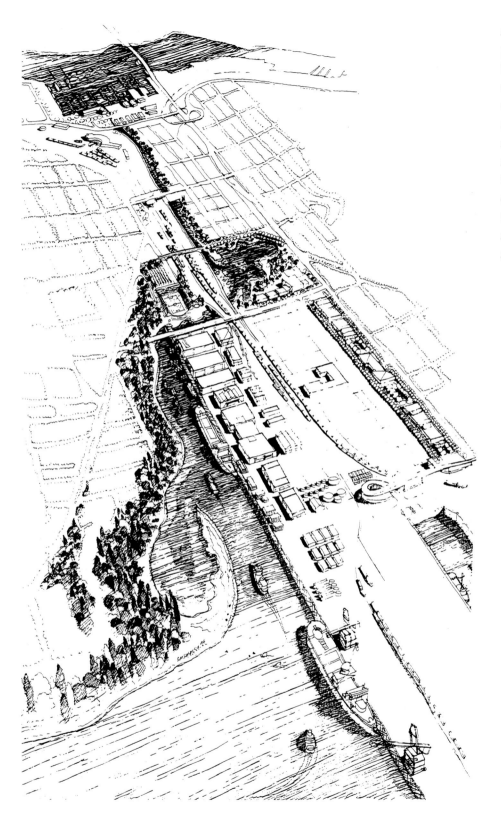

As shown in this aerial perspective by Ron Kasprisin, the "industrial estuary" of Scheme 2 penetrates deep into Interbay and forms the mouth of a salmon stream and pond system that connects to Salmon Bay. The hard side of the waterway is for berthing ships and boats and the soft side is a park and tidal marsh.

Smith Cove is restored to its historic shape and becomes a functioning estuary and habitat for fish and fowl. A salmon stream and greenbelt climbs to "Interbay"—a large pond, on which fronts a new elementary school and water purification laboratory. The stream turns into a slough and eventually terminates at Fisherman's Terminal.

The downtown trolley is extended northward next to the Burlington Northern railyard, and a network of bicycle paths is proposed.

Scheme 3

Like Team 2, this group wanted to maximize maritime industry and commerce. They first explored the possibility of moving the BN railyards eastward to 15th Avenue. The railyards would be covered with a lid which would carry 15th Avenue West. This move would aggregate a large parcel of land for development on the west side of the site and mitigate the noise generated by rail on the east side. Easily foreseeing the outcome of this strategy, however positive, they decided to pursue another less predictable scheme. Leaving the railroad tracks and marshaling yards at their present location, they treated them like a river, building earthen levees on each side for noise abatement.

Their scheme runs a trolley line along 15th in a transit or service lane, so as to create a grand boulevard with triple median strips, each with trees. They proposed replacing the Magnolia Bridge with a more sweeping and permeable viaduct. Its graceful arc is more northerly than the present alignment, and thereby frees up more space on Terminal 91. The Port property north of the bridge is platted in a Cartesian grid for industrial tenants, large ones in the center and smaller ones to the east and to the west. These smaller footprints would favor research and development over manufacturing and transshipment. The western water frontage of T88 is proposed to be purchased by the Port and made a working maritime terminal. The proposed Immunex site is designed for commercial office buildings and laboratories, with apartment houses across Elliott Avenue in front of Kinnear Park.

A salmon stream is proposed to start between T88 and T90 and rise to Salmon Bay in a series of long pools and intermittent runs to compensate for the flatness and the low head offered by the 15- to 25-foot fall from Salmon to Elliott Bay. A nine-hole golf course runs over the railyards on a lid. There is also a rail lid carrying a school and soccer field between Dravus and Bertona Streets. Like other teams, this one designed a residential village at the north end of the site, centered on Dravus Street.

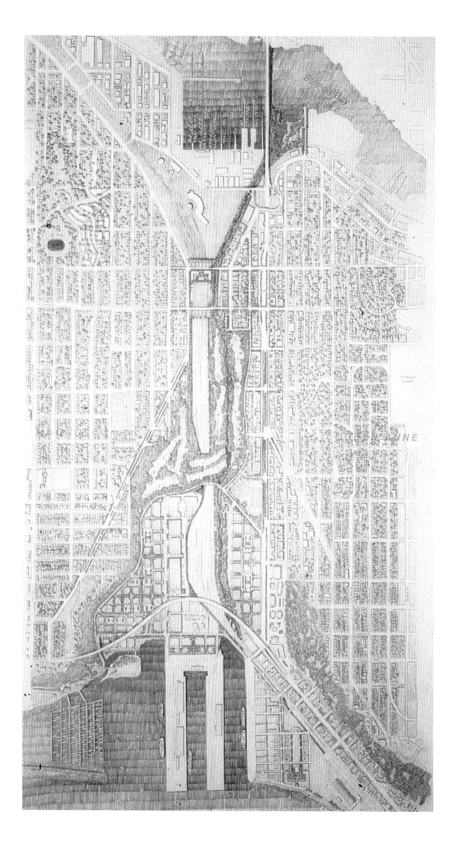

Scheme 3 Site Plan, as designed by the team led by Laurie Olin, Lorenzo Matteoli, and George Rolfe.

Scheme 4 Site Plan, as
designed by the team led
by Dave Sellers, Anne Tate,
and Rich Untermann.

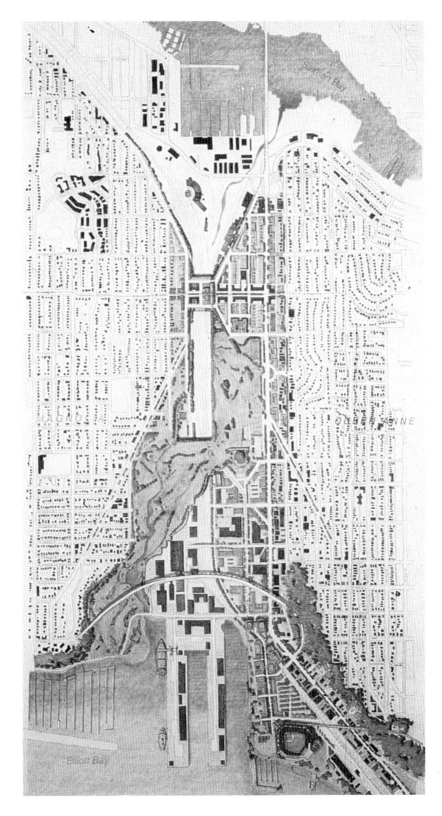

Gigantic sculptures such as "The Port Authority" could be inflated to celebrate important holidays and festive occasions, such as Seafair.

Scheme 4

This team emphasized the importance of jobs and of transit in their opening commentary. Not only did they propose commuter rail, trolley, and bus lines but also several stops of the Amtrak trains to Vancouver. They also suggested a funicular cable car run between Magnolia and Queen Anne, and an extension of the monorail to Terminal 88. Major lidded rail stations were designed, one at a bend where Elliott Avenue becomes 15th Avenue West and one at Dravus Street. A new curving bridge to Magnolia has a new alignment and a bicycle path suspended under its roadway.

A golf course crosses the BN railyard on a lid for the back nine of eighteen holes. A residential urban village occupies the Dravus Street corridor. It has a tree-lined median strip ending at the intermodal station on the landscaped lid over the tracks. There is also a new open-air ballpark for the Mariners proposed on T88, with the Immunex headquarters juxtaposed nearby. "High bank housing" over commercial backs up the slopes of Kinnear Park on Elliott Avenue.

Because of the many new uses proposed, this scheme devotes less land to industrial purposes than the three other visions. Indeed, it envisions the possibility that the piers may become less industrial over time and become populated with varied structures, such as a Ferris wheel and large inflatable colossus statue straddling the two piers.

This team reinforced the public domain with public art and proposed design competitions for "pin point buildings" at key spots in the study area. The public golf course and its clubhouse would be an active part of the public realm, hosting Fourth of July picnics and acting as a public arboretum. A salmon stream weaves its way through the golf course and ultimately to Salmon Bay.

Scheme 5: The Design Studio

The fifth design proposal was developed by a graduate architecture and urban design studio taught by the author and Bo Gronlund, visiting from the Royal Danish Academy of Fine Arts. They worked together with six students for ten weeks after the charrette, meeting three afternoons per week. There was an interim review, attended by Port Commissioner Paul Schell and other guests. After this review, the design was altered and adjusted to reflect comments by reviewers. The final design, illustrated below, was presented to the Port Commission and City of Seattle staff.

The fifth scheme focused more on Port of Seattle properties, although it necessarily had to include within its cone of vision the Burlington Northern, Northwest Industries, National Guard, and former Terminal 88 and 89 properties. The studio team, all of whose members had the benefit of participating in the charrette, gleaned what it considered the best ideas advanced by the four original teams. Specifically, it maintained the low-rise, high-density development pattern consistently espoused in the charrette, especially for housing. It consolidated T90 and T91, filling the waterway in between with dredge spoils, much as Team 2 had proposed in the charrette. It dredged out the estuary, and restored the shoreline to a configuration much closer to the former Smith Cove. This new estuary would significantly increase the water frontage of the park at the foot of the Magnolia embankment and the riparian habitat on both of its sides. It could also serve as the tidal mouth for the salmon stream to the Ship Canal, an idea which all four charrette teams recommended. Like Team 2, it eliminated the Magnolia Bridge (Garfield Street Viaduct) in favor of a more upland east-west connector. Its removal was based on the fact that it is in poor condition, looking like a cripple with so many knee braces, and the fact that it does not enter Magnolia at a central location. The fifth scheme also picked up on the inner city rail stop proposed by Team 4. The possibility of bus, trolley, commuter rail, and intercity rail all stopping at Interbay was one of the major reasons the fifth scheme chose to increase the intensity and density of development beyond any of the designs from the charrette.

In addition to the ideas that the fifth scheme combed from the four charrette proposals, it developed several new ideas. The most obvious at first glance is the Inner Harbor, a large circular tidal basin with transient moorage and a promenade along its edge. The perimeter includes an Inn, maritime sales and services, cafes, retail, and a hotel facing downtown across a drawbridge over the estuary. A canal connects this marina to the T90 waterway to the

east of the consolidated pierheads. This canal helps flush out the inner harbor, while providing additional water frontage and amenities. Another new proposal is to connect Magnolia and Queen Anne with a mixed-use Main Street rather than a limited-access viaduct. Also a grand boulevard is proposed running north to south, terminated at one end by Interbay Circle and the train station and by a middle school at the other end. This boulevard is built on a lid directly over the BN railroad tracks, no wider than necessary but as long as possible. Accordingly, the school could be built elsewhere in Interbay, allowing the lid and boulevard eventually to extend north to Dravus Street or beyond, thereby mitigating more railroad noise.

Higher Density

The increase in intensity of development may be the major difference in the fifth scheme. Density was increased for five reasons, the first of which—*to take better advantage of available rail transit*—has already been mentioned. The second reason was *to prevent and preempt suburban sprawl*, which is rapaciously gobbling up the region's countryside and leaving behind a social and physical monoculture that will remain on the ground for many decades to come. The 300-acre proposal accommodates more than 12,000 new residents and 12,000 new jobs and would prevent between four and five square miles of suburban sprawl (assuming a residential density of two units per acre, an average suburban household size of three, and a net commercial FAR of 0.15 and 300 gross square feet per employee; warehouse and industrial areas are kept

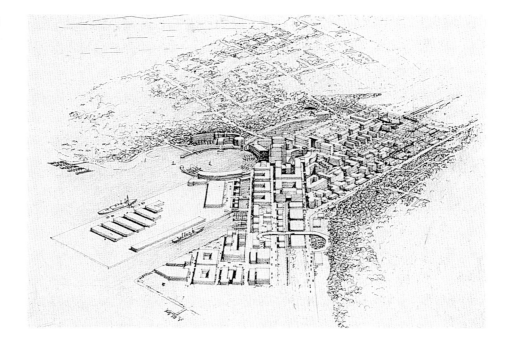

Looking toward Magnolia down Elliott Avenue. The street grid and the rail lid crank north at Interbay Circle, following the railroad and topography. (Prakit Phananuratana)

the same in both the urban and suburban models). As sprawl Los Angelizes our region, it has begun to bankrupt local governments, denature and pollute the environment, and decenter community. Low-density, mega-sized shopping malls, office parks, and gated residential subdivisions have taken the traditional parts of hometown America and placed them in giant, single-use zones that breed dependence on the automobile, social isolation, and environmental stress. The regional governments, including the City and Port, must forge policies that reward urban development and limit sprawl. Interbay represents the opportunity to build from scratch a model high-density, physically compact, walkable, mixed-use urban center that has a large amount of industrial uses and a sustainable jobs/housing balance. Infill at Interbay also reduces development pressure on Queen Anne and Magnolia hills.

The third reason for a more intensive development is *to justify and capitalize the high cost of lidding the railroad tracks*. Noise abatement is essential for the success of this project. Three of four of the charrette teams proposed lidding a significant part of the tracks, but none could justify the expense of lidding them for the full length of Interbay. Scheme 1 lidded the most track, but it did so with a lightweight parking structure. Even with a short-span lid with light loads, the cost would be hard to recapture in value added. The fifth scheme has a linear lid that parallels the railroad tracks, dog-legging at the Interbay Circle, the knuckle of the scheme. The top of the lid is 32 feet higher than the tracks, which yields headroom of 24 to 28 feet, enough for

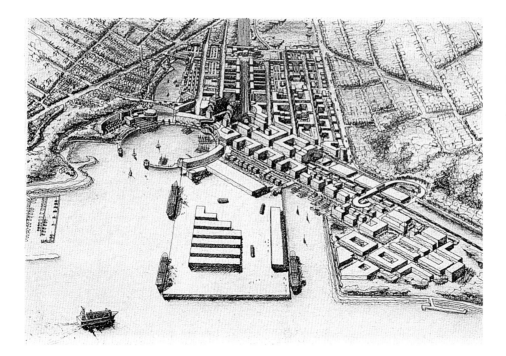

Looking north at the Urban Center nestled between the two hills and spreading out toward downtown. The landfill was extended into Elliott Bay earlier this century. (Muh-Huh Lu)

up to three levels of parking where the tracks do not take up the full width of the lid, which is typically 250 feet. By building higher (five to seven stories) and denser apartment houses along Interbay Boulevard and five-to-seven-story perimeter block offices between Elliott Avenue and Miller Street, the initial cost of the lid is absorbed more easily. Indeed, its cost can be spread among the capital costs of the entire project, along with other improvements and amenities, such as the canal, estuary, inner harbor, and parks. The more rentable and saleable square footage of commercial, residential, and industrial space that is built, the more feasible this infrastructure becomes.

The fourth reason is the *topography of the site* —a long, level valley between two hills—which allows for the erection of relatively high buildings without blocking views from the high ground. Both Queen Anne and Magnolia sit well above the site: the top of the former is about 400 feet higher than Interbay and the top of Magnolia is over 300 feet higher. The steep slopes rise to escarpments that are 150 to 200 feet higher than the valley floor on the Queen Anne side and 100 to 150 feet higher on the Magnolia side. This elevation allows buildings from seven up to fifteen stories, with little if any view blockage of Elliott Bay, Puget Sound, or the Olympic Mountains. (Obviously, views from buildings nearer the bottom of these slopes will be more compromised, but these units tend to be further north on the site, where the views are not as good.) Accordingly, two twenty-story office towers are included as both symbol and landmark at the heart of Scheme 5.

The marina and office
complex at water's edge.
(Jarrod Lewis)

The view of Interbay from above is important and guarded zealously by the respective neighborhoods. One of the prized amenities of the south slope of Queen Anne and to a lesser extent on Magnolia is the view of downtown Seattle's bristling skyscrapers. The view is made all the more vivid and dramatic by the contrast of high-rise towers in the distance set off against lush lawns and gardens of single-family homes in the foreground. Residents are understandably protective of these views and usually see any intervention in the viewscape as negative, just as they count any decrease in the suburban quality of their neighborhood as negative. Ironically, developing Interbay with two office towers and two senior citizen towers would actually make many views from Queen Anne and Magnolia more dramatic and would, by contrast, make both seem more verdant and more suburban. An example of topography especially favorable for mid- or high-rise development is along Elliott Avenue. Ten- to fifteen-story residential towers with stunning views of Elliott Bay and beyond could be built against Kinnear park without blocking views from Queen Anne above. If the towers had small floorplates, their slender profile would cast minimum shadow on the hillside park.

The fifth and last reason for more intensive development is *to provide a fuller array of alternatives from which the Port, the city, and the community could choose.* Like the charrette, the design studio is meant to generate illustrative designs. The results are suggestive not final, and are meant to stimulate ideas for discussion, modification, amalgamation, or rejection. The studio is

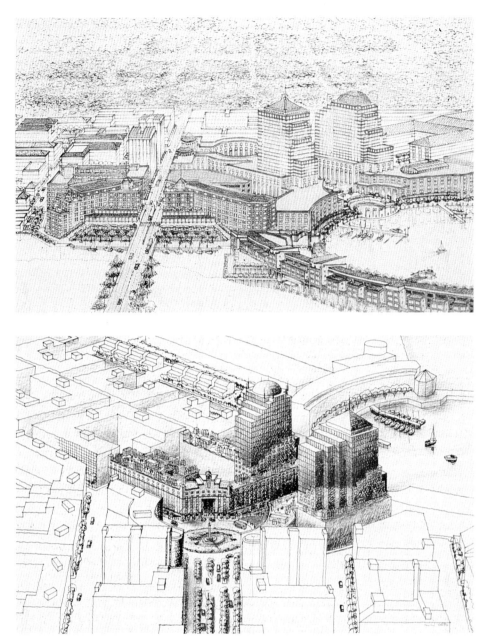

The view from above Magnolia, looking east along Main Street over the estuary and Inner Harbor to Queen Anne. (Peerachati Songstit)

Looking south at the transit station. (Muh-Huh Lu)

another relatively inexpensive way to test ideas and policies before committing to them.

Project Feasibility

Interbay is a huge and ambitious undertaking on a scale exceeding the Seattle Commons project. However, the impetus for the project is likely to come from public agencies rather than a group of visionary citizens. The Port of

Seattle, the city, and other public and private groups would need to collaborate closely. They would probably have to divide up the authority and responsibility for a project of this magnitude.

The following sequence lays out how the fifth scheme might develop:

Phase 1
   Immunex site development
   Filling in between Terminals 90 and 91
   NW Center and National Guard acquisition

Phase 2
   Relocation of Datsun to consolidated pier
   Trolley/light rail extension
   15th Avenue/Elliott Avenue redevelopment
   Relocation of Magnolia bridge
   Lidding and transit center

Phase 3
   Office and residential development

Approximate takeoffs of the quantity of public facilities and infrastructure required for each sector of the fifth scheme were generated. They included streets, bridges, dredging, lid, public facilities, land assembly, and air rights over RR tracks. The total cost of public improvements and infrastructure is preliminary, estimated in current dollars to be between $350 and $450 million—roughly the cost of public improvements proposed for the Seattle Commons. Some of the cost would be borne by the public sector, some by the private sector. The total cost of private development is estimated in current dollars to be between $1 and $1.5 billion, depending on the scope and quality of development of the proposed design.

The Port could expect revenues raised from land sales and leases to be in excess of $125 million. The annual government revenue from property tax is estimated to be about $3.9 million, plus about $1.5 million from sales, B&O, and hotel/motel taxes. With tax-increment financing, the property tax revenue jumps to approximately $15 million. In this case, public debt of approximately $156 million could be supported, which falls short of the projected public costs of $356 million. However, with revenue from Port of Seattle land sales/leases and with the Regional Transit Authority underwriting the transit station ($45 million), the gap is reduced to about $32 million. The most encouraging economic scenario combines tax-increment financing, Port land sales and leases, and the RTA and Road Improvement Fund contributions. In this case, the total public funds available are around $335 million,

	Square Footage of Development	Floor/Area Ratio
Scheme 1	2,834,000	0.24
Scheme 2	5,784,000	0.47
Scheme 3	2,880,000	0.29
Scheme 4	4,030,000	0.41
Scheme 5	12,220,000	0.98

which indicates in a preliminary way that the fifth scheme may be economically feasible. These numbers are very sensitive to assumptions and variables that are hard to predict, as well as sensitive to compound calculations that can quickly multiply false assumptions. Accordingly, despite their initially promising results, the economic analyses done for this project must be taken as a framework for and first cut at a longer and more involved process.

CONCLUSION

The Interbay area seems appropriate, feasible, and ripe for development. It represents one of the largest and most underutilized sites in the city. Minimal demolition and relocation are required to add thousands of residents and jobs, thereby saving square miles of agricultural and wild land elsewhere. It is a site that can compactly demonstrate the compatibility of mixed uses, including maritime industrial, office, retail, wholesale, institutional, recreational, and, most importantly, housing. It allows direct linkages to public transit, intercity rail, and freight transport. There is enough space for large-scale industry that is water-dependent, rail-dependent, or both. Terminals 90 and 91 can be consolidated into a single, very large import and export facility, especially for fish and apples. Development does not block views as it does with so many Seattle building sites. Because of its consolidated land ownership, topography, underutilization, and favorable tax revenues, it is a more feasible, viable, and exciting project than was the Seattle Commons. It could be the next urban project to capture Seattle's attention. Indeed, it could be a new and sustainable model of development for much of the Pacific Rim.

PART III POLICY

"Seattle is one of the last and best hopes for creating high quality urban life in America."

—Norm Rice, Mayor, City of Seattle

CHAPTER 10

What We Should Do A.S.A.P.
Seven Policies for the Region

"The government and the market are not enough to make a civilization. . . . There must also be a healthy, robust civic sector—a space in which bonds of community can flourish."—Senator Bill Bradley

The previous two sections have examined the complex knot of problems and opportunities facing the region. Part I presented the case for how high the costs of sprawl are; how the forces of homogenization and banalization can be resisted with Critical Regionalism; how important the typical building is in the urban fabric; and how these issues are being addressed by new urban design and planning models. Part II documented design charrettes and studios which suggest a specific blueprint for parts of the Puget Sound area. This vision is not without its ambitions and conceits, but it is a far cry from the grand 1909 plan for Chicago by Daniel Burnham with its monumental axes and golden skies. Nor is it the formalistic Bogue Plan of Seattle from early this century. It isn't the brave new world that Le Corbusier proposed in the 1920s for Paris or the Broadacre City that Frank Lloyd Wright envisioned for America in the 1930s. And it bears no resemblance to the futurism of either Archigram or Disney's Tomorrowland a generation later. Neither does it resemble the slum clearance and huge housing projects of 1950s and 1960s urban renewal. Instead, it is the beginning of a strategic patchwork of interventions at critical pressure points—places where opportunities are greater or problems are fewer or both. It is not a grandiose fin-de-siècle master plan, but rather an urban cookbook for the beginning of the twenty-first century.

The plans and designs in this book and many others like them need to be further developed and implemented if we are going to accommodate growth in ways that do not destroy our region. The public and private sectors must join forces behind these exemplary projects—Interbay, Lacey, Seattle Com-

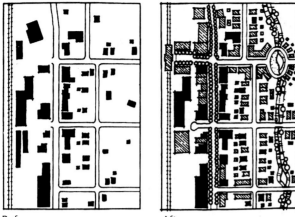

Before   After

mons (some more politically popular reincarnation of it), Sand Point, the Kingdome, and the University District. These charrettes all offer sensible, feasible but farsighted proposals that call for action. Interbay seems to offer especially great opportunities—its accommodation of 12,000 housing units and 12,000 jobs on a half square mile near downtown would preempt the most suburban sprawl and could be the most transit-oriented.

It will take scores of such projects to accommodate the growth expected in our region and state. The ways and means of originating such projects are many and complex, including design charrettes, which have proven to be among the most cost-effective and liberating ways to generate visions for a community. The practice of neighborhood and regional design requires lots of this kind of public process, as well as a solid grounding in theory and design.

Equally important, we need to promote the creation and maintenance of more livable, affordable, and sustainable communities through *public policy*. From the welter of ideas and proposals in this book, there are seven policy initiatives worth singling out for immediate action:

1. *Get development priorities right.* Make infill and redevelopment of existing urban centers and towns a higher priority than new suburban development. Investment in suburbia has often meant a disinvestment in our cities. To retain, reuse, and revitalize existing towns and cities should be a top local, state, and national priority. Existing communities, because their social, physical, and institutional infrastructures are already in place, should be given higher priority than building new communities. Although beyond the scope of this book, maintaining or rebuilding good K-12 public educational systems in existing communities is probably *the* most critical priority for neighborhood stability and health.

Rigorously enforce the landmark Washington State Growth Management Act. Maintain tight urban growth boundaries around all towns and cities.

Existing communities, because their social, physical, and institutional infrastructures are already in place, should be given higher priority than building new communities.

Cars, cars, and more cars. They may still be objects of desire and status in our society, but not only are they are less fun to drive on our congested streets and highways, they are bankrupting us in ways that we are only starting to understand at the end of a century they have come to dominate.

Pocketbook issues are often the most critical in a secular, consumerist society, where it has repeatedly been shown that even widely accepted social or environmental imperatives will not change behavior without economic incentives or penalties. Being morally right is not enough.

Ample open space and a well-defined edge of agricultural land and interconnected riparian and wildlife corridors should be protected in perpetuity as greenways and nature preserves. A network of pedestrian and bike paths should link existing population centers as much as possible. Urban villages, Pedestrian Pockets, TODs, and TNDs should be developed within existing urbanized areas to reduce sprawling development on the urban fringe and to save open space. The experience with design charrettes and studios has shown that it is easier to reach consensus for new development and growth located in underutilized parts of towns and cities than in existing neighborhoods. Accordingly, the least utilized sites should be used first, reducing the political turmoil and complexity of inserting new development into existing, more mature neighborhoods.

2. *Get automobiles under control.* Raise pricing; lower VMT; stop subsidizing the automobile. Adopt new and more robust taxes and regulations that will make market prices more commensurate with true and total costs. "Mobility is a means; it deserves no subsidy. Taxpayers have bankrolled the car and sprawl for decades, with money thrown in for transit as a palliative; the only

thing worth subsidizing now is the city."[1] It is society's ends—such as education, the arts, parks, housing—not its means that deserve tax dollars. Pocketbook issues are often the most critical ones in a secular, consumerist society, where it has repeatedly been shown that even widely accepted social or environmental imperatives will not change behavior without economic incentives or penalties. Being morally right is not enough. (As the Vietnam War protest movement and the solar and environmental movements learned, occupying the high moral ground does not necessarily have sufficient clout to carry the day.)

The primary economic policy to reduce VMT should be a much higher gas tax. No single legislative stroke would do more to reduce sprawl, fuel consumption, traffic congestion, and air pollution. There are secondary economic measures, such as congestion pricing and pay-as-you-drive auto insurance, which would reward vehicle owners who drive less. Also, there are home mortgage policies that would provide homebuyers with credits for low auto ownership and usage. Lenders need to recognize that households in certain neighborhoods depend less on automobiles and, accordingly, have greater discretionary income to devote to mortgages. The policy could be administered by statistically rating neighborhoods according to transit availability and proximity to workplaces. This policy should also extend to discounts for energy-efficient housing and for home offices, both of which can significantly reduce monthly expenses.

In addition to these economic policies, there are several regulatory policies that will help. Adopt low and zero-emission vehicle requirements for a percentage of the automobile fleet in the region and state. Increase fuel standards and deregulate shuttle vans and taxis.

Lastly, there are technological policies that would encourage the development of hypercars, station cars, automated highway tolls, and niche vehicles, such as bicycles, golf carts, niche cars, vans, and jitneys. Hypercars, championed by Amory Lovins, are ultralight, high-performance electric drive vehicles that can get well over 150 miles per gallon. Station cars are small electric rental cars made available at transit stations for transit riders to drive to their homes, to work, and to shops and to run errands. Automated highway tolls electronically record and charge drivers according to time and distance of travel. Niche vehicles are smaller, cleaner, cheaper, and more efficient vehicles that can be substituted for the conventional automobile, which is oversized and overpowered for most household trips. Because niche vehicles may increase VMT by satisfying pent-up or latent demand and because station cars, like park n' ride, may extend the radius of sprawl, both should be thought of as temporary solutions until we better integrate land use and transportation.

3. *Get transit on track.* Proceed as quickly as possible with a comprehensive

Interstate 90 near Factoria—a hellish environment in the making?

regional transit system. We will need all the help we can get: more van pools, LINC vans (Local Initiative for Neighborhood Circulation), jitney taxis, local buses, express buses, busways, trolleys, light rail, commuter rail, high-speed intercity rail to Portland and Vancouver, and passenger ferries on both fresh- and salt-water routes. The RTA plan approved by voters in November 1996 is a good, modest start. The light-rail system will help reduce the projected increase in congestion and is the best way to move the largest number of people during the busiest hours in the most crowded corridors. It will also encourage more walkable densities and mixes of use at the stops between the airport and Northgate, to which the line should be extended in Phase I. Phase II will be needed to shape new development in patterns of greater density within other population corridors. More express buses, especially ones with direct access ramps to HOV lanes, may be needed in lower-density areas.

The price of building and Phase II will be high, but the cost of an incomplete system will be higher. When evaluating the costs, we must remember how high the total, true cost of the automobile is—about $500 per month to buy, maintain, park, insure, and operate one, plus the societal costs of rights-of-way land, roads, bridges, police, gasoline subsidies, congestion, noise, pollution, and highway deaths. One estimate for all monetary and nonmonetary costs both to the driver and to society is $1.05 per mile.[2] If this is reasonably accurate, the region is incurring close to $25 billion in total automobile costs each year (based on annual VMT in the four-county region of over 23 billion vehicle miles). Other studies, which make more conservative assumptions and do not quantify as many of the nonmonetary costs, estimate approximately $14 billion total costs for King, Snohomish, Pierce, and Kitsap counties.[3] In either case, it is a large and growing tumor in the regional economy. Suddenly, transit costs don't look so high.

We must also remember that when we invest in rail transit we are buying far more than a transportation system. We are buying a land use pattern that will structure our region in more livable, affordable, and sustainable ways and that will impart a greater regional consciousness and common identity in a way that asphalt and rubber tires never will. Rail is the skeletal system of the region. Bus lines and HOV lanes are the sinew and neighborhoods and districts are the flesh and muscle. In the best of all worlds we wouldn't have to subsidize transit, but as long as the deck is so heavily stacked in favor of the automobile, we must spend tax dollars on bus and rail to keep their ticket prices competitive.

4. *Get planning.* Develop Urban Design Guidelines for all parts of the region—ones that codify in clear and simple ways design principles espoused here or generated in the community. These ideas include but are not limited to such concepts as mixed-use zoning, typological zoning, walkability, bikeability, compact site designs and community plans, infill housing, bounded and legible centers, neighborhood schools and places of worship, main streets as opposed to shopping malls, zero–lot line and town housing, accessory units, alleys, recyclable and reusable building materials, regional building materials and practices, regional architecture, regional architectural types, and community empowerment. Municipalities should also adopt Neighborhood Plans, also referred to as Specific Area Plans or Sub Area Plans, as an overlay to existing zoning ordinances and comprehensive plans. Together with the Comprehensive Plan already required by the state, Urban Design Guidelines and Neighborhood Plans form a three-legged base for stable and effective planning. Design charrettes, as illustrated in Part II and as dissected in Appendix A, are helpful in turning all three legs and especially powerful in developing Neighborhood Plans.

The cost of rail transit is very high, but the cost of no action is higher . . . we are buying more than a transportation system.

Citizens should always be encouraged and given the chance to play an active role in generating and adopting these guidelines and plans. Citizen participation is a practical matter of defusing obstructionism and developing strong ideas and shared ownership as much as a moral matter of common decency and democracy. The best and most potent ideas often come from citizens. (*Planning to Stay*, by William Morrish and Catherine Brown, is a particularly good guide on involving residents in planning and designing their neighborhoods.) The charrette is an effective way to involve citizens.

Although beyond the scope of this book, similar guidelines and plans should be developed for lower density suburbs and rural areas beyond the urban growth boundary to help ensure that low density development is also environmentally, socially, and economically sound and sustainable.

5. *Get more Granny flats.* This may seem like a secondary issue, but it's such a win-win-win scenario that it should be first-order business. Seattle's existing ordinance empowers owners of single-family homes to add an accessory apartment within or attached to their home, but does not allow detached or garage units. Municipalities like Seattle, which have compromised the intent of the state law, should allow and encourage garage apartments and other detached accessory units. Accessory units are probably the single most cost effective and quickest way to provide affordable housing units. The region needs tens of thousands of them. Indeed, for many decades, they were a common source of low-cost housing—one that a whole generation of lower-income Seattleites has been denied. There are many large homes, built when family households were larger, whose owners now could be not only allowed but encouraged to convert spare rooms into accessory units. There are also many garages in our region on top of or in which accessory apartments could be built. These garage apartments, a.k.a. granny flats, home offices, studios, and teen lairs, can be large and private. They also provide crime surveillance along the many alleys with which our region is blessed. In both cases, the additional income stream makes the primary dwelling more affordable. Banks should be required to recognize this additional income in their mortgage underwriting.

6. *Get funding right.* Tie the allocation of government funds for transportation, energy, clean air, clean water, housing, neighborhoods, and public works to local land use, transportation, and development that nurtures compact, affordable, typologically coherent, and more pedestrian-, bicycle- and transit-oriented communities. Enforce criteria that require localities to achieve a more balanced mode split, i.e., use of more transit, bicycling, walking, and car pooling to reduce VMT. Energy and clean air enforcement should also encourage this type of transportation and land use planning. The EPA, for instance, should allow the region and the state to count emissions that are decreased by certain urban policies towards meeting their federal clean air standards. This policy would lead metropolitan regions to strengthen their transit-rich cores and corridors to reduce air pollution. Provide funding for model and pilot projects. Also, provide fast-track processing, with required turn-around times, for development projects that comply with these principles and policies.

7. *Get governance right.* Reconfigure government to empower to a greater extent both the region and the neighborhood. These are more appropriate and effective scales of governance than the municipality, which is an increasingly arbitrary and awkward unit for planning and operations. Formally shift more power down to the neighborhood. Consider subdividing the City of

Seattle into boroughs, which, in turn, would be divided into official neighborhoods of 5,000 to 10,000 people. With its dwellings, school, stores, community center, library, firehouse, church, synagogue, or temple, the neighborhood is the optimum and natural social and physical unit for building community. At the same time, shift power up to a new regional unit of government. Shifting power up to the county is not optimum, because counties have outdated and arbitrary boundaries like municipalities. Also, counties simultaneously act as both competitor and referee to municipalities on matters such as planning, sewage, and transportation when an unincorporated area competes with an incorporated area. We need a more truly regional government—one that corresponds to the region's populated area, transit system, and urban growth boundaries—perhaps a three- or four-county consolidation or at least a heavily beefed-up Puget Sound Regional Council. Representation on such a regional council should reflect the fact that the older and more central cities, such as Tacoma and Seattle, play a greater cultural, institutional, and employment role than their residential population count might suggest. In fact, formally recognize the increasing international fame and importance of the Seattle region by making that the official name of the regional government or council. Retain the boundaries and names of existing cities and towns but slowly and deliberately shift appropriate decision making from the increasingly obsolete mosaic of municipalities up to a regional entity and down to neighborhood units.

Getting these seven initiatives right would have a very salutary effect on community making in the region, dramatically improving it at the macro and the micro scale. Many of them could be implemented at the regional level. Others will require the state to act, and some, like the gas tax, are only fair and effective if enacted at the national level. Although they are recommended as incremental steps that work within the existing system, taken in concert they would constitute a sea change in the way government helps to make community and to solve problems.

THE CONSEQUENCES OF NOT ACTING

As stated in the Introduction, there is fundamental dissatisfaction and alarm with the direction that metropolitan development has taken here and elsewhere in the country in the second half of the century. Despite the recent rise of property rightists, there is fairly broad consensus that we cannot endlessly sprawl ourselves in large houses across the countryside in auto-dependent patterns. Although most citizens are against sprawl and rapacious development, they are also bothered by density and over-regulation—leaving society with a difficult dilemma. This dilemma is political and ethical in

Flash Gordon cartoons and Marvel Comics overstated and oversimplified what the 1950s thought the 1990s might be like, but they also reveal America's abiding and sometimes naive faith in technological deliverance.

nature and must be addressed by lawmakers, policymakers, civic leaders, and the citizenry a.s.a.p. It cannot be left to government technocrats or the vicissitudes of the marketplace.

Shelter is the largest economic investment made by the typical household and buildings are the biggest economic investment made by society as a whole. Investments in the built environment are usually decided by the marketplace. As discussed earlier, the marketplace has a poor record in assessing and assigning the cost of externalities, such as environmental and social costs. Uncoordinated attempts to regulate the market through laws, taxation, and subsidy have frequently exacerbated problems of community making. On the other hand, there has been considerable environmental progress through regulation in the U.S.A. over the last quarter century. This success story has resulted in a great irony. The environmentalists are reluctant to acknowledge progress for fear of complacency and rollbacks, while political conservatives are loath to give credit for fear of the call for more environmental legislation. If we don't break this deadlock, there are some alarming possible scenarios ahead:

- There will be more and more air pollution associated with the increasing frequency, delays, and length of automobile trips, with consequent increases in greenhouse gases, global warming, and other climate changes—not to mention an increase in health problems and the loss of clear skies and views. More efficient cars, including niche cars, station cars, smart cars, and hypercars, might mitigate energy consumption and air pollution but will do little for congestion, trip generation, and VMT.
- There will be more and more water pollution with the increased water run-off (Houston already has thirty parking spaces per resident![4]) and waste products associated with sprawling development, with consequent loss in fish and wildlife, as well as an increase in health risks and a loss of recreational space.
- There will be more and more traffic congestion, with more gridlock and lost time, necessitating increasingly drastic corrective measures, such as commuting taxes, toll roads, much higher parking fees and the regulation, even prohibition of driving at certain times and places. Also, the high number of deaths and injuries that result from automobile accidents will climb.
- There will be less and less open space to farm and wilderness to enjoy, with a commensurate loss in agriculture, wetlands, wildlife habitat, and flora, resulting in loss of animal and plant species and ecological diversity and sustainability.
- Housing will become prohibitively expensive, with the consequence of more homelessness, less home ownership, and further deterioration in the quality of construction, materials, and craftsmanship.
- As the built environment is put at a competitive economic disadvantage relative to less and less expensive electronics and other new technologies, there will be more substitution of ever cheaper fake materials and mediated reality (such as TV, video, virtual reality, and computers), as well as more architecture of artifice and entertainment (such as Disneyesque shopping malls and theme parks).
- As a technoworld equips everyone with Star Trek–like command modules to do electronic shopping, banking, reading, and communicating, there will be more personal isolation and more crime in a public realm that is increasingly stark, abandoned, and Huxleyesque.[5]
- There will be more placelessness, social alienation, and civil unrest, sometimes accompanied by violence, with an escalation of governmental measures in the name of law, order, and survival ecology.
- With sprawl and consumption continuing to absorb funds needed for such items as research and education, our country will become less and less competitive in the international arena, with a consequent downward spiral in the physical standard of living and in international standing.

Although it is unlikely that all of these scenarios will happen, none of them is out of the realm of possibility. These changes are often hard to measure. Sometimes we can't even agree on the terms of measurement, much less the amount of quantitative or qualitative change. Some change will reduce our standard of living *relative* to faster growing and more industrious parts of the world; others will result in *absolute* cuts in our physical living standards, especially for the poor and disadvantaged. Some changes are unfolding all across America, some more dramatically in our region. Much scarier scenarios are, alas, being lived out in places like Somalia and Rwanda.

The chronic differences between wealth and poverty, between management and labor, between landowners and tenants will be made all the more dire by ecological imperatives. There are social pundits who are already warning of the dangers of fascist and totalitarian political movements rising to institute draconian measures and countermeasures as environmental and socioeconomic problems reach crisis proportions—much as extremists have always seized such moments and curtailed human rights in the name of a greater cause. While these predictions may be alarmist, the inexorable trends of population growth and global limits presage more governmental taxes, regulations, and takings, as well as a social climate of less environmental, economic, and personal freedom. The right-wing upsurge in personal freedom, especially property rights, will eventually have to reckon with this unavoidable arithmetic.

"The fact is the United States, by world standards, has very light land use regulations."[6] They will no doubt increase over time, despite last-ditch attempts by well-intentioned property rights advocates to turn back the clock to an era of lower population and environmental laxity. Property rightists must come to grips with the fact that rights attached to land ownership are part of a social contract and not inalienable, absolute, natural, or God-given. (If God gave land and property rights to anyone in our region, it was to the Native Americans.) Their desire to roll back laws and compensate property holders for government regulation is reasonable in certain cases. However, if applied to all government actions that diminish property value, it would effectively emasculate government and its ability to govern. Moreover, those who cry loudest about government "takings" can be monumentally silent about "givings" that accrue to them as a result of government actions. If we are going to compensate landowners for their every loss, we should tax them for their every gain. A guarantee of risk-free land ownership and absolute protection of private property would ultimately rescind community and repeal civilization itself.

As we bump up against our planet's finite size and resources, new models for shelter and community are needed in this and other regions. While it is true that new technical inventions and scientific breakthroughs will deliver us from some of our existing and upcoming problems, they will not spare us from many of the hard decisions and trade-offs that await us. As always, American ingenuity will help, but we also have to rally our collective discipline and political will before it is too late. If we don't act soon, sensible incremental change will no longer suffice and the end-of-millennium door will be opened to massive crises and to violent cataclysmic change that could ravage the country on an unprecedented scale, as it already has begun to do in less fortunate parts of the world.

Some of the answers lie in traditional models of shelter and community and patterns of ecology and life that have been sitting under our noses all the time; others embrace new ideas and technologies as our society takes social twists and technological turns never even envisioned. We should be careful never to lose sight, touch, smell, and feel of place. It is the primordial tie that binds. Place is more fundamental than nationhood or government itself. Only kinship can produce stronger human bonds.[7] We can no longer muddle along and defer action on the basic questions of where and how we make place and community. To default is to follow Phoenix and Los Angeles, and ultimately Jakarta and Calcutta, into the abyss. We are not as far behind these places as we like to think and the future comes more quickly than it used to.

Placemaking and citymaking are local acts. Despite the gnashing-of-teeth and pulling-of-hair on a national and global scale, we must continually remind ourselves that we can only *act* in our home locale. This book has attempted to outline in words, drawings, and photographs some ways to make place at the neighborhood and regional scale. We have neighborhoods and a region that reverberate with natural and human resources, as well as a multitude of good intentions. Sustainability has as great a chance in the Pacific Northwest as anywhere on earth.

The Pacific Northwest is important beyond the 1 percent of the earth's land surface that it covers. Rising consumption, growing populations, and increasingly powerful technologies challenge societies everywhere to provide for their people while living within the earth's means. The Pacific Northwest is poised to lead in the quest for sustainability. Though the region's economy is badly out of balance with the ecosystems it draws upon, its environment is probably less degraded than any populated part of the industrialized world. No place on earth has a better shot at reconciling people and nature than the Pacific Northwest, the greenest corner of history's richest civilization. And with most of the planet's people aspiring to our North American standard of living, no one has a greater responsibility to set a new standard for an ecologically endangered world.[8]

As stated at the end of the Introduction and worth repeating at the end of the last chapter, this state is destined to grow very quickly—by an estimated 2.7 million people—between 1994 and 2020. Population growth in Washington State is predicted to be the fourth highest in the nation, after California, Texas, and Florida. According to U.S. Census Bureau estimates, only Texas and Florida will have more net in-migration of new residents. In other words, there may be more people moving to this relatively small state with few large cities than to all but two other states. Many if not most of the new residents will descend upon the Seattle region, with potentially horrendous implications. Some experts claim that this region may become *the* fastest growing region in the nation. Although these claims may be exaggerated and these predictions may prove inaccurate, the consequences of growth in this region will be widespread and dramatic. They are beginning to sink into our consciousness. To give an idea of how much development is needed for 2.7 million people: the nine projects illustrated in this book would only accommodate between 45,000 and 65,000 new residents in total. To accommodate 2.7 million people would take about 500 such projects or their equivalents. We have our work cut out for us in Washington State and especially in the Seattle region. All the forces and determinants for continued sprawl and auto dependence are in place. As the author of *Edge Cities*, Joel Garreau, has said, if we want sprawl as far as the eye can see, all we have to do is sit back and do nothing. It could also be said that, if we want more and more cars driven more miles per year, with all the additional congestion, pollution, and energy consumption, we need only sit back and watch.

The Declaration of Independence established our right to "life, liberty and the pursuit of happiness" and the Constitution our right to settle anywhere in the country that we choose to. While these rights may sometimes conflict—as they do when a state like ours absorbs far more than its fair share of national population growth—they remain inalienable. We cannot stop new residents at the state line. We have no choice but to accept this flood of new Washingtonians and Seattleites. The question is whether we can do it without ruining the qualities that have brought people here in the first place. Indeed, can we do it in a way that will enhance our community and personal lives? We need to find ways, including the theory, design, and policy espoused in this book, to maintain and improve our quality of life as our relative and sometimes our absolute physical standard of living drops.

It will be hard for Americans to give up private space for common space and private worlds for common ground and public realm. It will be challenging to relinquish some of their personal freedoms and property rights for a greater sense of community. It will be painful to give up automobility for more shared means of conveyance. It will be hard to repeal consumerist dreams and break subsidized habits for smaller lifestyles. It will be difficult to resist economic pressures to settle for cheaper and shoddier buildings as regional authenticity and local nuance get more expensive. (It will also be hard for design professionals and their clients to give up some of their personal expression for a more regionalist and more typological architecture and urbanism). More equitable distribution of wealth and opportunity will be taxing in more ways than one. Diversity and gender issues will be both socially and psychologically troubling; environmental issues will continue to be politically divisive. Neighborhoods will resist their fair share of society's costs and burdens and municipalities will be glacially slow to yield to regional governance. To shift our tradition of rugged individualism to a civic humanism may prove the biggest challenge of all. We must do all of this and more, if we are to sustain community and civilization for future generations. It won't be easy, but we have overcome problems of this magnitude before; and we can do it again. It will be worth the efforts because the alternatives are stark, even apocalyptic. And, if we are not too careful, we may build better lives and common places for ourselves along the way.

Acknowledgments

More than five hundred people contributed to these endeavors over a ten-year period. So these acknowledgments will be longer than usual. First, there are the hundreds of University of Washington students who participated in the seven design charrettes and four studios included in the book. There are more than fifty design team leaders, who came to campus, sometimes more than once, from different backgrounds, professions, and places around the country and abroad. Then there are the many sponsors who had the gumption and faith to underwrite the charrettes themselves. There are also many University of Washington administrators, faculty, and staff who worked in various ways at various times. There are supporters-at-large, citizens and community leaders who volunteered many hours of time. And there are the people who collaborated on the book itself and those who have influenced my thinking and values over the last decade. Lastly, there are the two foundations, namely the Graham in Chicago and the Narramore in Seattle, that helped fund the book.

There are obviously far too many charrette participants to acknowledge here, but I must cite some. Two design team leaders, David Sellers and Mike Pyatok, are *charrettiers extraordinaire*. Dave was born to lead charrette teams and was always the most fun and imaginative presence in the six charrettes in which he participated. Mike, a member of the University of Washington faculty, was always the most focused and productive designer on any of the many teams that he led. Many of the charrette drawings in this book are from his hand. Don Prowler was one of the steadiest and most insightful team leaders in the four charrettes in which he participated. He has always been my first choice as a team co-leader.

I would like to acknowledge my intellectual debt to Peter Calthorpe, my professional associate and long-time friend. His lightning-quick mind and lucid revelations have always been an inspiration. He is the originator and master of the Pedestrian Pocket concept, an idea on which I have capitalized and for which I am personally and professionally indebted to him. I am also grateful to him for many images and ideas that are laced through this book and through *The Pedestrian Pocket Book,* which he coauthored and coedited with me. Like him, Harrison Fraker and Dan Solomon were repeat participants in the charrettes—each of them intelligent and fun to work with. Speaking of intellectual debts, Ken Frampton, whom I was able to bring to campus to lecture and jury several times, inspired much of the chapter on Critical Regionalism, and Leon Krier cast a big shadow in the chapter on typology.

Ron Kasprisin, a member of the University of Washington faculty, was a particularly accomplished and productive charrette designer and delineator. Other faculty colleagues who co-led design teams were Rich Haag, Phil Jacobson, Elaine LaTourelle, Dave Miller, George Rolfe, Rich Untermann, Anne Vernez-Moudon, and Dave Wright. The faculty of architecture's dynasty of photographers—Chris Staub, Dick Alden, and especially John Stamets—did an enthusiastic job of shooting slides of drawings and models under perennially rushed circumstances. Students Will Glover, Son Vuong, and Lynn Simon each handled the logistics for one of the events.

Trina Deines deserves special mention for the thoughtful and precise editing of the first draft and her unselfishness in helping on projects which are not her own. Despite her personal spin, she helped make the writing more my own. Jennifer Dee was a reader of chapters in Part I. These two colleagues have exercised their formidable intellectual and moral powers over me since I arrived in Seattle over a decade ago and have reformed much of my world view, if not my behavior.

Thank you, Dean Jerry Finrow, as well as Chairs Doug Zuberbuhler and Jeffrey Ochsner, for your support, and especially for the grant from the Dean's Fund. Without the budgetary and moral support of these two, this book might still be in search of a publisher.

There are numerous University of Washington staff to acknowledge. First and foremost is Ciara Hanley, who typed letters, press releases, programs, mailing labels, and reports *ad nauseum,* without ever showing how sick of it she was. Over the years Program Managers Toni Franklin and Caroline Orr were supportive with their own and their staff's time in the Department of Architecture. Louise Eaton typed the index. In the dean's office, Sandy Houser, Erin Menna, Lyn Firkins, and Sarah Phillips were always helpful when needed on charrette matters. Nedra Pautler and Mary Levin of *University Week* covered the charrettes handsomely for the press.

As essential as they were, there are too many charrette sponsors and clients to name. The City of Seattle, thanks to Gary Lawrence and Denice Hunt, was a willing underwriter and cosponsor of several of the University of Wash-

302

ington charrettes and should be singled out. The other sponsor and funders are credited elsewhere in the book.

Steve Clagett and George Rolfe were very helpful in the Interbay study. Rick Mohler co-taught the Lacey studio and helped write the follow-up booklet with his usual conviction and clarity. Daniel Glenn was an enthusiastic and eager collaborator in the Sand Point charrette, studio, and booklet.

There are other people without whom the charrettes would not have happened so well or would not have been published locally or nationally. Peter Katz is only one of the former and Don Canty and Clair Enlow only two of the latter. Among the many community participants, Tom Byers was especially supportive and an articulate juror. Steve Matthias was frequently willing to lend his gifted drawing hand.

Names of these and hundreds of other participants and contributors are listed in Appendix B. Apologies to those participants whose names are absent or misspelled on these rolls or elsewhere in the text.

I also thank Forrest Murphy for ably executing the early design and layout of the book and for helping me compose my thoughts and words. Shane Ruegamer was a hawk-eyed and enthusiastic proofreader, researcher, assistant, and word processor, who knows more than anyone how many time it took me to get the words the way I wanted them. I could not have made it without them. Bob Horsburgh and Herschel Parnes, social as well as architectural friends, were perceptive and helpful reviewers, as was Ann Thorpe, editor and publisher of the fledgling, excellent periodical *On the Ground*.

At the University of Washington Press, I have several people to thank. First Naomi Pascal, the *sine qua non* of the book. She slowly convinced her colleagues that this was a publishable book. Marilyn Trueblood was a supportive, patient, and painless editor. Bob Hutchins brought to the images and text the same kind of legibility and coherence that this book advocates for our cities.

The last person I would like to thank in this roll call is my wife Kathleen, who graciously put up charrette guests and patiently put up with my extended absorption in this project and my self-absorption in general. She was understanding throughout and always provided wise counsel, the perspective of a non-designer, and the security of a loving home. Thank you, Kat.

The actual writing of a book is a lot like being an architect for a building—something in which I have more experience. They both take several years, involve a surprising amount of teamwork, and require many iterations, painstaking attention to details, and a willingness to make changes late in the game, when they send unpredictable and unwanted ripples throughout the work. Both are slow to deliver gratification and both defy shortcuts. There are, however, two major differences. A book, unlike a building, is self-com-

ACKNOWLEDGMENTS

303

missioned. Although it needs a publisher and a printer, it doesn't need a client with a lot of capital or a contractor and many subcontractors. Nor are there the many regulations, codes, and inspectors, although some editors, fortunately not mine, can be demanding. There is, without so many second and third parties, more freedom when writing than when designing. It's pretty much you and language. With nothing but your own words to hide behind, an author is more naked than an architect, who is removed from his or her audience by an abstract language and the acts of many other people.

The other difference is dimensional. If architecture is three-dimensional and urban planning two-dimensional, a book could be seen as one dimensional—a long string of words and thoughts that depend entirely on being in the right order. Because a building is 3-D, a designer can behold it in her mind as a totality. You cannot behold a book as a whole. It is linear and additive, serial rather than simultaneous. There are no axonometric or perspective views, only a long and sequential narrative. When writing this book, I never knew if it added up to a whole. I'm still not sure. Friends who read the manuscript helped integrate it, pointing out omissions and suggesting ideas so obvious that they never occurred to me. Now it's time for the reading public to glean whatever truth and to find whatever fault that may lie herein.

Doug Kelbaugh
January 1997

APPENDIX A

Organizing a Design Charrette

The University of Washington design charrette started in 1985, when I was Chair of the Department of Architecture. Wanting to invite a visiting design teacher for each academic quarter but unable to afford it, I seized on the idea of getting several guests to come for a week. The assumption was that, if they felt they might learn from and enjoy the company of other guest designers, they would be willing to come despite their busy schedules and the low honoraria. The assumption proved true, and for the last ten years the department has brought a remarkable number of distinguished guests to campus. The charrettes have changed over the years, but only slightly. It was an idea, born of adversity, that worked better than anticipated.

There have been some problems. In the early years willing clients were hard to find. Budgets were tight. Recently, some student participants have complained about being overworked, undervalued, or exploited by the process. Some faculty members feel a charrette is a superficial exercise; some resent the fact that it reduces attendance in their classes for a week; others may be jealous of the attention and publicity it gets. Nonetheless, the positive aspects outweigh the negative. Many students have commented very favorably on the experience; some have described it as a highlight of their academic careers. Budgets have improved over the years, as more and more community groups and agencies seek involvement and demonstrate a willingness to pay their share. Indeed, groups sometimes now compete to be selected for a charrette.

The UW design charrettes have received considerable local and national acclaim. Most have received a good deal of local press and several have been featured in the national architectural journals. Some charrettes have helped garner publicity and support for subsequent local projects, such as the Seattle Commons, the development of the Kingdome parking lots, and the conversion of the Sand Point Naval Air Station. Others have kindled possible new projects, such as public restrooms for downtown Seattle and the Interbay Urban Center—both of which may someday be realized. The University District and Winslow charettes and the Lacey studio aided ongoing local planning efforts, contributing ideas, consensus and publicity.

INTENT

The UW design charrette is meant to advance creative but feasible solutions to a real problem on behalf of a sponsor, client, and user group. The problem addressed is usually an urban design issue of social, civic, and environmental importance. It is often a topical and controversial problem. Sometimes the charrette tests a new theory or policy on a real site; or it attempts to solve a problem or opportunity presented by a specific place; other times it provides planning and design services requested by a neighborhood. Although it possesses aspects of theory and teaching, the charrette is not a hypothetical or pedagogic exercise per se. It is community outreach and service. The client or sponsor has always been a public agency, organization, or institution. Because the department donates resources, it has limited its service to public causes as befits a public university.

PROJECT AND SITE SELECTION

Each site and project was carefully chosen. They were not chosen simply because a willing sponsor had a site and a budget. Several criteria have been fixed: the charrette has to deal with a problem of significant enough size and scope to warrant the use of so many designers and resources, the location and subject have to make environmental and planning sense, and the sponsors have to be not-for-profit. If the charrette is likely to have an impact on actual development and/or responds to an urgent need or opportunity, so much the better.

The projects addressed so far have included housing for the homeless, an urban riverfront revitalization, saving a small Italian hilltown, new models of suburban design, public restrooms, urban redevelopment, New Town development, park design, recycling a military base, a new town in town, and a university district. They have been projects set at the scale of urban design rather than architecture. The sites have ranged from 50 to 500 acres in size. Often, open or underutilized sites have been selected. They are usually less architecturally, socially, and politically intricate and conflicted, although every site is part of some community, which must be included in the planning and execution as much as possible. Some require less community participation, some more, depending on the proximity to and impact on the community of the proposed designs. Also, relatively blank sites tend to allow design charrettes to exercise their full range of imagination and creativity. Constraints are usually welcomed by designers, but only a limited number of them that can be dealt with during a week.

STRUCTURE

The UW charrette is competitive. Each team develops a separate design proposal. The work is not secretive, but teams don't collaborate with each other. It is unlike some charrettes or RUDATs (Rural and Urban Design Assistance Teams) in which a single design proposal is developed by one or more teams. Usually there are four teams, although there have been as few as three and as many as five. Three or four teams seem to work the best. More than four teams results in a public presentation that is too long and confusing for the audience. Less than three alternative designs usually doesn't result in a wide enough range of potential solutions.

Team leadership is critical. It is essential to select team leaders who are hardworking, convivial, and talented in urban design, and who can be there for the entire event. Mutual respect among the leaders is helpful in attracting professionals who otherwise might not be inclined to join a long and arduous workshop. If possible, it is helpful to get names that are known and respected among the students and in the community, whether they be local or out-of-town guests. This respect can reduce the amount of time devoted to jockeying among team members for power and position at the outset of the charrette. It is best to have two leaders for each team. This greatly reduces the pressure on the leaders, who invariably need a break from continuous work. Recently, we have appointed three team leaders, often to add a specialist such as an artist or economist. It is essential that out-of-town guests be coupled with local design professionals, whether local practitioners or faculty members. This mix obviously combines fresh, outside perspective with local knowledge. It is also good to mix different design professions, for example, to pair architects with landscape architects. Personal chemistry must, of course, be carefully taken into account when grouping team leaders. Values can vary, but it is not good to have 2 or 3 team leaders who are particularly strong-willed or particularly deferential. Each leader should have urban design experience, at least for the scale of projects typical of UW charrettes. Gender and ethnic diversity are desirable, especially if the student body is diverse or if the project is set in a diverse neighborhood. Although the event is not designed to be a pedagogic or academic exercise per se, it can be a very powerful learning experience for the students. Team leaders are role models for many of the students, a fact which must be considered when choosing them.

Team size is also critical. The ideal is between 8 and 12 members, including 2 or 3 team leaders. Teams as small as a half dozen and as large as 15 have worked, but production has fallen short in the former case and management has become problematic in the latter case. Team size, of course, depends on the caliber of the team members. Experience with community charrettes outside the University of Washington suggests that teams of students need to be larger than teams of design professionals. For one thing, some students lose interest and drop out; other students, particularly undergraduates, lack the requisite design skills to keep up with the fast pace. Accordingly, it is advisable to start out with a larger team roster than desired. If a team starts out with 12 to 15 students, it is likely that a solid core of about 8 to 10 will emerge, which is a good, workable size.

Team composition is less critical than might be expected. It is, of course, best to have students from two or three disciplines represented. For many urban design projects the ideal mix has been about 6 to 8 architecture students, 2 to 3 landscape architecture students, and 1 to 2 urban planning students. Some projects, like the Seattle Commons and Sand Point charrettes, benefited from having more landscape architecture students, because of the large parks involved. Generally, students should be advanced, preferably in their final design studio. The ability to draw and render quickly and convincingly is desirable, but strong design and analytical skills and sensibilities are even more in demand. It is important to make sure the best design students are as evenly distributed among the teams as possible. Graduate students are usually superior to undergraduates, but a mix will work, especially if graduate students predominate.

SCHEDULE

The annual charrette happens during the first week of spring quarter, approximately the first week of April. It lasts from Monday to Friday, although there is a dinner for the team leaders on the Sunday evening before. This dinner allows the leaders to get to know each other and some of the charrette ground rules to be laid out and discussed.

Monday starts with a morning bus and/or walking tour of the site for all participants. After lunch on their own, team leaders and members assemble for a briefing session. Presentations are made by invited stakeholders, experts, sponsors, community representatives, municipal representatives, etc. There are usually a half-dozen to a dozen presentations of 5 to 10 minutes each. A welter of programs, background maps, photographs, and written information is distributed to each team, who repair to their individual rooms to begin organizing and brainstorming.

Tuesday, Wednesday, and Thursday are devoted to team work. Teams work each afternoon and evening, to increasingly late hours as the week wears on. Working in the morning is optional, particularly for students, who sometimes have classes then. On Tuesday and/or Wednesday evenings, there are public lectures delivered by out-of-town guests. If the guest is famous, these events will be well-attended, occasionally more heavily than the public presentation at the end of the charrette. Mid-week there may be the need to have a meeting of the team leaders to discuss such items as the graphic format, scale, and color palette of the final drawings or to deal with some unpredictable question or problem that arises.

Early Friday morning, say 7:00 A.M., all drawings are due at a studio in which they can be photographed. Each team is allowed up to 25 images, including close-ups of larger drawings. Ektachrome slides are processed by 2 or 3 P.M., at which time they are distributed to team leaders. The public presentation is scheduled for 4:00 P.M. in a large auditorium, which must accommodate audiences of up to 300 or more people. (Some are sent invitations; others are interested students, faculty, and community residents who have heard about the event through posters or word-of-mouth.) Each team is allowed 20 to 25 minutes to present its scheme, accompanied by slides. Typically, one or two team leaders speak. After the last team has presented, the floor is opened to comments and questions from the audience. Discussion is often lively. (If there is no clear constituency for a project, a panel of invited experts can be convened to critique the work before opening the discussion up to the audience.) By 6:30 or so, people have left or are ready to leave. Many charrette participants attend a party that evening.

A tour of the city, on the Saturday and/or Sunday before the workshop is helpful for visiting team leaders. Also, the Saturday night stay-over reduces their airfare considerably.

The schedule for community and university charrettes elsewhere is usually shorter, often only a weekend. Some start Friday evening, others Saturday morning. In these cases, the public presentation is often the following week, to allow time for making photographic slides of the work. Since the purpose of these meetings is to present the results to the community, it is best to schedule the public presentations in the late afternoon or in the evening.

LOCATION

The UW charrettes are held on campus, in one building. Each team needs a studio with at least six to eight drafting desks and a large table or tables. The Public Restrooms charrette, which is not included in this book, was held downtown, at vacant space at Pike Place Market. In this case, all teams worked in one space. Some team leaders prefer this arrangement. It encourages more interaction among teams, but because of crossfertilization, it is likely to produce a narrower spectrum of ideas. A pin-up of all work halfway through the charrette also tends to reduce the breadth of ideas because teams sometimes pick up on each other's ideas.

The public presentation can be on-campus or off-campus, perhaps at the project site. The Kingdome Connection charrette held its public review in the Kingdome. The Public Restroom charrette ended in a large downtown church, with food served by a local homeless shelter.

PROBLEM STATEMENT

A written program is necessary. Often the client already has one. In some cases it must be generated by paid or volunteer consultants, which may take months of lead time and additional budget. The program document can be brief, as in the Pedestrian Pocket and Kingdome charrettes, each of which had less than one page of requirements. The level of detail depends on the client's or sponsor's needs and expectations, which vary widely.

PRESS AND PUBLICITY

A press release is sent out to the local media one to two weeks before the event. The press is invited to both the Monday site tour and briefing and the Friday public presentation. They rarely attend the former and frequently attend the latter. Often, several newspapers have followed up with illustrated articles. Occasionally a national journal will run an article about a charrette. Most clients value this publicity, although a few have shunned it. If a booklet is produced about the charrette later, it can be sent to the press and other interested parties. Written invitations to the Friday presentation are sent to selected guests. The Friday presentation is also advertised in the College Lecture Series flyer, along with the mid-week lectures.

PRODUCTS

Each charrette produces a set of color slides for the client. Budget permitting, a booklet is produced afterwards. The Seattle Commons, the Sand Point, the University District, and the Interbay charrettes all produced booklets. They are 11" x 17" horizontal or 8 1/2" x 14" vertical, spiral-bound photocopy studies, 50 to 100 pages in length, with a limited number of color pages. *The Pedestrian Pocket Book* was published by a national press after the charrette and is now in its fourth printing.

FOLLOW-UP DESIGN STUDIOS

Because the UW charrette is held the first week of an academic quarter, there is the possibility for one or more design studios to continue working on the problem. This continued study can either build on one or more of the charrette schemes, focus on part of the problem, or investigate the whole problem anew. In the case of the Seattle Commons, the University District, and the Sand Point charrettes, a follow-up studio generated more detailed housing designs for subareas of the project. The Interbay charrette was followed by a studio which developed a fifth scheme, quite different from the original four. A financial and fiscal analysis of the alternatives was also included in the booklet for this project, the most expensive and ambitious to date.

BUDGET

The budgets have varied widely. The first charrette had only three team leaders and was done for under $5,000. The charrette in 1987 in Turin, Italy, was the most expensive one ($50,000), primarily because there were many guests and they came a great distance. At the University of Washington, it has cost approximately $20,000 to underwrite the event itself, depending on the number of visitors. A follow-up booklet adds $5,000-$15,000, depending on its scope and length. The charrette costs can be borne by a single client or sponsor or a consortium of them. The University of Washington contributes faculty, student, and administrative time, as well as space.

Originally, visiting professionals were paid $1,000, plus expenses. The honorarium has since been raised to $2,000. This is a modest fee when their normal rates and the hours of work are taken into account. Team leaders must prepare before the event by studying the project literature, work 10 to 15 hours a day for four days, present to the public on the fifth day and later write up a summary of their work. If a team leader delivers a public lecture during the week, a supplementary fee is usually paid. Local guest professionals are usually paid $1,000, because they are not expected to work as many hours and they do not incur travel time and as much interruption in their personal and professional lives. Sometimes local professionals work pro bono.

The budget must allow for honoraria, travel, and room and board for the visitors, and meal expenses for local guests. Each team needs money for supplies and reproduction, often amounting to hundreds of dollars. Food and drink are occasionally provided to the student participants during the week and at a final party. Sometimes complimentary food and other services, such as photography, are provided by local vendors. A student assistant is budgeted to help with logistics before, during, and after the event. Clerical services are also necessary during the planning and followup periods.

The shorter weekend charrettes cost less. The Winslow charrette had a budget not to exceed $10,000, which covered the cost of preparation, facilitator, publicity, reproduction, food, and some city staff time. All the team leaders and members were volunteer architects and citizens from the community.

The North Beacon Hill and Rainier Avenue charrettes, run by the Seattle AIA chapter, were done entirely with volunteer labor assisted by city staff.

The value of the charrette exceeds the cost by a wide margin if there are students and/or volunteers involved. A university charrette can produce results that would probably cost two or three times as much if produced by conventional consulting. The chemistry of a charrette, competitive between teams and collaborative within the team, usually results in a synergy that is hard to duplicate in professional practice. Although hard to measure, charrettes almost always generate imaginative and unexpected ideas that linear, conventional professional consulting would be unlikely to produce. They also develop many unusable ideas, which should be pointed out to potential sponsors in advance.

COMMUNITY INVOLVEMENT

Community participation is a critical aspect of design charrettes. There are always invitations to community representatives for the Monday briefing and to all community residents for the Friday presentation. Volunteer design professionals from the community may join the teams during the week, especially if they can be there every day. Having lay citizens on the design teams can be unwieldy. However, in cases where an existing neighborhood or community is being studied, it is good to have residents on the teams, despite the logistical difficulties. In charrettes that propose new neighborhoods or new towns, community involvement is less critical, although neighboring communities should be involved in some way.

Most of the UW charrettes have focused on new neighborhoods or communities, which has greatly reduced the complexity of citizen participation. However, the Kingdome Connection, the University District, and the Public Restroom charrettes were set in well-established neighborhoods and enlisted more citizen involvement. The last included, for example, a twenty-four hour survey of homeless people on the street that was administered by students. The Winslow charrette, a non-UW charrette held on site without many students, successfully included three or four lay members on each design team— as did the North Beacon Hill and Rainier Avenue charrettes.

The results of a charrette should be seen as a sort of gift to the community from the design world—one that is neither perfect nor final, but the best designers could do with the available information and within the available time. It is illustrative rather than definitive and is not meant to be complete. Like any vision, it must be reworked by others until it is either discarded or adopted. A charrette is a collective brainstorm, not a master plan. It should be seen as a beginning, not an end.

Credits

Unless otherwise noted, photographs and drawings are by the author or belong to the University of Washington College of Architecture and Urban Planning archives or slide library. Wherever possible, attribution is given in the text or captions to drawings and photographs from other sources.

In the spirit of teamwork that pervaded the design charrettes (and because I am not able to identity every contributor to a drawing or model), individual attribution is only occasionally given to team leaders for this work. In the case of design studios, individual students are credited in the caption of a drawing or photograph. What follows is a list of everyone who contributed to the charrettes and studios, which are listed in chronological order.

THE KINGDOME CHARRETTE, 1990

Team 1	Team 2	Team 3
Leaders:	**Leaders:**	**Leaders:**
Susan Boyle	Dave Miller	Elaine LaTourelle
Mike Pyatok	Don Prowler	Dave Sellers
Students:	**Students:**	**Students:**
Kari Anne Bergersen	Lisa Barnes	Dan Blake
Benjamin Black	Jim Beley	Norton Ching
Jeannie Chow	Slade Blanchard	Elizabeth Clark
Donna Colley	Craig Corbin	Gibby Dammann
Scott Faulkner	Jeff Gutheil	James Grafton
Terry Findeisen	Keith Hayes	Konrad Hee
Rhonda Fuller	Michael Hlastala	Gregg Johnson
Liz Granryd	Brett Lamb	Dirk Kilgore
Justin Hill	Ilkka Pauniaho	Ed Leonen
Theresa Julius	Cathi Scott	Steve Maekawa
Bill Kurtz	Lisa Scribante	Leila Ramac
Pete Lorimer	David Seely	Stephanie Schwab
Bernie O'Donnell	Diana Wogulis	Julie Wendt
Bill Sowles		Kendall Williams

Team 4

Leaders:

Galen Minah

Stef Polyzoides

Students:

Susan Busch

Theresa Dir

David Dykstra

Jill Goodejohn

Terri Hirt

Chris Keyser

Diane Kirby

Brian Maugh

Frank Nickels

Hirokazu Shimosaka

Gail Suzuki-Jones

Michael Wheeler

Andrew Williams

Robert Wright

Special thanks to: Steve Badanes, Tom Byers, Carol Darby, Allan Black, Jeff Harris, Denice Hunt, Greg Nickels, Jim Olson, Bill Reams, John Savo, Lynn Simon

THE NEW COMMUNITIES CHARRETTE, 1991

Team Leaders:

Mike Pyatok

Dave Sellers

Students:

Anna Bastin

Christopher Beza

Michael Braden

Gary Fuller

Wei-chan Hsu

Timothy Jewett

Brian Kaminski

Bruce Macon

Tibor Nagy

Patrick Nakamura

Aaron Schmidt

Brian Schumaker

Team Leaders:

Phil Jacobson

Ed Kagi

Students:

Kari Brown

Joseph Donnette-
Sherman

Paul Eberharter

Melissa Evans

Jerome Fellrath

Stewart Gren

Larus Gudmunson

Eric Hong

Danielle Machotka

Tristin Pagenkopf

Jennifer Sim

Slava Simontov

Team Leaders:

Doug Kelbaugh

Stefanos Polyzoides

Students:

Marci Bryant

Cynthia Esselman

Holly Godard

Suraiya Khan

Peter Lian

Robin Murphy

Hyun Paek

Kathleen Shaefers

Paula Shill

Toshiaki Takanohashi

Ted Van Dyk

Elizabeth Wakeford

Team Leaders:

Harrison Fraker

Dan Solomon

Students:

Max Anderson

Scott Becker

Thomas Conway

Carreen Heegaard-Press

Douglas Ito

Molly LaPatra

Mary Lawor

Bunda Pongport

Caterina Provost

Robert Renouard

Rob Trimble

Judith Walker

Special thanks to: Stu Blocher, Carter Bravman, Bill Carey, Keith Dearborn, Julie Enderle-O'Neil, Peter Katz, Steve Matthias, Barbara Winn

THE LACEY STUDIO, 1992

Instructors:
Doug Kelbaugh
Rick Mohler

Students:
Amy Avnet

Susan Busch
Marcie Campbell-McHale
Cynthia Esselman
Alan Farkas
Tom Jordan
Olivier Landa

Sarah Meskin
Tamara Pankey
Robert Raasch
Amy Shulman
Gretchen Van Dusen
Louise Wright

Special thanks to: Loren Brandford, Ben Bonkowski, Tony Ford, Daniel Glenn, David Maurer, Susan Messengee, Sarah Phillips, Mike Piper

THE SEATTLE COMMONS CHARRETTE, 1992

Team Leaders:
Daniel Glenn
Elizabeth Moule
Mike Pyatok

Students:
Thea Bennett
Douglas Breer
Royal Dumo
Jun Galsim
Allan Farkas
Andrew Fauntleroy
Roger Hodges
Singh Intrachooto
Olivier Landa
Renee Roman
Mitch Romero
Kirsten Saterberg
Scott Schramke

Team Leaders:
Lee Copeland
Jack Dunn
Peter Staten

Students:
John Arnold

Dennis Arechevala
Greg Bishop
Michael Dorcy
Salone Habibuddin
Leah Hall
Linda Moran
Carol Olbert
Pinet Punyaratabandhu
David Sowinski
Jacque Smith
Khaisri
   Thyammaruangsri
Dana Walker

Team Leaders:
Doug Kelbaugh
Tony Walmsley
David Wright

Students:
Stephanie Adams
Christy Barrie
Barbara Brandt
Thomas Carver
Kim Clements
Colin Gilligan
Thomas Isarankura

Tom Jordan
Kirsi Leiman
Marcie McHale
Jennifer Meisner
Brian Neville
Tamara Pankey
Louise Wright

Team Leaders:
Linda Jewell
Ron Kasprisin
Anne Vernez-Moudon

Students:
David Barkelew
Brian Bennett
Margaret Berman
Ellen Cecil
Amy Hartwell
Kate Kulzer
Vincent Law
David Maurer
Mike Mora
Natalie Peters
Brian Ross
Amy Schulman
David Wilder

Special thanks to: Ben Bonkowski, Tom Byers, Elizabeth Connor, Eliza Davidson, Rich Haag, Joel Horn, Tom Jordan, Gary Lawrence, Chris Leyman, David Maurer, Paul Mortensen, Holly Miller, Dick Nelson, Mike Piper, Cynthia Richardson, Ellen Sollod, Helen Sommers, Tayloe Washburn, Gary Zarker

THE SAND POINT CHARRETTE AND STUDIO, 1993

Team Leaders:
Jorge Andrade
Daniel Glenn
Linda Jewell

Students:
Madzy Besselaar
Michael Cannon
Otto Condon
Gerson Garcia
Mary Little
Amata Luphaiboon
Brian McWatters
Patrick Nopp
Margo Peterson
John Stoeck
Sarah Tarr
Aaron Wegmann
Jens Wegner

Team Leaders:
Doug Kelbaugh
Stacy Moriarty
Mike Pyatok

Students:
Lisa Churchwell
Jeanne Denker
Barbara Freeman
Patrick Hewes
David Hunsberger
Mitch Kent
Catherine Maggio
Tom Paladino
Michael Read

David Saxen
Jim Sheldrup
Jacqui Smith
Paul Tognotti
Danh Vu

Team Leaders:
Cheryl Cronander
Rich Haag
Ron Kasprisin

Students:
Sai Chaleunphonph
Tom Eanes
Tim Gass
Roger Hodges
Bradshaw Hovey
Jean Joichi
Martha Koerner
Patty McHugh
C. Mungthamya
Simone Oliver
Harry Ray
Paul Roybal
Clarence Secright
Ranleigh Starling

Team Leaders:
Dave Sellers
Ellen Sollod
Rich Untermann

Students:
Christine Carr
Susan Clark

Drew Giblin
David Gilchrist
Matthew Lane
Jennifer Mundee
Forrest Murphy
Chip Nevins
Paul Ormseth
Jonathan Pettigrew
Deb Ritter
Ron Rochon
Matthew Sullivan
Mike Usen

DESIGN STUDIO
Instructors:
Daniel J. Glenn
Michael Pyatok

Students:
Christie Carr
Tom Eanes
Gerson Garcia
David Gilchrist
Jean Joichi
Matt Lane
Mata Luphaiboon
Jennifer Mundee
Chanitpreeya
    Mungthanya
Forrest Murphy
Paul Roybal
Jim Sheldrup
Ranleigh Starling

Special thanks to: Marty Curry, Daniel Glenn, Luther Green, Margherita Gudenzi, Denice Hunt, Christine Knowles, Gary Lawrence, Christopher Malarkey, Forrest Murphy, Karen Porterfield, George Scarola, Bonnie Snedeker, John Stamets, Keehn Thompson, Tallman Trask III, Bob Watts, Jeanette Williams

THE WINSLOW CHARRETTE, 1993

Design Profesionals:
Bruce Anderson
Gerardo Aguuayo
David Balas
Amy Beierle
Bart Berg
Jim Burford
Mick Davidson
Allan Ferrin
Jeff Foster
Jeff Garlid
Holly Godard
Becca Hanson
Bill Isley
Jerry Jay
Frank Karreman
Charles Kelley
Tom Kuniholm
Richard LaBotz
Roger Long
Peter O'Connor
J. Mack Pearl
David Roth
Andy Rovelstad
John Rudolph
David Swenson
Josie Varga
Paul Von Rosenstiel
Tom Von Schrader
Peter Watson
Sherry Wellborn
Miles Yanick

Priscilla Zimmerman

UW Student Volunteers:
Tom Eanes
Brendan Kelly
Kerry Morgan
Jennifer Mundee
Ken Pirie
Sandra Strieby

Citizen Participants:
Tom Ahearne
Bess Alpaugh
Brenda Bell
Dick Bowen
Bob Burkholder
Pauline Deschamps
Tom Haggar
Jessie Hey
Darlene Kordonowy
Wayne Loverich
Andy Mueller
Don Nakata
Liz Taylor
Ron Tweiten
Pat Wyman

Sponsors:
Bainbridge Bakers
Bainbridge Broadcasting
Bainbridge Public Library

Custom Printing
The Far East Cafe
Island Exposures
Pegasus Coffee
Picnics Plus
Pizza Factory
Safeway
Saint Cecelia's
That's-A-Some Pizza
Thriftway
Town and Country

Public Relations:
Jeff Brein
Laurel Caplan
John Hough
John Ratterman

City Staff:
Jane Allan
Jenny Shemwell

Facilitator:
Doug Kelbaugh

Graphic Designer:
Rachel Ruud

Artist/Architect:
Andy Rovelstad

THE INTERBAY 2020 CHARRETTE AND STUDIO, 1994

Team 1
Leaders:
Stephanie Bothwell
Andres Duany
Denice Hunt

Students:
Tim Andersen
John Burke
Chuan-Tsung Cheng
Teresa Hsin
Jarrod Lewis
Michael Naylor
Prakit Phanuratana
Jorge Planas
Mark Sharp
Aubrey Summers

Team 2
Leaders:
Bo Gronlund
Ron Kasprisin
Doug Kelbaugh

Students:
Mauricio Castro
Colleen Dooley
Richard Davis

Rob Doyle
Tzu-Jyh Lee
Uli Lemke
Janet Longnecker
Takeshi Okada
Peerachati Songstit

Team 3
Leaders:
Lorenzo Matteoli
Laurie Olin
George Rolfe

Students:
I-Chen Chao
Ann Dunphy
Theodros Gebremichael
Catherine Johnson
Lara Normand
David Peterson
Deborah Ritter
Thomas Rooks
Cheryl Smith
Rachel Stevenson

Team 4
Leaders:
Dave Sellers

Anne Tate
Rich Untermann

Students:
Virginia Brumback
Nixon Golla
Dan Hazzard
Jennifer Hing
Yao-Hsin Hsieh
Muh-Huh Lu
Paul Moon
Adriana Veras
Bryan Woodruff

DESIGN STUDIO
(SCHEME 5)
Instructors:
Bo Gronlund
Doug Kelbaugh

Students:
I-Chen Chao
Chuan-Tsung Cheng
Jarrod Lewis
Muh-Huh Lu
Prakit Phananuratana
Peerachati Songstit

Special Thanks to: Terry Adams, Dan Carlson, Keith Christian, Steve Clagett, Alex de Guzman, Dave Forseth, Eric Friedli, Ciara Hanley, Fritz Hedges, Paul Hess, Denice Hunt, Ann Kastel, Peter Katz, Ying LaPierre, Gary Lawrence, Jarrod Lewis, John McAllister, Betty Jane Narver, Alan Potter, Charlie Sheldon, Paul Schell, Paul Sommers, John Stamets.

UNIVERSITY DISTRICT CHARRETTE AND STUDIO, 1995

Team 1
Leaders:
Lee Copeland
Don Prowler
Mary-Ann Ray

Students:
John Curtis
Harris Davernas
Prentis Hale
Adrian Higson
Ian Leader
Emma Platt
Alissa Rupp
David Sarti
Nina Sia
Tara Siegel
Phillip Twilley
Community Rep:
John Deeter

Team 2
Leaders:
Peter Hasselman
Cynthia Richardson
Gordon Walker

Students:
Janet Dovey
Tamara Dyer
Damian Fifeld
Mette Greenshields
Douglas Ito
Walter Martinez
Thomsa Maul
Andrew Miller

Daniel Ruiz
Tracy Shriver
Terri Smith
Paul Stefanski
Albert Torrico
Emma Trumon
Community Rep:
Sue Fleming

Team 3
Leaders:
Yoshi Ii
Mike Pyatok
Ken Schwartz

Students:
Rachel Berney
Dace Campbell
Matt Giles
Peter Goodall
Tom Hall
Robert Hutchison
Kenneth Last
Joyce Maund
William Nash
Kevin Tabari
Elizabeth Tobey
Community Rep:
Tim Rood

Team 4
Leaders:
Doug Kelbaugh
Michael Shaw
Jill Stoner

Students:
Daniel Gray
Thomas Hemba
Renee Jankuski
Brendan Kelly
Robert Kiker
Mark McCarter
Sarah Mitchell
Ann Okada
Simon Rennie
Lydia Ruddy
Scot Starr
Maya Wahyudharma
Woody Woodward
Delphine Yip
Community Rep:
Christine Cassidy

DESIGN STUDIO
Instructor:
Doug Kelbaugh

Students:
Matthew Giles
Prentis Hale
Michelle Kandi
Kenneth Last
Ian Leader
John McNicholas
Andrew Miller
Daniel Ruiz
Alissa Rupp
Theresa Smith
Paul Stefanski
Elizabeth Tobey
Michele Wang

Special Thanks to: Bob Cross, Sue Fleming, Fred Hart, Christine Knowles, Rick Krochalis, Nedra Paulter, Cynthia Richardson, Tim Rood, Lydia Ruddy, Michael Shaw, Scott Soules, Tallman Trask III, Patty Whisler

Notes

NOTES TO INTRODUCTION

Chapter epigraph. This was related to me by Rich Haag, FASLA, Professor of Landscape Architecture at the University of Washington, who heard it from his father, who heard it from a tenant farmer.

1. Wendell Berry, "Global Management," *The Ecologist*, July-Aug., 1992, p. 180.

2. Bart Giamatti, *Take Time for Paradise*, Princeton University Press, Princeton, NJ, 1966, pp. 51-52.

3. Judith Martin, "The New Urbanism Meets the Market," Lincoln Institute of Land Policy Seminar on "The Influences of New Urbanism," Cambridge, MA, Dec. 1995, p. 5.

4. Paul Hawken, *The Ecology of Commerce*, Harper Business, New York, NY, 1993, p. xv.

5. Robert Searns, "What's in a Name? The Concept of Greenways," and William Moorish, "Beautiful Infrastructure," *On the Ground*, Winter/Spring 1995, pp. 9, 15-18.

6. "Global Report on Human Settlements: An Urbanizing World," as reported in *The Seattle Times*, Nov. 6, 1995, p. A7.

7. Jane Jacobs, *Systems of Survival*, Vintage Books, Random House, New York, 1992.

8. John C. Ryan, *State of the Northwest*, Northwest Environment Watch, Seattle, WA, 1994, p. 1 of attached flyer.

9. *Seattle Times*, Sept. 14, 1995, p. 22.

10. Jane Jacobs, *The Economy of Cities*, Random House, New York, 1969.

NOTES TO CHAPTER 1

1. Robert Fishman, "Space, Time and Sprawl," *The Periphery*, Architectural Design, London, 1994, p. 45.

2. Ira Bachrach, "The World of Product Names," lecture, Chicago, Nov. 1993.

3. *Modern Odysseys: Heroic Journeys We Make Everyday*, METRO Rail Transit Artist Project, Seattle, 1992.

4. Peter Calthorpe and Henry Richmond, *Changing America: Blueprints for the New Administration*, New Market Press, 1992, p. 699

5. Elmer W. Johnson, *Avoiding the Collision of Cities and Cars*, American Academy of Arts and Sciences, 1993, p. 3.

6. Genevieve Giuliano, "The Weakening of the Land Use/Transportation Connection," *On the Ground*, Summer 1995, p. 12.

7. McGinnis and Foege, "Actual Causes of Death in the United States," *Journal of the American Medical Association*, Nov. 10, 1993.

8. Alan Durning, *The City and the Car*, Northwest Environment Watch, distributed by Sasquatch Books, Seattle, 1996, p. 24.

9. Kevin Kasowski, "Suburban Sprawl: Land Use and Economic Costs," *On the Ground*, Fall, 1994, p. 5.

10. John C. Ryan, "Greenhouse Gases on the Rise in the Northwest," *NEW Indicator*, Northwest Environment Watch, Seattle, Aug., 1995, pp. 3-4.

11. See Guiliano, "The Weakening," p. 2 (several of the statistics in this paragraph come from E. W. Johnson's *Avoiding the Collision of Cities and Cars*).

12. *Modern Odysseys*, METRO Rail Transit Artist Project, 1992

13. Michael John Pittas, "The City after the Info Age," *Loeb Fellowship Forum*, Harvard University Graduate School of Design, Spring/Summer 1995, p. 3.

14. Yi-Fu Tuan, *Topophilia*, Prentice-Hall, Englewood Cliffs, NJ, 1974, p. 226.

15. Anthony Downs, "Creating More Affordable Housing," *Journal of Housing*, July-Aug. 1992, vol. 49, p. 179.

16. Ibid.

17. Cited in a lecture on neighborhood revitalization by Oscar Newman at the Federal Office Building in Seattle, July 7, 1994.

18. Timothy Egan, "Closed-off Communities Multiply, Spur Concerns," *Seattle Times*, Sept. 3, 1995, pp. A1 and A12.

19. Delton W. Young, "Suburban Disconnect—Human Needs Overlooked When Growth Is Unplanned," *Seattle Post-Intelligencer*, Nov. 12, 1995, p. E1.

20. *Vision/Reality*, Office of Community Planning and Development, U.S. Department of Housing and Urban Development, 1449-CPD, March 1994, p. 36.

21. Camille Paglia, *Vamps and Tramps*, Vintage Books, New York, 1994, p. 27.

22. Peter Calthorpe, *The Next American Metropolis*, Princeton Architectural Press, New York, 1993, p. 18.

23. Peter Katz, "Housing vs. Neighborhoods," *On the Ground,* vol. 2, no. 1, 1996, p. 15.

24. Philip Langdon, "The Urbanist's Reward," *Progressive Architecture*, Aug. 1995, p. 84.

NOTES TO CHAPTER 2

Chapter epigraph: Victor Papenek, *The Green Imperative*, Thames and Hudson, New York, 1995, p. 139.

1. John C. Ryan, *State of the Northwest,* Northwest Environment Watch, Seattle, 1994, pp. 10-11.

2. Ibid., pp. 13, 45, 47, 65.

3. Jeffrey Ochsner, "The Missing Paradigm," *Column 5*, 1991, pp. 4-11.

4. Jeffrey Ochsner, ed., *Shaping Seattle Architecture: A Guide to the Architects*, University of Washington Press, Seattle and London, 1994, pp. xli-xlii.

5. Colin Rowe, *The Architecture of Good Intentions*, Academy Editions, London, 1994, p. 42.

6. Alan Plattus, personal communication, May 23, 1995.

7. Vincent Scully, Charles Moore Gold Medal Presentations, Feb. 6, 1991, Washington D.C. (as quoted in Stewart Brand, *How Buildings Learn*, Viking Penguin, 1994).

8. Brand, *How Buildings Learn*, p. 88.

9. Margali Sarfalti Larson, *Beyond the Post Modern Facade*, University of California Press, Berkeley, CA, 1993, p. 181.

10. Alex Krieger, "The Eye as an Instrument (Again) of Urban Design," *Progressive Architecture*, Feb. 1992, p. 102.

11. Kenneth Frampton, "Critical Regionalism," *The Anti-Aesthetic,* ed. by Hal Foster, Bay Press, Port Townsend, WA, 1983, p. 17.

12. Ibid.

13. Jacques Barzun, *The Columbia History of the World*, Harper and Row, New York, 1992, p. 1165.

14. Nicholas Humphrey, "Natural Aesthetics," *Architecture for People,* Cassel Ltd., London, 1980, p. 159.

15. Brand, *How Buildings Learn,* p. 113.

16. Alan Balfour, "Education—the Architectural Association," *Journal of the Indian Institute of Architects,* Oct. 1994, p. 51.

17. Peter Eisenman, "Confronting the Double Zeitgeist," *Architecture*, Oct. 1994, p. 51.

18. Larson, *Beyond the Post Modern Facade*, p. 252.

NOTES TO CHAPTER 3

Chapter epigraph: Leon Krier, "The Reconstruction of Vernacular Building and Classical Architecture," *Architectural Design*, London, Sept. 13, 1984, p. 63.

1. Allan Bloom, *Love and Friendship*, Simon and Schuster, New York, 1993, p. 211

2. Jacques Barzun in *The Columbia History of the World*, Harper and Row, New York, 1972, p. 1159.

3. John Passmore, "The End of Philosophy," *Australasian Journal of Philosophy*, vol. 74, no. 1, March 1996, pp. 1-19.

4. Mark Gelernter, "Teaching Design Innovation through Design Tradition," *Proceedings,* 1988 ACSA Annual Meeting, Miami, 1988.

5. Bryan Appleyard, *Richard Rogers: A Biography*, Faber and Faber, London, 1986, p. 65.

6. Rafael Moneo, "On Typology," *Oppositions,* Summer 1978, no. 13, p. 32.

7. Anthony King, *The Bungalow*, Oxford University Press, New York, 1995.

8. Leon Krier, *Architectural Design,* p. 61.

NOTES TO CHAPTER 4

Chapter epigraph: Alex Krieger, "The Eye as an Instrument (Again) of Urban Design," *Progressive Architecture*, Feb. 1992, p. 102.

1. F. A. Hayek, *The Fatal Conceit: The Errors of Socialism*, University of Chicago Press, Chicago, 1991.

2. Wendell Berry, "Conservation Is Good Work," *The American Journal*, Winter 1992, p. 33

3. Jane Jacobs, *Systems of Survival*, Random House, New York, 1993.

4. Charter, Congress for the New Urbanism IV, Charleston, SC, May 1996.

5. John Kaliski, "The New Urbanism: Vocational Excellence Versus Design Paradox" (draft), Lincoln Institute of Land Policy seminar on "The Influences of New Urbanism," Cambridge, MA, Dec. 1995.

6. Genevieve Giuliano, "The Weakening Land Use/Transportation Connection," *On the Ground*, Summer 1995, pp. 12-14.

NOTES TO CHAPTER 5

The Kingdome Charrette

1. Jeffrey Ochsner, ed., *Shaping Seattle Architecture: A Historic Guide to the Architects*, University of Washington Press, Seattle and London, 1994, p. xxxviii.

2. Murray Morgan, *Skid Road, An Informal Portrait of Seattle*, University of Washington Press, Seattle, 1982 (originally published in 1951).

3. David Hewitt, Jim Daly, Jim Olson, Gordon Walker, Dick Hobbs, David Fukui, Dan Calvin, Barnett Schorr, and Jeremy Miller.

The Seattle Commons Charrette

1. "The Day the Commons Died: A Lose-Lose-Lose Decision," *Seattle Weekly*, May 29, 1996, p. 4.

NOTES TO CHAPTER 6

The University District Charrette and Studio

1. N. John Habraken, "Cultivating the Field: About an Attitude When Making Architecture," *Places*, Winter 1994, p. 19.

2. This section is based on edited excerpts from *The Ave.*, an unpublished planning study conducted by the University of Washington's Department of Urban Design and Planning, Spring Studio, 1994.

3. The balance of this chapter is excerpted from *Where Town Meets Gown: Visions for the University District,* ed. by Doug Kelbaugh, University of Washington Department of Architecture, 1995.

NOTES TO CHAPTER 7

Chapter epigraph: Barbara L. Allen, "Ranch-Style House in America: A Cultural and Environmental Discourse," *Journal of Architectural Education*, Feb. 1996, p. 164.

The Lacey Studio

1. Robert Geddes, "Jefferson's Suburban Model," *Progressive Architecture*, May 1989, p. 9.

2. This subchapter is based on writings by Rick Mohler and Doug Kelbaugh in *Designing for Density,* University of Washington Department of Architecture, 1992, pp. 90-127.

3. Philip Langdon, "The Urbanist's Reward," *Progressive Architecture*, Aug. 1995, p. 88.

NOTES TO CHAPTER 9

The New Communities

1. Ian McHarg, *Design with Nature*, The Natural History Press, Garden City, New York, 1969.

NOTES TO CHAPTER 10

Chapter epigraph: Bill Bradley, speech to National Press Club, Feb. 1995.

1. Alan Durning, *The Car and the City*, Northwest Environment Watch, distributed by Sasquatch Books, Seattle, 1996, p. 62.

2. Ibid., pp. 48-49.

3. Transportation Pricing Task Force, Puget Sound Regional Council, final draft, Oct. 10, 1996.

4. Victoria Eisen and Deborah Hopkins, "Advancing Niche Vehicles and Infrastructure Design," *On the Ground*, Summer 1995, p. 27.

5. Glenn Pascall, "Team Spirit, The New Economy," *Seattle Weekly*, Nov. 8, 1995, p. 16.

6. Neal Peirce, "Among Voters, 'Takings' Laws Don't Pass Muster," *Seattle Times*, Jan. 7, 1996, p. A5.

7. Gary Synder, "Readings," Elliott Bay Bookstore, Seattle, Dec. 13, 1995.

8. John C. Ryan, *State of the Northwest*, Northwest Environment Watch, Seattle, WA, 1994, p. 5

Bibliography

SUGGESTED READING

Alexander, Christopher. *A Pattern Language*. New York: Oxford University Press, 1977.

Berry, Wendell. *The Unsettling of America: Culture and Agriculture*. San Francisco: Sierra Club Books, 1986.

Brand, Stewart. *How Buildings Learn*, New York, Viking Penguin, 1986.

Calthorpe, Peter. *The Next American Metropolis: Ecology, Community and the American Dream*. New York: Princeton Architectural Press, 1993.

Duany, Andres, and Elizabeth Plater-Zyberk, with Alex Kreiger, ed. *Town and Town-Making Principles*. New York: Rizzoli, 1991.

Durning, Alan. *The Car and the City*. Seattle, WA: Northwest Environment Watch, distributed by Sasquatch Books, 1996.

Hawken, Paul. *Ecology of Commerce: A Declaration of Sustainability*. New York: Harper Collins Publishers, Inc., 1993.

Jackson, Kenneth T. *The Crabgrass Frontier: Suburbanization of the United States*. New York: Oxford University Press, 1985.

Jacobs, Jane. *The Death and Life of Great American Cities*. New York: Vintage Books, 1961.

———. *The Economy of Cities*. New York, NY: Random House, 1969.

———. *Systems of Survival: A Dialog on the Moral Foundations of Commerce and Politics*. New York: Random House, 1992.

Johnson, Elmer W. *Avoiding the Collision of Cities and Cars*. American Academy of Arts and Sciences, 1993.

Katz, Peter. *New Urbanism: Towards an Architecture of Community*. New York: Mc Graw Hill, Inc., 1994.

Kelbaugh, Doug, ed. *The Pedestrian Pocket Book: A New Suburban Design Strategy*. New York: Princeton Architectural Press, 1989.

Kunstler, James H. *The Geography of Nowhere: The Rise and Decline of America's Man-Made Landscape*. New York: Simon and Schuster, 1993.

Larson, Margali Sarfatti. *Behind the Post Modern Facade*. Berkeley: University of California Press, 1993.

Morrish, William R., and Catherine R. Brown. *Planning to Stay*. Minneapolis: Milkweed Editions, 1994.

Norberg-Schulz, Christian. *Genius Loci: Towards a Phenomenology of Architecture*. New York: Rizzoli, 1980.

Nyberg, Folke. "Logo-Architecture and the Architecture of Logos," *Column 5*, vol. 8, pp. 2-9, University of Washington, 1994.

Porphyrios, Demetri. *Leon Krier; Houses, Palaces, Cities*. London: AD Editions, 1984.

Rowe, Colin. *The Architecture of Good Intentions*. London: Academy, 1994.

Ryan, John C. *State of the Northwest*. Seattle: Northwest Environmental Watch, 1994.

Sale, Roger. *Seattle, Past to Present*. Seattle: University of Washington Press, 1976.

Solomon, Daniel. *Rebuilding*. New York: Princeton Architectural Press, 1992.

Van der Ryn, Sim, and Stuart Cowan, *Ecological Design*. Washington, D.C., and Covelo, CA: Island Press, 1996.

Vision/Reality. Washington, D.C.: U.S. Dept. of Housing and Urban Development, Office of Community Planning and Development, 1994.

ADDITIONAL READING

Appleyard, Donald. *Livable Streets*. Berkeley: University of California Press, 1981.

Borgmann, Albert. *Crossing the Postmodern Divide*. Chicago: The University of Chicago Press, 1992.

Fishmann, Robert K. *Bourgeois Utopias: The Rise and Fall of Suburbia*. New York: Basic Books, 1987.

Frieden, Bernard, and Lynn B. Sagalyn. *Downtown, Inc.: How America Rebuilds Cities*. Cambridge, MA: The MIT Press, 1992.

Jacobs, Allan B. *Great Streets*. Cambridge, MA: MIT Press, 1993.

Kelbaugh, Douglas. *Housing Affordability and Density: Regulatory Reform and Design Recommendations*. Seattle: Washington State Dept. of Community Development, Department of Architecture, College of Architecture and Urban Planning, University of Washington, 1992.

———. *Designing for Density: Ideas for More Compact Housing and Communities*. Supplement One of *Housing Affordability and Density*.

———. *Envisioning an Urban Village: The Seattle Commons Design Charrette*. Supplement Two of *Housing Affordability and Density*.

———. *Interbay 2020: Terminal 91 and Beyond*. Seattle: Dept. of Architecture, College of Architecture and Urban Planning, University of Washington, 1994.

———. *Reinvesting the Peace Dividend: Visions of Sand Point*. Seattle: Department of Architecture, College of Architecture and Urban Planning, University of Washington, 1993.

———. *Where Town Meets Gown*. Seattle: Dept. of Architecture, College of Architecture and Urban Planning, University of Washington, 1995.

Langdon, Philip. *A Better Place to Live: Reshaping the American Suburb.* New York: Harper Collins, 1995.

Lynch, Kevin. *The Image of the City.* Cambridge, MA: MIT Press, 1960.

MacDonald, Norbert. *Distant Neighbors: A Comparative History of Seattle and Vancouver.* Lincoln: University of Nebraska Press, 1987.

MAKERS Architecture and Urban Design. *Residential Development Handbook for Snohomish County Communities.* Prepared for Snohomish County Tomorrow, Everett, Washington, March 1992.

Mohney, David, and Keller Easterling, ed. *Seaside: Making a Town in America.* New York: Princeton Architectural Press, 1991.

Morgan, Murray. *Skid Road.* Seattle: University of Washington Press, 1982. (Originally published in 1951.)

Moudon, Anne Vernez. *Built for Change: Neighborhood Architecture in San Francisco.* Cambridge, MA: MIT Press, 1986.

Ochsner, Jeffrey, ed. *Shaping Seattle Architecture: A Historical Guide to Architects.* Seattle and London: University of Washington Press, 1994.

Peirce, Neal. "The Peirce Report," A *Seattle Times* Special, reprinted from October 1-8, 1989.

Puget Sound Council of Governments/Puget Sound Regional Council. *Vision 2020: Growth and Transportation Strategy for the Central Puget Sound Region.* Seattle, Washington, October 1990.

Puget Sound Regional Council. "Vision 2020: Multicounty Planning Policies for King, Kitsap, Pierce and Snohomish Counties," Seattle, Washington, March 1993.

San Diego Metropolitan Transit Development Board. *Designing for Transit: A Manual for Integrating Public Transportation and Land Development in the San Diego Metropolitan Area,* July 1993.

SNO-TRAN's Public Transportation Plan Technical Advisory Committee. *SNO-TRAN's Guide to Land Use and Public Transportation,* vol. 1, 1989.

Sucher, David. *City Comforts: How to Build an Urban Village.* Seattle, WA: City Comforts Press, 1995.

Tuan, Yi-Fu. *Topophilia: A Study of Environmental Perception, Attitudes and Values.* Englewood Cliffs, NJ: Prentice-Hall Inc., 1974.

Washington Growth Management Acts of 1990 and 1991 (Chapter 17, Laws of 1990, First Extraordinary Session) and (Laws of 1991, First Extraordinary Session). Olympia, Washington, 1990 and 1991.

Index